THE BIBLE NOW

Contributors

CECILY BENNETT

LAURENCE BRIGHT, OP

BRIAN DAVIES, OP

JOHN GREEHY

ADRIAN HASTINGS

DORIS K. HAYES

HANS KÜNG

JOHN L. McKENZIE, SJ

N.D. O'DONOGHUE, O. CARM

TIMOTHY RADCLIFFE, OP

BERNARD ROBINSON

LIONEL SWAIN

HAMISH F. G. SWANSTON

GEOFFREY TURNER

HENRY WANSBROUGH, OSB

HAROLD WINSTONE

THE BIBLE NOW

Essays on its Meaning and Use for Christians Today

PAUL BURNS and JOHN CUMMING, Editors

THE SEABURY PRESS · NEW YORK

1981
The Seabury Press
815 Second Avenue
New York, N.Y. 10017

Printed in the United States of America

Library of Congress Cataloging in Publication Data

Main entry under title:
The Bible now.
1. Bible—Addresses, essays, lectures.
I. Burns, Paul. II. Cumming, John, 1915—
BS475.2.B44 220.6'1 81-5691
ISBN 0-8164-2335-0 AACR2

Contents

Acknowledgements
The chapter by Laurence Bright, OP, first appeared in *Getting to know the Bible,* and is reproduced by permission of Living Parish Pamphlets.

The chapter by Hans Küng is based on a Christmas radio broadcast and incorporates material from *On Being a Christian* and *Does God Exist?,* both published by Collins.

Introduction

The Bible is still a somewhat equivocal asset. A plethora of new translations, each more 'readable' than the last, and an increased emphasis on the liturgy of the word make one feel that one ought to be reading, studying and praying Scripture in the 'right' way. But what does that mean? Almost everyone is aware that the modern church and academic ideas about the Bible are less restrictive and much more exciting than in even the recent past, when for Catholics the Bible had to be approached with care and under the strict guidance of the teaching Church, and many Protestants kept to a 'fundamentalist', even literal understanding of it. But few people apart from specialists have any real idea of what research has told us.

Nineteenth-century debates on the historicity of Old Testament 'myths', and a widespread conviction that the creation account had to be defended against the theory of evolution, have given way to a recognition that acceptance of different categories of writing in the OT does not detract from but enhances its message. But what happens to faith if the same principle is applied to the NT? Recent publications seem even to cast doubt on the validity of applying the name 'Son of God' to Jesus, or at least to question his divine self-consciousness – whether he thought he was God – and so to reduce the content of the original Gospel. Cherished doctrines such as the virgin birth and even the resurrection seem then to be relegated to an 'extra-historical' dimension. Is this an attack on the essential revealed 'deposit of faith', or simply a winnowing-away of historically-conditioned accretions from the kernel of truth?

In the Roman Catholic tradition the Bible was for many centuries an ecclesiastical possession. Its use for private reading and devotion was a major issue in the debates of the Reformation and Jansenist quarrel; its immediate accessibility to the faithful was not really established as a matter of church principle till the second Vatican Council. Yet the Church has long enjoined on its pastors the tasks of preaching the Gospel and expounding the Scriptures – a task given fresh emphasis with the new cycle of readings and the stress on preaching on the readings in 'homily' form rather than on offering general edification.

While evangelization has always been central to the Church's mission, the Bible, as opposed to the teaching the Church derived from it, has not. In this the Roman Catholic Church has been at variance with Protestant missions, and the two wings of Christian evangelism have often devoted more energy to attacking one another than to evangelization. The effect of the more direct use of the Bible in one-time missionary lands can best be seen today in Latin America, where the central message of the Bible (as interpreted) and the exodus narrative in particular have become a justification and historical precedent for the Church's commitment to social and political liberation. The Bible has a dynamism it never possessed in the days of its church-guarded interpretation. This gives urgency to questions like the relevance of the OT to Christian belief and practice, and the use of the Bible in liturgy and education, all of which should lead to a better appreciation of what the Bible is. This in turn implies some knowledge of more technical aspects such as its chronology and the literary categories it employs.

By examining these and related questions this book sets out to bridge 'the gap between the scholars and other Christians', which is the first sub-heading of its first chapter. It brings together a group of distinguished scholars who are also proficient teachers, broadcasters, pastors, lecturers and counsellors, able to mediate their scholarship in accessible and practical ways. Together they show what the Bible is, how it came into being, what it means, and how it should be used.

The way in which it is often used today leaves much to be desired. Public examinations in 'Religious Knowledge' encourage young people to learn passages in virtual isolation, with little critical historical background. The fundamentalism of many teachers is illustrated in the chapter by Doris Hayes (pp. 167-77). In parish churches the situation is little better, if at all: 'A practising Christian hears the text of Scripture week by week in church, and is supposed to be given some explanation of it. Yet even where this is not replaced by appeals for money, or slanted by dogmatic considerations from reformation or counter-reformation theology, it is seldom informed by a modern critical approach' (Laurence Bright, pp. 13-14). The reformed liturgy of the Roman Catholic Church and the corresponding Anglican scheme of readings give churchgoers access to a wider range of scripture readings than before, but it is very doubtful if most congregations even today have had the reasons for the reforms explained to them in an intelligent or even intelligible form; the 'new liturgy' is in danger of fossilizing into yet another rite handed down from above.

We are sure that the essays in this book will help teachers, catechists, pastors and religious to remedy such inadequacies. Our main aim, however, is to bridge that gap, to bring the basic facts and speculation of modern biblical scholarship within the reach of students and interested lay people, to enable them in their turn to 'study the texts as critically as (they) can . . . to respond to their message' (p. 22), and to see how richly fascinating they are. The structure of the book is designed to help this process: after the first chapter, which sets out general principles for reading the Bible, chapters 2-5 deal with themes affecting the whole Bible, chapters 6-9 concentrate on relevant aspects of the OT, chapters 10-13 tackle the major problems of the NT, and the last three chapters deal with the Bible in relation to the three main processes through which it can make its presence in the world felt: teaching, liturgy and evangelization.

Laurence Bright sets out the basic principle of biblical criticism: 'Any passage of Scripture can only reveal its meaning when related to its historical background'. Until the Bible ceases to be regarded as beyond the reach of the principles normally applied to any literary criticism, because it is 'sacred' and therefore in some measure untouchable, passages will not be seen in context, the work will not be seen as a whole, and 'the effect is shattering'. Bernard Robinson examines inspiration and revelation – two basic concepts whose historical understanding has long been a barrier to an investigative approach. Outlining the course of the development of biblical criticism (defined as 'the application to the interpretation of the Bible of the scholarly disciplines used in secular academic research'), he shows how Catholics in particular have lagged behind other denominations, hindered by definitions of Trent and Vatican I. These barriers were removed only in 1943, with the encyclical *Divino Afflante Spiritu,* which means that not a few parents, pastors and teachers of today spent their formative years in the context of papal teaching that the gospels contained the actions and sayings of Jesus 'intact and unchanged'. The process by which the Church (as opposed to scholars) came to revise its concept of its guardianship of the sacred writings is set out by Timothy Radcliffe.

In a more detailed examination of the literary forms and images used in the Bible, Hamish Swanston shows how far one form depends on another and one culture on another, so that, for example, the passion narratives in Matthew and Mark use the theme of the suffering servant in Isaiah, which in its turn draws on the figure of David. 'The range of forms and images in the scriptural writings is both an acknowledgement that the divine cannot be adequately expressed unless the literary devices of many peoples are brought into service, and an announcement that the order insinuated by such literature is finally discoverable in Jesus' (p. 60). If we are to discover a meaning in the Bible for ourselves, we need to discover the intention behind the forms and words used, which a superficial reading of them as 'history' in the modern sense will not reveal. Noel O'Donoghue shows what discovering a meaning for ourselves is, and examines the spirituality of the Bible from a Christian standpoint, one 'rooted in the death and resurrection of Jesus'. He finds 'a spirituality which has its roots in the ethical, in everyday justice and decency, but which goes far beyond it. Yet it goes beyond it *in its own direction* . . . '(p. 64). It transcends the everyday, but does not forsake it; the disciple who follows Christ does not forsake his fellow man; what he forsakes is the world as 'possessed and possessive'. If he frees himself from the world, it is in order to save it.

Turning specifically to the OT, Lionel Swain applies the principle that if we are to understand it, we need to set it in its historical context. He shows its writers as witnesses to Israel's faith, and its compilation as the fruit of a long and complicated process. Unravelling some of the main aspects of this process, John L. McKenzie picks out three dominant modes of ethical writing: the law, the prophets and the wisdom literature. There is, he says, no uniform overall code of ethics discernible in the OT – as would be expected from 1000 years of history and such a multiplicity of authors; to impose a moral code on it would mean intruding one's own theology and ethics. The law contains little of general ethical interest or originality – hence Jesus' oppositions between what the men of old said and, 'But I say to you . . . '; the wisdom literature preaches a courtly ideal for later generations of Israelites, which 'may not be profound morality, but rises above the combative behaviour which seems to have become characteristic of modern cities' (p. 96); the prophets, on the other hand, proclaim the collapse of a community, attacking the society of the Monarchy as contrary to the will of Yahweh – the God of the exodus and therefore the liberator of the oppressed.

Examining the theme of prophecy in more detail, Geoffrey Turner sets the prophets in their historical background: a variety of crises from the ninth to the sixth centuries. Essentially men of their time, they 'spoke an urgent message which was not meant to survive the crisis to which it was addressed'; their function was 'forthtelling rather than foretelling', reminding the Jews that they had a covenant and that they were breaking their part of it, for which they would be punished. They addressed their times, but their voice has lived on in the Christian Church: Archbishop Romero and Ernesto Cardenal are surely two of their successors today.

Cecily Bennett asks how the OT is relevant to Christians today, and shows how, for all its apparent alien-ness, it is talking about 'our' God. If we are to find him in its pages, she says, we have to take them whole, because they are 'human literature, with all its failings and limitations, *being* God's word to us, not God's word wrapped in a detachable shell of human literature'. The God of the Bible is a God of history, but that should not lead us to seek some form of 'salvation history' in his 'mighty deeds' as recounted in the Bible. We will never know what is fact and what is not, and God's word cannot depend on something so inaccessible. God's work in history is the books themselves; we meet his self-revelation, '*in* these writings, not in a salvation history behind them'.

The authors of the NT had met their God '*in* these writings'. Henry Wansbrough asks who those authors could have been, what literary processes they used, and why, concluding that modern scholarship reveals the variety and richness of Christian witness spread wide in the Mediterranean world by an early date: a Christian society 'which treasures the memory and the words of Christ and turns to them for guidance when occasion arises'. John Greehy examines the guidance we can find in the message these authors handed on, and finds ideals become reality in the person of Christ, total response to the love of the Father, even to death on the cross. It is this death on the cross, says Hans Küng,that distinguishes Jesus from founders of other religions. The crib and the cross go together; the infancy narratives show the community of the Easter faith looking back to its origins, and explaining its response in story form, and proclaiming 'the nature of being "Son of God" and therefore true man'. The truth of Jesus' humanity has implications for ours, which Brian Davies draws out in his consideration of the perpetual mystery of the resurrection. The NT writers are in no doubt that 'the risen Christ is the Christ who died', and, if the NT is right, then 'what we value most, our humanity, is pregnant with its own glory'.

Writing from practical experience that what teachers need is good basic theology, Doris Hayes echoes this continuity between the historical Jesus and the exalted Christ. The significant aspects of the person of Christ are also encountered in the liturgy, which, Harold Winstone shows, is totally dependent on the Bible, because Christ depended on Scripture and because the most significant thing in his life echoed the most significant event in the history of Israel. There can be no liturgy without the Bible; and there can be no Church without the Bible: this is the burden of the concluding chapter by Adrian Hastings, in which he examines the 'central ambiguity' of Christian history: the relationship between the Bible and the Church, an oscillating tension between the 'scriptural finger' and the 'ecclesiastical finger', with the twin dangers of fundamentalism and 'domestication' of the Bible. The Bible challenges the Church to be free; only in a listening, self-questioning Church can it truly make its voice heard, as it did in the little community of Solentiname in Nicaragua, and does in basic communities in Brazil and elsewhere. Restored to its place, perhaps now possible for the first time in Christian history, it can do its work, because: 'It belongs to the Church, yet stands over and above the Church. It is in daily use, but it judges. Ignored at one's peril, its use seems often as dangerous as its reverent ignoring. The Church changes, the Bible remains the same'.

February 1981

PB
JC

On reading the Bible

LAURENCE BRIGHT, OP

1. The gap between the scholars and other Christians

Biblical criticism today rests on as firm a foundation as any other scholarly discipline. Behind it lies a vast work of collaboration between people of every Church, in every part of the world, over nearly a century and a half – even though one has to add that until recently it has mainly been by men of European extraction, from the Protestant Churches, and this has inevitably given it a certain imbalance. Like every living study it has developed, so that much of the pioneer work is now outdated. But over time and space there is wide general agreement on the main principles of study – without which, indeed, the differences of detail could not emerge and be stated.

Yet to the Christian public at large the work is still unfamiliar. The large number of books and articles by scholars and popularizers aimed precisely at this general public has still not succeeded in familiarizing them with it. With Roman Catholics this is understandable, since it is only comparatively recently, in the main since the publication of Pius XII's encyclical *Divino Afflante Spiritu* in 1943, that Catholic scholars have been able to play a full part in the shared research.

There is also a quite considerable Christian body, the Evangelicals in the Anglican communion and many of the Free Churches, who are still excluded by their commitment to a selectively literal 'fundamentalist' approach. But this does not account for the lack of knowledge of the majority of Christians in every Church, who continue to read, hear, and study the text as if this work had never been done. This ignorance is strikingly reflected in almost any mention of the Bible in the mass media, which put forward views that no scholar has held for many years in order to tell us they have been refuted by archaeologists or computers.

Much of the blame for this lies with preaching. A practising

Christian hears the text of Scripture week by week in church, and is supposed to be given some kind of exposition of it. Yet even where this is not replaced by appeals for money or slanted by dogmatic considerations from reformation or counter-reformation theology, it is seldom informed by a modern critical approach. Since we must assume that, in some cases at least, the preacher is aware of this, it would seem that he is reluctant to share his knowledge lest he should 'upset the faithful'. What kind of truth is this that is too dangerous to pass on? In fact, as everyone who studies Scripture in this way comes to see, what emerges carries far more conviction than fundamentalist accounts, which in the end are literally incredible.

I do not wish to claim more for the study of the Bible than it can give. I am certain that Christianity is a matter of life more than of knowledge, and stands or falls by how men act more than by what they believe. But of course it is distorting to separate the two like that. Tradition of an understanding plays an important role, and a central place must be accorded to the tradition of what is written in Scripture. The widespread misunderstanding that still exists today, by comparison with the consensus of scholarly opinion, is therefore very alarming.

2. *Reading in context*

Any passage of Scripture can reveal its meaning only when it is related to its historical background. This is the basis of any serious biblical criticism. It can be a rather complicated matter, since the passage may have a long history of adaptation to differing needs. There is also the unavoidable difficulty that the main knowledge of these historical contexts has to come from the Bible itself. This is because Israel was comparatively obscure, and so has left less mark on the larger world over the period than we might wish, and also because we have little written data until quite late other than in the Bible itself. We can use the results of archaeological discovery in Palestine, and we can use our growing knowledge of the life and thought-forms of cultures contemporary with Israel, but these remain secondary to the Bible itself.

Even with the utmost critical care, using evidence from all parts of Scripture, drawing on such things as the etymological study of lists of tribes and genealogies, there is therefore a risk of the arguments being somewhat circular. But there is no way out of this. The actual historical background to a passage is often very different from the apparent one, yet it is only through a critical study of the passage itself, together with many others just as misleading on their surface, that this emerges.

As a result of long collaboration between scholars, we now have a reasonably accurate picture of the changing background against which the Bible was written. It changed considerably over the period, from the semi-nomadic world of the patriarchs, through the conquest and feudal-style kingdom, to the long experience of being a conquered people under a series of world empires, accompanied always by dreams of revolt, until the end came under the Romans.

We also know a good deal about the complex way in which Israelite religion developed in response to this changing context. It was not, of course, a simple linear evolution. It went forward and regressed. It moved differently in different places – round various shrine centres in the early period, for instance, or in North and South under the kingdoms, in town and country at every time, and over the Greek world at the dispersal. There was a good deal of interaction between the lines of thought. The same is true, over a shorter period, of the rapid Christian expansion into the gentile world. New needs produced new responses, and new insight into the activity of God within history and its complex of human relationship. They still do.

To treat the Bible like this is obvious enough once we have learned to do it. It is the way we look at any literary or historical text. Yet the Bible is still so often treated differently, as though from beginning to end it was revealing, flatly and uniformly, one single eternal truth. People feel that because it is sacred it escapes normal human categories, just as they incline to the heresy that the humanity of Jesus is not quite like ours. The effect is shattering.

3. Chronology

Because biblical passages have to be related to their historical setting we cannot move a step without having a rough chronological picture in our heads. We would get an odd idea of Shakespeare if we thought he wrote *Love's Labour's Lost* after completing *The Tempest;* no odder than supposing Ezekiel wrote before Isaiah, or Thessalonians came after Colossians. The picture need only be roughly sketched; it is a mistake to get bogged down in the minutiae of dating. So many tables in books are confusing by their irrelevant detail. The one below is designed to give an overall idea in simple form.[1]

OLD TESTAMENT			NEW TESTAMENT		
Writings (approx. date of first versions)	Events and people BC		Writings (All dates approx. ? indicates very uncertain	Events and People AD	
	1800	?Abraham		10	
		?Jacob			
	1600			20	
		?Joseph			
	1400			30	Crucifixion
		?Moses, exodus			
					Paul
	1200				Missionary
		Conquest			expansion
		Judges		40	
		Saul	Thessalonians		
J	1000	David			
		Solomon	Galatians	50	
		Elijah	Corinthians		
	800		Romans		
E		Amos, Hosea, Isaiah			
Amos, Hosea	722	Fall of Samaria	Colossians	60	
Isaiah			Philippians		
D					
		Josiah,	Mark		Death of Paul
		Jeremiah, Ezekiel	? Q		
Judges-Kings	600/597	Deportations		70	Destruction of
	587/	2-Isaiah	?Ephesians		temple
		Return			
P		Ezra, Nehemiah			
			Luke-Acts	80	
Many psalms	400		?Hebrews ?Matthew		
Chronicles			?Revelation ?Timothy		
		Septuagint			
Wisdom				90	
writings	200				
Daniel		Maccabees	John		
	0			100	

A glance at this table shows that on the whole the writing by no means corresponds in date with the event it concerns. Paul's letters are an obvious exception, and some prophecies were probably recorded within a generation; the 'succession document' (2 Sam. 9-20, 1 Kg. 1-2) embedded in later writing, is thought to be nearly contemporary with its story. But J wrote centuries after the patriarchs, and the evangelists decades after the ministry of Jesus. In each case there was a period of oral tradition in all probabibility connected with the liturgy in which the stories were recounted, took shape and became connected together roughly as we have them.

Placing the OT and NT in parallel, even though the time-scale is so different, brings out the close similarity between the two processes. In each case the accounts have undergone this development by the community, and by the groups who committed them to writing, in order to express as clearly as possible what they believed to be the theological meanings of the events. There are no grounds in any part of the Bible to satisfy the positivist longing for 'factuality' – a blow-by-blow account of what occurred. Instead we are given understanding, which is more important.

4. Literary dependence

This was the first thing to be recognized when scientific biblical criticism began in the last century. The strands of writing in the first five books were picked out relatively easily, and it was realized that later writers were often consciously modifying earlier ones, as well as using new material from the oral tradition. Scholars saw that the evangelists had other writings, especially Mark, in front of them as they wrote, and modified these in conformity with their own theological purposes.

There is in later parts of the OT, and in the NT, considerable reference back to earlier events and patterns of writing, whose theological meaning is thereby continued with modifications in the later account. To recall one central example, the exodus formed a basic experience for Israel of the saving power of God in history. It lies behind the structure of second Isaiah's prophecy of the return from exile, and of Jesus's journey to Jerusalem, even of his passage from death to new life. Details of the story, especially in the Deuteronomic version, form a background pattern to more detailed later accounts, such as the temptations of Jesus in Luke and Matthew.

Sometimes there is an explicit citation, as often in Matthew; more often it is by allusion to a key-word or image, picked up more readily by the original readers than by most of us today, working as we do with translations that often paraphrase the

Hebrew or Greek text. Yet once the allusion is pointed out by scholars who know the language and methods of the authors, the truth of what is being said comes home to us — it must be so, we say.

5. The breakdown of the text into units

After the discovery of the literary strands came the recognition that these were by no means homogeneous but were made up of units of various lengths and possibly quite different pre-histories even when adjacent to one another in the edited version. The previous history might have been oral or literary. So incorporated in the J history are accounts of local gods, explanations of puzzling features in nature and culture, records of who owned land and wells, as well as ancestor stories ranging from folklore to the great covenant accounts. These have been woven together into a narrative with overall purposes related to Israel's history before Yahweh, seen as the one God.

Similarly a gospel is made up of the most various material from different traditions — parables, miracles, conflict stories, justifications of church customs, 'sayings of Jesus' from the hypothetical collection known as 'Q', and so on. In the course of transmission they may well have formed larger units before reaching their present position in a gospel. So for instance it seems likely that the passion story, which differs less than other material from gospel to gospel, existed as a single unit quite early on. Groups of parables are found linked by connecting key-words, probably for the convenience of the preacher. Even in Paul we find fragments of earlier material embedded in the text — hymns or creeds which may have been used in the liturgy common to him and his readers.

Sometimes it is possible to get behind the written material in this way, and so reach towards the early patriarchal communities or the first days of the Christian Church. At the same time this provides a check and a caution about accounts whose literary form is that of eye-witness to an earlier time, but are in fact shaped by later theological intentions. For example, the story of the conquest of Canaan in the earlier chapters of Joshua must be treated very cautiously, since it in no way agrees with the piece-meal conquest account of Judges 1; it reflects Deuteronomic theories of the holy wars of Yahweh. The early history of the Church in Acts is also somewhat suspect where it differs from Paul, shaped as it is by Luke's theological schema.

6. Editorial structures

At one time there was a tendency on the part of scholars to play down editorial creativity. It seemed sufficient to break the text into its units and explain these, without considering why they had been arranged into the particular patterns of the larger context. Today we realize that the editor (or a series of editors) played an important rôle in the construction of the whole. Naturally we cannot always be certain about this, especially where we have little idea about the sources used. But comparison with other accounts, examination of editorial link passages, recognition of characteristic theological emphases and so on, can tell us a good deal.

For example, the fact that the parallel northern history E seems never to have contained an equivalent to J's pre-history, now part of Gen. 1-11, leads us to suppose that the pre-history had a special rôle in expressing J's theology, not present to the sources available to him and E. By using mythological stories current in the Near East, he introduced a universal element into Israel's history under God; Yahweh ruled all mankind. Moreover the universal sinfulness of men, culminating in the Babel story, is matched by Yahweh's plan to save them through the faithfulness of Abraham. The name God gives him (Gen. 12: 2) is in deliberate contrast with the name men tried to seize at Babel (Gen. 11: 4).

Again, we can examine the work of the Deuteronomist editors who compiled the history running through Joshua, Samuel and Kings. Some sources, such as the 'succession document' and the cycle of tales about Elijah and Elisha were simply incorporated; others, such as the lost chronicles of the kings, frequently mentioned, may have been heavily selected from. We could not guess, without knowledge from outside sources, the importance of King Omri in the North, since the editors have almost eliminated him from the history. Their aim, among other things, is to attribute the decline and fall of the kingdoms to the somewhat anachronistic reason that the kings failed to concentrate worship at the central Jerusalem temple ('high-place' worship was considered orthodox by everyone in the earlier period covered by the history), and yet at the same time to show that despite this God would remain faithful to his promise to the house of David (2 Sam. 7: 12-16).

It is the same with the NT. The gospel editors are probably responsible for the Mosaic patterns into which their work is cast in various ways — so the baptism corresponds to the Sea of Reeds, the transfiguration to Sinai, and so on. Luke and Matthew arrange the material they incorporate into Mark in quite different ways. Matthew puts it in five 'discourses' that break the narrative (Moses traditionally had five books), while Luke puts it into the context of a single journey to Jerusalem (Lk. 9: 51 — 18: 14). Jerusalem is very important for him as the centre to which all converges before once more radiating out in Acts, and he conveys what he is about to do in the highly condensed editorial phrase at 9: 51: 'When the days drew near for him to be received up, he set his face to go to Jerusalem'.

7. Interpretation

Study of the author's methods goes a long way to clarifying the meaning of these ancient texts, constructed in a manner so different from any we would use. But a further barrier has still to be overcome. The Semitic languages and thought-forms that lie behind all these writings (even where the actual language is Greek) are very different from those of modern western men and women. In the past too much may have been made of this, in relation to outmoded anthropological ideas about 'the primitive mind', but the fact remains that we still have to interpret these texts from a very unfamiliar culture.'

Hebrew, for instance, is a language without tenses; only context determines whether present or future is in question, an important point when dealing with prophetic literature. Again Hebrew has a liking for concrete imagery. This can be over-emphasized, but it is still true that much more is conveyed about God through his activity in history than seemed natural to later theologians. The distinction between body and soul that we get from the Greeks was not common among the Hebrews, and when, late on in the OT, the idea of surviving death began to grow, it was in terms of personal resurrection, not the soul's immortality. The far greater significance of a person's name, the use of an individual to stand for a group, number symbolism (the declining ages of the patriarchs in the late P sections of Gen. 1-11, for instance, represents their increasing distance from God) — all this and much more can mislead us until we become familiar with it through experience. It is all part of the process of reading an ancient text as its authors meant it to be understood.

The fundamentalist will no doubt object that God could never have concealed his revelation from ordinary people in this complicated way. To those of us who feel less sure about knowing the mind of God there is no simple answer. But two points are worth making. First, that no one who has worked through the process of understanding Scripture by these methods will doubt that he or she has come closer to the truth. So many difficulties and puzzles will have been cleared away, together with the specious solutions that were used to account for them in the past.

Second, a lot of the difficulty arises from the fact that we start the process too late in life. Our childhood approach to the Bible has usually been such a childish one that we have an unnecessary amount of lumber to get rid of before we can start. If the modern approach to the Bible were introduced to children from the start, it would be as natural to them as the literal approach seems to be now, and it would have the advantage that the contents would reveal their true fascination to young people, rather than appearing as a collection of improbable moral tales.

8. Application

The familiar question, 'Why bother to read this ancient document today?' is clearly not one that can be answered here in full. The reason is that its single form falsely conveys the idea that there should be a single answer, whereas bible study has had a number of very different functions in Christian communities in every age. Those who have begun to look at the text with fresh eyes will find it affecting their prayers, their church-going, their everyday lives in innumerable ways. Study groups, especially in the recent past, were often urged to make a specific application of their conclusions to the contemporary situation, so something needs to be said about this question of application.

A typical question, in a student bible-reading guide, was 'What does Ephesians have to say to us about university chaplaincies?' I hope it is quite clear that the only possible answer is: 'Nothing whatever, since such matters were completely remote from the author's mind.' Similarly we have to resist the assumption that the best guide to conduct is to work out what Jesus would have done in the situation. We can never know. Such an approach is akin to the view that in Scripture we are being given factual history, or a psychological insight into the minds of the characters.

We must be far more reluctant to make any direct transition between the ancient text and the modern situation. The Bible itself indicates a better procedure. As times changed the biblical authors did not try to 'apply' their sources, they rewrote them, retaining what they needed of the original. To be stuck in the past was more often the subject of condemnation than of praise (cf Jer. 7: 4). I believe that our task today is to study the texts as critically as we can, and to respond to their message, just as we learn (also with the help of the critic) to respond to poems and novels and music. The experience needs no further justification.

But something more comes from it, though we might find it hard to specify exactly how. We begin to write our own modern texts; not (though this may be included) a poem or novel or a new religion, but a life. In terms that are less metaphorical, we learn to act in our human world in ways that are more sensitively human. It is this that the Christian Church has always tried to do, admittedly without conspicuous success. The continuous reading of Scripture down the years has surely played its part in what success there has been, but I doubt if it could be spelled out exactly how. 'Application' does take place, but not in too literal a way.

Note

1. A more detailed account of the chronology of the OT will be found in the chapter on 'The OT in the history of Israel' (pp. 73-85).

Inspiration and revelation

BERNARD P. ROBINSON

'This is the word (or, the gospel) of the Lord'. In what sense is, say, a passage about Jacob from the book of Genesis or a genealogy from the book of Chronicles – neither of which is likely to be factually very accurate – God's word? Again, are all parts of Scripture equally God's word, the fulmination of a minor prophet against one of Israel's inveterate foes as much as an excerpt from the Sermon on the Mount? Further, if the true light illuminates every man (Jn 1: 9) at a supernatural, salvific, not merely a 'natural' level, as seems to follow from the teaching of Vatican II that 'the Holy Spirit offers everybody the possibility of sharing, in some way known to God' in the salvific work of Christ *(Lumen Gentium* 22), how is God's revelation of himself in Scripture to be related to this universal revelation? And why was there a sort of cut-off point, some time around the end of the first century AD, to the operation of God's scriptural inspiration and revelation? In what follows, I shall be trying to show the sort of answers to such questions that a Roman Catholic who seeks to hold fast to the faith delivered once for all to the saints (Jude 3) but is also responsive to the insights of biblical research can offer in the early nineteen-eighties. I shall consider the two concepts of inspiration and revelation separately, although they are closely related.

1. Inspiration

Present-day thinking about biblical inspiration needs to be seen against the background of the history of the development of Catholic attitudes to biblical criticism over the last century.

Biblical criticism, that is to say the application to the interpretation of the Bible of the scholarly disciplines used in secular academic research, dates effectively from the nineteenth century, and was originally a predominantly Protestant pursuit. In 1893 Pope Leo XIII felt constrained while calling on

Catholics to make more use of the Bible, to warn them against the new way of studying it. This 'higher criticism' (so called to distinguish it from textual criticism), in its attempt 'to judge the origin, integrity and authority of each book from internal indications alone', would not, Leo asserted, throw any real light on the Bible, but would only eliminate from Scripture 'everything that is outside the natural order' and 'give rise to disagreement and dissension' (encyclical *Providentissimus Deus*). To treat holy Writ like any other book was to ignore the fact that, as Trent and Vatican I had taught, it had God for its author. The human writers were 'instruments' of the Holy Spirit. The Pope quoted Augustine and Gregory the Great as teaching that Scripture was 'dictated' by God, and concluded that the idea that any error could be present was unthinkable, although he allowed, as indeed had some of the Fathers, that in scientific matters the Holy Spirit accommodated himself to the ideas current at the time of writing even if these lacked scientific accuracy. Sadly negative as Pope Leo's judgment must now seem on a study that has in the event brought the Bible alive for countless thousands of men and women, one must set it in its historical context. Some of the biblical critics must have seemed to the church authorities more anxious to demonstrate their own ingenuity in the analysis and exposition of biblical material than to serve the Gospel. Thus in the eighteen-thirties and forties the view had emerged in Tübingen that the story in Acts 8 of Simon Magus' offer of money to Peter and John in order to buy for himself the power to confer the Holy Spirit was only a covert attack on Paul and his collection for the poor churches. In general, many scholars seemed keen to find as little historicity in biblical narratives as possible: they were far more reluctant to allow Genesis, the gospels or Acts to be historical than ancient historians were the secular texts that they studied. Given the conception of inspiration with which the church authorities had grown up, a conception of 'verbal' or 'literal' inspiration which survives today only among fundamentalists, it is small matter for surprise that Pope Leo took fright at the excesses of some of the critics and slammed the door on the whole notion of the historico-critical study of Scripture. His aim was to encourage the study of the Bible, but he forbade Catholic scholars the chief means for them to do this effectively.

The hostility to biblical criticism shown by Leo XIII persisted in the Church of Rome for half a century. During the pontificate of Pius X, 1903-14, the 'Modernists' who *inter alia* flirted with biblical criticism were roundly condemned, and the Pontifical Biblical Commission began a decade (1905-15) of oracular judgments alerting the faithful to the danger of such notions as that Moses did not write the Pentateuch (1906), that the fourth evangelist was not John son of Zebedee (1907), that Isaiah 1-66 was not a literary unity (1908), that Mark's gospel might have been written before Matthew's (1911), and that Paul might not have written the pastoral epistles to Timothy and Titus (1913). In 1920, Pius X's successor, Benedict XV, echoed in his encyclical *Spiritus Paraclitus* the teachings of *Providentissimus Deus* and re-asserted the historicity of biblical narratives, in particular those of the fourth gospel: the gospels, according to Benedict, contain 'intact and unchanged' the sayings and actions of Christ with no admixture of the thinking of a later generation.

The revolution in Catholic attitudes came with the publication in 1943 (reputedly at the instigation of Cardinal Bea) of Pius XII's great encyclical *Divino Afflante Spiritu,* in which he emphasized the need to study the literary forms in use at the time of the composition of the biblical books. 'To express what they had in mind the ancients of the East did not always use the same forms and expressions as we use today; they used those which were current among the people of their own time and place: and what these were the exegete cannot determine *a priori,* but only from a careful study of ancient oriental literature' (39). 'The sacred books' he added, 'need not exclude any of the forms of expression which were commonly used in human speech by the ancient peoples, especially of the East, to convey their meanings, so long as they are in no way incompatible with God's sanctity and truth' (41). This teaching had the liberating effect that henceforth it was no longer obligatory to suppose that everything in the Bible that was expressed in the form of a third person account was intended as history. Also it allowed for the possibility of the Pentateuch and other passages of Scripture being composite works incorporating at the same points several variant and partly contradictory accounts, if this could be shown to be consistent with ancient ways of writing. Again, if pseudonymity was a literary convention in Israel, the possibility could not be excluded that books such as the pastoral epistles were not the work of the men whose names they bore.

From 1943, Catholic scholars were free to practise, both on their own and in co-operation with non-Catholics, the historico-critical method which Leo XIII had proscribed, as also the newer form critical method.[1] They were still obliged to accept the idea of inerrancy, but it was widely accepted opinion that it was the *assertions* of the human author that were preserved from error, and that not everything which an author wrote was intended as an 'assertion'. Within a decade, scholars felt free to state, what most of their Protestant counterparts had been saying for upwards of half a century, that Gen. 1-11 does not purport to retail history (the Biblical Commission itself stated as much in a letter to Cardinal Suhard in 1948), that the first gospel was that of Mark, that the three synoptic gospels derived from two sources (Mark and the collection of Jesus' sayings known to scholars as Q), that the pastorals were non-Pauline, and such like notions which had been actively discouraged by Pius X's commission. The commission of Pius XII in 1955 legitimated such opinions through a declaration that, where faith and morals were not at issue, scholars had 'complete freedom' to dissent from the judgments of 1905-15.

In 1964 Benedict XV's simplistic view that the gospels contain 'intact and unchanged' the words and deeds of Jesus was, in effect, set aside by the Biblical Commission in an *Instruction on the Historical Truth of the Gospels,* which came to terms with the findings of the historico-critical method, form criticism and redaction criticism.[2] The instruction allows, for example, that the apostles in preaching the Gospel preached Jesus in terms influenced by their newly-acquired recognition of his divinity, and that the apostles sought to give their listeners, and evangelists their readers, a selection of Jesus's deeds and sayings which did not always follow their chronological order in Jesus's life and which, in the case of the sayings, was often 'not literal but different', in that the sayings were handed on in a form that had undergone re-interpretation according to the needs of the listeners and readers. 'The doctrine and life of Jesus were not simply reported for the sole purpose of being remembered', the commission says, 'but were "preached" so as to offer the Church a basis of faith and morals.' It was not possible to get at what the sacred writers intended and actually said without recourse to 'the laudable achievements of recent research'.

The Vatican II constitution on revelation, *Dei Verbum,* of 1965, makes interesting reading alongside *Providentissimus Deus.* The council fathers retain the key notions of Leo XIII – Scripture is inspired by God and has God for its author – but they elevate the importance of the human writers, whom they assert to be not inert tools in God's hands but 'true authors' (11), and they treat biblical criticism as an ally rather than an enemy. They emphasize too the fact that Scripture uses many different literary forms, and they adopt the formula 'all that the inspired authors or sacred writers assert is to be regarded as asserted by the Holy Spirit' *(ibid.),* a phrase quite compatible, in the view of most Catholic critics, with the notion of the presence of historical error in Scripture. The concept of inerrancy has not been dropped, but it occurs in what may well be an intentionally ambiguous sentence: 'the books of Scripture teach certainly, faithfully and without error the truth that God for our salvation willed to be recorded in holy Writ' *(ibid.).* This, as the American Catholic exegete Raymond Brown has pointed out, 'has made it possible to restrict inerrancy to the essential religious affirmations of a biblical book made for the value of our salvation'.[3] At the same time as giving a seal of approval to biblical criticism (and to ecumenical co-operation in the biblical field: *Dei Verbum,* 22) church pronouncements have stressed that the Bible is the Church's book. This does not mean that the Church is superior to the Bible, nor that the authority of the Bible derives from that of the Church. What it does mean is that the Bible was written, under God's direction, by members of the people of God for use by the people of God, and that the Church 'has the divine commission and the office of preserving and explaining the Word of God' *(Dei Verbum,* 12). This notion is important since it distinguishes the Catholic viewpoint from that of the sort of critic who regards scholars as having a proprietary right to expound the Bible without reference to any ecclesiastical teaching authority.

The new attitude of the Catholic Church to biblical criticism is clearly reflected in the writings of Catholic scholars. A

Catholic today no longer begins with a presumption that, for example, the patriarchal narratives of the Acts of the Apostles are totally reliable historical records. He is quite likely to take the view that the authors did not intend to write scientific history, and to find their assertions to lie in the area of theology rather than of historiography. Or he may take the line that the author is indeed setting out to tell things as they actually were but that the result is an admixture of fact and error, as with all historians, since although the Holy Spirit protects the religious message, he does not underwrite inessential details in the story. After all, Leo XIII himself quotes St Augustine to the effect that 'the Holy Spirit did not intend to teach men things in no way profitable to salvation', and this principle, if valid, can surely be applied to details of history as much as to the physical sciences. If God allowed the human writers to speak as if the Ptolemaic cosmology were true, why should he not have allowed St Luke to have erred, as the evidence strongly suggests that he did, on the dating of Quirinius' census (Lk. 2: 2)?

Most Catholic critics would also say that although the human author 'wrote all that God willed and only what he willed' *(Dei Verbum,* 11), with the implication that all biblical books have something of God's salvific truth to teach the reader, the context within which an individual book or passage testifies to God's truth is the Bible as a whole. Even when it is making theological judgments, absolute truth cannot be predicated of an individual passage. God does not guarantee the truth of the denial of rewards and punishments after death that we find in many OT passages (eg, Job 14: 7-22, Ps. 88: 10, 115: 17) nor the cynicism of Ecclesiastes. Each book or passage has its contribution to make and has its place within the single whole, but as Rahner says *(Foundations,* p. 376): 'We must read every individual text within the context of this single whole in order to understand its true meaning correctly. Only *then* can it be understood in its real meaning, and only then can it really be grasped as "true".' This relativism, so to call it, in respect of separate parts of the Bible goes beyond what is stated about Scripture in any church definition or declaration but it seems sound enough in the light of what we know about the nature of truth and of human speech; it explains — rather than, as was not unknown in the past, explains away — a number of 'awkward' passages in the Bible;

and it is fully consonant with what is said in a pronouncement *(Mysterium Ecclesiae,* 1973) of the Congregation of Doctrine about a related subject, namely dogma. This states that church definitions express the truth in an historically limited and conditioned way and may later need to be rephrased or developed. If this is so, it is reasonable to suppose that the human authors of Scripture too see through a glass darkly and their assertions are historically conditioned.

In speaking of the 'inspiration' of the human authors, the Church does not mean to imply that the authors were always, or even normally, conscious of the work of the Spirit in them. They ordinarily had to work for their information and they acquired their ideas and data by the ordinary human means. But their writing was part of a divine master plan: they were being used by God for a greater purpose than they were aware of, and if necessary he will have prevented them from writing anything that would not ultimately subserve that end. Whether inspiration operated chiefly in a directional way (God moving the authors to inform themselves and to write) or whether a degree of illumination of their judgments was also involved (as to the ideas to be communicated and/or the ways in which this was to be done) is disputed. Scripture itself gives little away on this point.[4]

After his reunion and reconciliation with his brothers, Joseph is said to have told them, speaking of the time when they had sold him into slavery: 'You intended evil towards me, but God intended it for good' (Gen. 50: 20). The idea found here, that a human action can have divine purpose that differs from the purpose of the human being performing the action, has broad implications for biblical exegesis. It means, for example, that apart from the intention of the human writer of a passage (its 'literal sense') there is always a divine intention involved and the divine intention may not be identical with the human author's. This divine intention constitutes what is called the 'spiritual sense' of a passage. Thus in the scheme of the divine purpose the story of the exodus from Egypt may have a meaning as an anticipation, a foreshadowing, a 'type' of the 'paschal' work of Christ. Similarly, predictions that the throne of the Davidic monarchy would last for ever (eg 2 Sam. 7: 12-3), or that a new Davidic king woud arise from Bethlehem (Mic. 5: 2), or Second

Isaiah's description of the Servant of Yahweh, can be seen as intended by God, through a *sensus plenior* (a 'fuller sense', a specific kind of spiritual sense) to have a future reference to Christ not intended by the human author. In the past the idea of spiritual senses was often overworked and spiritual senses were sometimes attributed to passages *in place of* the literal sense, because the evident literal sense was hard to square with the 'hot line' ideas of inspiration current at the time. The thinking today on the spiritual sense is that it is secondary to, and can never replace, the literal sense ('interpreters should bear in mind that their chief aim must be to discern and determine what is known as the literal sense': *Divino Afflante Spiritu,* 28), and that where there is a spiritual sense that is to be distinguished from the literal it will be evident from the NT and/or church tradition.

2. Revelation

How is all that I have said above to be related to the concept of revelation? If by revelation one means God's disclosure of information to which man has no natural access, the inspiration of Scripture – except perhaps so far as the spiritual sense is concerned – has little to do with it, since normally, as we have seen, the human authors arrived at their ideas and information in natural ways. In another sense of the word revelation, however, biblical inspiration has everything to do with it. The Bible is about God's self-disclosure, his revelation of himself, and it is for this very purpose that he uses the human authors.

But surely God discloses himself all the while and through everything that he does. What, then, is so special about the scriptural revelation?[5] God does indeed communicate himself, on a supernatural not just a natural level, to all men at all times, and countless men and women have responded to this salvific encounter. Many, indeed, have not only experienced God's grace but have been able to account for God's gracious dealings with themselves and other human beings. The OT and NT are such accounts, with much in common with others, but differing from them in that they are divinely authorized as official, definitive, normative accounts. But why are these two collections of books given this special rôle? Because of their relationship to the one and only instance of the self-disclosure of God that was complete and unqualified, namely the incarnation. Let us now see how this applies to each of the two Testaments.

The NT is perhaps best understood as an articulation of the apostolic Church's experience of the Christ-event. It was of the essence of an apostle that he should witness to his experience of the historical Jesus's life, death and resurrection (Acts 1: 21-2), which is why the supply of apostles soon ran out and they were not replaced. Significantly, the apostles are twice referred to in the New Testament (Eph. 2: 20, Rev. 21: 14 and 19) as a 'foundation'. A foundation-stone is laid once and for all, and the whole building rises up on it, a point made by Paul in 1 Cor. 3: 10-7, where the foundation in question is Christ himself. The apostles were not just the first bishops, there was something unique, unrepeatable and normative about them that derived from their special relationship to Christ. They had handled the Word of Life, they had seen his glory, and they knew God's truth not in the form of a set of propositions, but as an experience, a 'master-vision' in Newman's phrase. This experience they left behind in a set of texts (diverse in nature — gospel accounts, occasional letters, a series of visions and an account of some of their own endeavours — the better to express the many-sidedness of their experience), a set of texts that constitutes an authorized and official version of their experience of the one total divine self-communication.

What, then, of the OT? The authority of the OT does not derive merely from the fact that members of the people of Israel encountered God in situations of disclosure and grace and expressed this in writing, for the same could be said of other nations too. If the OT is the Word of God in a sense that the Vedas are not, it must be by virtue of its relationship to the Christ-event. The apostolic Church recognized the OT as 'God-breathed' because of its relationship to the Christ-event. The OT is the articulation of the faith and experience of a people whose encounter with God culminated in the definitive encounter, the encounter different in kind and not merely in degree from all other encounters. As Rahner puts it (*Foundations,* p. 168), it is only in view of Christ that the OT has any special significance for us, and 'it can really have a religious meaning for us only as the most immediate and proximate pre-history of Christ himself, and it is only in this way that it can be our own history of revelation and our own tradition'. The Christian accepts the OT as God's word not because the Jews canonized it – in fact, the Church's canonization of it may well precede the Synagogue's (*Jerome Bible Commentary* 67:15), and in any case the Catholic Church accepts a wider canon than does Judaism – but because it is part of the normative apostolic experience that the OT is integral to the Christ-event.

Let us push this line of thinking a little further.[6] The NT is clear that the Christian community is the 'Israel of God' (Gal. 6: 16). In other words, the story of Israel and the story of the Church constitute one story. It is a story of how a people learnt of God in and through the vicissitudes of history, now as an ethnically heterogeneous collection of desert wanderers, now as a loosely-knit association of tribes, now as a nation-state, now as a band of homeless exiles, now as a people of a book, and eventually as a people that is no people but a Church. On the way, this people frequently lost one identity and found a new one, and through this process of finding life by losing it the people was constantly reborn to new forms of awareness of God as gracious, loving and free.[7] This experience Israel articulated in the writing of the OT; in fact, the writing of many of the books was an actual stage in the process of this rebirth. The apostolic Church, in accepting the OT as inspired, was confessing that the articulation of experience that it comprised was underwritten by God as an authentic part of the process whereby Israel became the Church by virtue of the Christ-event.

A word or two should perhaps be said here about the relation of Scripture to tradition. The theory was much in vogue at one time that these two constituted two separate 'sources of revelation'. St Thomas More very clearly expressed this view when he wrote that 'the traditions of God are partly inserted in the scriptures themselves, partly transmitted by the living word of God'. This is as much as to say that the revelation of God contained in Scripture is incomplete and needs to be supplemented by oral traditions handed down to us from the time of the apostles. This 'two-source theory' seems to have originated in the fourteenth century. The Council of Trent was asked to endorse it but declined to do so, although the council fathers' preferred formulation (that God's truth is contained 'in written books and unwritten traditions'; the rejected formula had 'partly in written books, partly in unwritten traditions') does not exclude it, nor does that of Vatican II. There is, I think, little doubt that the view expressed at Trent by the General of the Servites, 'I consider that all evangelical truth is in Scripture', is more representative than that of More of the standpoint both of the church Fathers and of present-day theologians. Certainly the proposition that the doctrines of the immaculate conception and the assumption (to take two of the more difficult doctrines to 'prove' from Scripture) were taught explicitly in an oral form by the apostles and were handed down, generation after generation, as part of the deposit of faith until they were defined as dogma in modern times raises even more problems than the alternative idea that those doctrines are in some way implicitly contained in Scripture. It is sometimes said, however, that it is not possible to dispense entirely with the concept of supplementary apostolic traditions since the knowledge of what books constitute Scripture could only have come to the Church in this way. But if there had been an unwritten apostolic tradition on this subject, why was the early Church at first uncertain about the canonicity of Revelation, Hermas and Barnabas? Is it not rather the case that in writing the books of the NT the Church articulated its experience of the Christ-event, and having written them it recognized them, after some reflection, to be the word of God because it could discern in them a reflection of that experience that it continued to enjoy, in a sacramental form, in its daily life?

3. Conclusion

When, then, we say after a scripture reading, 'This is the word of the Lord', we do not mean that the passage was verbally inspired or dictated by God. We recognize that it was written by a man, or men, who probably had to work things out in the ways that all human writers do. We accept that any statement it makes about science or history may contain inaccuracies, and that even its religious affirmations will be historically-conditioned and will need to be read in conjunction with other passages. We are conscious that the excerpt in question may well be using literary forms that have no exact literary counterpart and that specialist knowledge may need to be called upon if we are to discover what the author is trying to say. We take into account also, of course, the possibility that the words read may not accord perfectly with the text that God inspired, either because of the fallibility of the translator or because the transmission of the original text has been defective. So much for what we are *not* affirming. What we are affirming, in saying 'This is the word of the Lord', is that there was a divine impulse behind the writing of the passage, that we are in a position to read this passage because God willed us to have it, and that if it is read in the context of God's whole strategy of inspiration, namely his gift of Scripture in its totality, it has the power to make us wise unto salvation through the faith which is in Christ Jesus (2 Tim. 3: 15).

Notes

1. Form criticism is concerned with the transmission of material in the pre-literary stage, and the different forms or categories in which the various traditions were handed down according to the function that each had in the life of the community (its *Sitz im Leben,* 'life-setting').
2. Redaction criticism, the newest discipline of the three, examines the work of the writers of the various books of the Bible in shaping and selecting the traditions, oral and written, that reached them. In particular it focusses on the theological ideas of the writers which they sought to express through their work as authors.
3. R.E. Brown, *Biblical Reflections. . .*, p. 115 (see Further reading).
4. *Jerome Bible Commentary* 66: 42-57 (see Further reading).
5. I find Karl Rahner particularly helpful on this point, and the answer I offer owes much to my reading of the books of his listed in the bibliography.
6. In this paragraph, I am indebted to Timothy Radcliffe, OP, for insights gained from a recent article of his (details in Further reading).
7. I do not mean, however, that Israel's history saw a linear progression of insight into the nature of God, so that he was better understood in the time of Jeremiah than in that of Solomon, and better understood in the time of Malachi than in that of Jeremiah.

Ecclesial authority and biblical interpretation

TIMOTHY RADCLIFFE, OP

On 13 December 1979 Edward Schillebeeckx, the Dominican theologian from Nijmegen, arrived at the headquarters of the Congregation for the Doctrine of Faith in Rome for what were politely called 'conversations' about the orthodoxy of his book *Jesus, an Experiment in Christology.*[1] Five days later the same Congregation declared that the Swiss theologian Hans Küng 'can no longer be considered as a Catholic theologian nor function as such in a teaching role.' In both cases what was at issue was the relationship between ecclesial authority and the interpretation of the Bible. Everyone would agree that not *every* interpretation of Scripture is acceptable. If the Church is a community of faith then it must be able, in the end, to define itself as such through the exclusion of some interpretations. For example a theologian who maintained that Jesus never existed or that the resurrection was an invention of the early Church would, *de facto,* have put himself outside the community of the Church and the Church would be obliged publicly to recognize this fact. But the question remains: Who is to decide what is an unorthodox reading of the Bible and how is a decision to be reached? We must honestly admit that these are issues which currently divide the Church.

The Congregation for the Doctrine of Faith is the body which has the official mandate to investigate alleged departures from orthodoxy. It used to be called The Holy Office until Paul VI, in 1965, decided to change its name, revise its procedures and give it a more constructive role. It seemed then that the days of heresy hunts were over. There is a widespread lack of confidence in the ability of this body to perform its task of maintaining the Church in the truth. It has made too many mistakes in the past. Often it seems incapable of discerning the difference between the new and the unorthodox. It represents an understanding of the relationship between ecclesial authority and theology that has been called into question. But to understand the crisis of authority in the Church, faced with the return to the Bible by theologians like Schillebeeckx, we must first glance at the history of the Church during the last century and a half.

In 1847 the British archaeologist Layard discovered Assurbanipal's library near Niniveh. In the following year Pius IX was forced to flee from Rome, an event that transformed him from being an open-minded and liberal pope into a fierce conservative, determined to strengthen the fortress of the Church against the Modern World. It is true that Pius was not chased out by irate archaeologists but by revolutionaries, but the two events are not unrelated. Fergus Kerr has said: 'The single most revolutionary idea of the nineteenth century (it certainly bore fruit in Marxism) is that meaning and truth are, to some extent at least, relative to the society, or to the historical perspective, in which they are affirmed or presumed.'[2] The French revolution had shown that political structures are not immutable. The archaeologists toiling away in the Middle East showed that the way that people think and perceive the world can change dramatically, and that we cannot understand the Bible as if it had dropped word for word from heaven, but as the product of individuals whose ways of thinking were formed by civilizations very different from our own. In 1872, for example, George Smith translated an Assyrian version of the story of the Flood that was very close to the biblical account. The reactions of the Church to political revolution and to this discovery of the ways in which the biblical texts are culturally relative were intimately related. It had to defend itself as an eternal and unchangeable society in possession of eternal and immutable truths that have come direct from God. In 1864 Pius declared in the *Syllabus Errorum* that it was anathema to say that 'the Roman Pontiff can and should reconcile himself with, and accommodate himself to, progress, liberalism, and modern civilization'.[3] The declaration of papal infallibility was intended to support the Church's claim to be the guardian of the sole, true and unchangeable interpretation of the Bible, and the grand opponent of political revolution for, as Mgr Nardi said: 'he who believes in a Pope believes in God, and he who believes in God would never conspire to overthrow a government'.[4]

The accession of Leo XIII in 1878 seemed to promise a more open and liberal Church. He even opened the Vatican Library to non-Catholic historians. There was a renaissance of Catholic biblical studies. In 1890 Lagrange, a French Dominican, founded the *Ecole pratique d'études bibliques* in Jerusalem which, two years later, started to publish the *Revue biblique*. In 1891 the Abbé Vigouroux started publication of the *Dictionnaire de la Bible* though this was less enlightened and, for example, gave the same amount of space to the article on *foi* (faith) as it did to the following entry on *foie* (liver). In 1895 it was followed by the *Biblische Studien* from Freiburg. Catholic scholars nervously returned to the Bible and tried to take stock of the results of the century's historical research and of the more adventurous Protestant exegesis. In 1893 Leo published *Providentissimus Deus* which encouraged biblical scholarship, admitted that we should not look for scientific information in the texts of Genesis, allowed the study of non-Catholic scholars, even though they know only 'the bark of Sacred Scripture and never reach its pith'.[5] But this new scholarship must not challenge the Church's claim to be the sole and true interpreter of the Bible, for in matters of faith and morals, 'that is to be considered the true sense of Holy Scripture which has been held and is held by our Holy Mother the Church, whose place it is to judge of the true sense and interpretation of the Scriptures; and therefore none should interpret Holy Scripture in any other way or contrary to the unanimous opinions of the Fathers'.[6]

The truth was that Leo could welcome the new biblical scholarship only because of his supreme confidence that the Church already knew, in all essentials, what the Bible said. All that one could expect was clarification. And the Church possessed, in neo-scholasticism, a petrified nineteenth-century version of the philosophy and theology of Aquinas, the *philosophia perennis* and a theological system that was not time-bound, a conceptual system as perfect as man could devise. Neo-scholasticism was the Church's intellectual fortress against the threat of historical relativism, and one of Leo's first acts had been, in *Aeterni Patris,* to make its study mandatory throughout the Church.

This theological system was based on the assumption that revelation was the divine communication of a number of true propositions. These propositions, extracted from the Bible, provided theologians with the axioms for a process of deductive reasoning that was the only valid theological method. Like its rival, science, it claimed to lead the mind of man, darkened by sin and ignorance, to objective truth. Daly says: 'The truths revealed were eternal and immutable but they subsisted in the flux of history untouched by its vagaries and particularities. The massive objectivity of this system reduced the role of the historian to one of simple communicator. Whatever interpretation was needed would be provided by a divinely guided magisterium. The theologian, whose task it was to deal speculatively with revealed truths, needed no historical skills or training for the adequate performance of that task. Dogma, not history, provided him with the material necessary for the pursuit of his craft; and a stern magisterium was there to see that he reached the correct conclusions'.[7] So there was relative peace during Leo's pontificate, since the dogmatic theologians considered the new biblical scholarship to be of no fundamental significance, and the biblical exegetes mostly shied away from considering the theological consequences of their new understanding of the Bible.

In 1900 the German Protestant Harnack published *Das Wesen des Christentums,* in which he maintained that there was a radical discontinuity between the simple message of Jesus, which proclaimed the coming of the kingdom and our relationship to God the Father, and the theology of the Church. Hellenistic philosophy, especially, had led the Church to betray the Gospel. Two years later a French priest, Alfred Loisy, defended the Church in *L'Evangile et l'Eglise*. He accepted there was a discontinuity, but believed that it was inevitable and necessary if the Gospel was to go on being preached. Continuity is given not in the possession of a number of eternally true propositions but in a renewed encounter with God which the Church's teachings make possible. 'Dogmas are symbolic utterances designed to strike answering chords in the human spirit.'[8] There are no eternal truths for 'truth. . . is no more immutable than man himself. It evolves with him, in him, by him; but that does not prevent its being truth for him. . .'[9]

When the Vatican finally understood what Loisy was saying it reacted with hysteria. In 1907 Pius X published *Lamentabili Sane Exitu,* which condemned 65 propositions, of which Loisy was the author of 53. Even the mode of attack is significant since it was precisely a propositional concept of truth that Loisy was qustioning. It rejected any suggestion that Scripture was not objectively true, that the Church's interpretation of the Bible was open to correction or that there was any discontinuity in the Church's teaching throughout its history. So, for example, it condemned the proposition that: 'The chief articles of the Apostles' Creed did not have the same sense for the Christians of the first ages as they have for the Christians of our time' (no. 62). The Pontificial Biblical Commission, founded by Leo in 1902, issued a series of directives affirming the Mosaic authorship of the Pentateuch (against the view that it was, as a French exegete put it, '*une mosaïque de textes*'), the apostle John's authorship of the gospel of that name, the substantial historical truth of the first three chapters of Genesis and the literal historical truth of the others, etc. It is paradoxical that the Church had to defend the authority of its official neo-scholastic theology by asserting the historical accuracy of Scripture, while asserting that this claim was not open to historical investigation. Furthermore it defended the authority of the Church by claiming that the Church had done no more than clarify what was there from the beginning, while Loisy, who believed that he was legitimizing the Church's reformulation of the Gospel, was seen as undermining the Church's authority.

Two months after *Lamentabili* came the encyclical *Pascendi Dominici Gregis.* This was a more reasoned, coherent analysis and refutation of the new heresy of 'Modernism'. There was no such systematic heresy but it had to be invented if it was to be disproved by a strictly logical theology like neo-scholasticism. This lack of system is identified as 'one of the cleverest devices of the Modernists. . . so as to make it appear as if their minds were in doubt or hesitation, whereas in reality they are quite fixed and steadfast'.[10] Their opponents agreed that the source of all the 'modernist' errors was Kant. It was Kant who had taught them to distrust any concept of objective truth and to appeal to experience and the will rather than trusting in the intellect. It was *il veleno kantiano* – the Kantian poison. Pius X called it the *'mal franchese* of the Church', a euphemism for venereal disease. To the Roman theologians of the time there seemed only the choice between Aquinas, and the possibility of hanging on to eternal and immutable truths, and Kant, which led one to subjectivism and relativism and the impossibility of a revelation that was given once and for all. 'To the cry. . . "Back to Kant" let us anwer defiantly with the cry of Leo XIII, repeated by Pius X, "Back to Thomas".'[11]

George Tyrrell, one of the accused, complained that they were being condemned not for not being Catholics but for not being scholastics. That is true, but most theologians could have seen no other way of hanging on to 'the deposit of faith'. But the severity of the reaction to 'Modernism' frightened theologians and biblical scholars away from even attempting to think their way before this alternative of either an immutable ahistorical propositional truth or historical relativism. Any attempt to take historical criticism of the Bible seriously led to suspicions of heresy. An unofficial and secret society, *La Sapinière,* was formed to track down teachers infected with 'Modernism', until it was formally censured by Benedict XV in 1914. It even invented its own coded language, referring to the Pope as *'Maman'* and the bishops as *'tantes'*. It was a hard time for serious scholars like Lagrange, who was accused of dishonouring 'the white wool of St Dominic' which 'he daily profaned with his sacrilegious, sophisticated piety.'[12]

The first significant sign of a thaw in the attitudes of the church authorities was with the publication of *Divino Afflante Spiritu* by Pius XII in 1943. It recognized that any interpretation of the Bible must take seriously the particular literary forms that were employed at the time of its composition. We must discover who the author was and how he thought if we are to understand what the text means. This encyclical has been greeted as the 'Magna Carta' of Catholic biblical scholarship and as a charter of freedom. And so it was, but it is clear that scholars were to receive this new liberty only for a defensive purpose, rather than to open the Church to new interpretations of the Bible. We must pursue new ways of showing that the Bible is, as the Church has always taught, true. By these new analyses 'confidence in the authority and historical truth of the Bible which, in the face of so many attacks had in some minds been partially shaken, has now among Catholics been wholly restored'.[13]. It is clear from *Humani Generis,* 1950, that neo-scholasticism was to remain the sole guardian and test for orthodoxy. It vigorously attacks the 'hot-headed supporters of appeasement' with the modern world and those with 'an unwholsesome itch for modernity'. Thomist philosophy is founded on 'those principles of thought which impose themselves, in their own right, on the human mind' (para. 17).[14] Thomas' teaching 'seems to chime in, by a kind of pre-established harmony, with divine revelation — no surer way to safeguard the first principles of the faith, and turn the results of later healthy developments to good advantage' (para. 18). Unless we retain this system, we shall be caught up in relativism: 'the whole of dogma would thus become no better than a reed shaken by the wind' (para. 17). The old fears were there but the modern world could not be held at bay for much longer. In 1955 the Pontifical Biblical Commission wrote that its directives issued during the Modernist crisis could no longer be considered binding, except where they concerned matters of faith or morals.

The original draft document on revelation was thrown out by the second Vatican Council in November 1962. Three years later it passed the Constitution *Dei Verbum.* This represented the defeat of an exclusively neo-scholastic and propositional concept of truth. In the original draft the truth of Scripture had been understood in terms of the truth of all its propositions. In *Dei Verbum* it is a truth that is salvific, and our salvation lies in our fellowship with the Father in Christ. Bishop Butler has written: 'We are not in the schoolroom where a divine philosopher, himself unseen, dictates abstract ideas to pupils of high intelligence. We seem rather to be in the original paradise, where an infinitely loving God calls to us, accosts us as his friends, woos us to his friendship'.[15] Revelation is not in the first place the disclosure of a number of truths but God's self-gift in Christ. The tenor of the whole document is given in the second paragraph: 'In his goodness and wisdom, God chooses to reveal Himself and to make known to us the hidden purpose of His will by which through Christ, the Word made flesh, man has access to the Father in the Holy Spirit and comes to share in the Divine nature. Through this revelation, therefore, the invisible God out of the abundance of His love speaks to men as friends and lives among them, so that He may invite and take them into fellowship with Himself.'[16] This mystery of salvation is made known to us not only in what is said but in what God has done in salvation history and in Christ. It is a truth that Christ not only speaks but does and is, as the Word made flesh. 'By this revelation then, the deepest truth about God and the salvation of man is made clear to us in Christ, who is the Mediator and at the same time the fulness of all revelation' (para. 2).

This shift in the Church's understanding of truth clearly has important consequences for how one understands the relationship between the magisterium, i.e. the pope and the bishops, and the interpretation of the Bible. If the truth of Scripture is only given in fellowship with God in Christ then it is not a truth that we can be said simply to possess. It is a truth that we must move towards and reach out for. 'For, as the centuries succeed one another, the Church constantly moves toward the fulness of divine truth until the words of God reach their complete fulfilment in her' (para. 8). This is clearly a process that has not been completed. There is a fulness of truth that we do not yet behold. The Church therefore not only interprets Scripture but is judged by it. *Dei Verbum* explicitly recognizes that the Church is not above Scripture but serves it. But this open and dynamic concept of truth is counter-balanced by another understanding of the relationship between the magisterium and biblical interpretation that leaves the former very much in control. 'The task of authentically interpreting the word of God, whether written or handed on, has been entrusted exclusively (*soli*) to the living teaching office of the Church, whose authority is exercised in the name of Jesus Christ' (para.10). So at one and the same time the magisterium is presented as judged by a fulness of truth which it has not succeeded in articulating, and yet as the sole judge of what counts as a valid interpretation of Scripture. This tension between an open attentiveness to a new understanding of Scripture and a closed, conservative and defensive attitude can be seen in the careful balance of this statement: 'This teaching office is not above the word of God, but serves it, teaching only what has been handed on, listening to it devoutly, guarding it scrupulously, and explaining it faithfully by divine commission and with the help of the Holy Spirit' (para. 10).

Such a tension between a sense of the truth of Scripture as that which is known, possessed and so to be guarded, defended and passed on, and the truth as that which is to be discovered and listened to, is necessary for a proper understanding of the relationship between the Church and the Bible. A Church that believed that it had already and finally laid hold of the whole truth of God's self-revelation would reduce God to a function of its own intellectual system; it would fall into idolatry. This has been the temptation of the ecclesial authorities in the last hundred years in their fight against relativism. The Church has tended to lose a sense of how God transcends our own perception of him, and to succumb to what Matthew Arnold called 'the licence of affirmation in our Western theology'[17]. In such a Church there can be no place for biblical scholars except as the defenders of an already established position. But a Church that could in no sense maintain that it had the truth, that it would only be given eschatologically, would have nothing to say and no authority. It might be a community of hope but hardly of faith.

This balance between the magisterium as the guardian of a truth that is found and as the servant of a fulness of truth to be sought is admirable, but it will not lead to a resolution of the crisis of authority in the Church unless there is also a radical re-appraisal of the relationship between authority and the whole community of the Church. Since the early Middle Ages, when the division of the Church into clergy and laity hardened, the authority of the Church has been seen as located in just one section of the community, 'the teaching office of the Church', the pope and the bishops. The community of the Church consisted of those who teach and those who are taught, the *ecclesia docens* and the *ecclesia discens*. This authority was believed to derive from a direct commissioning of the apostles by Christ, who passed on their authority to their successors, the bishops. The Church remained in the truth so long as it was obedient to those whom God had appointed, through Christ, to speak on his behalf. This understanding of the authority of the Church is open to criticism on two scores. First of all authority is seen as that which stands over against the community, the authority of a mysterious, transcendent and absent God whose will must be imposed on a corrupt humanity whose salvation must lie in submission and obedience. So there must be those who command and those who submit. This model is justified by an unbroken handing on of authority from one generation to the next, back to the moment at which Christ commissioned the apostles immediately before his ascension.

That was why the Church reacted so violently to any suggestion that there was a discontinuity between Christ and the early Church. We had to know the names of every single pope back to St Peter. But a careful reading of the New Testament would suggest that the authority of the Church does not derive from the absence of Christ but from the presence of his Spirit. The Church can speak with authority about Christ because it is the Body of Christ, the community of Pentecost which having received his Spirit can speak in his name, the Spirit 'who will guide you into all truth' (Jn 16:13). Authority is that which the Church possesses, in the first place, as a whole. This is not to deny the authority of the magisterium but to locate it as an authority which comes from hearing the Word of God from within the community of those who are reconciled to each other and to God in Christ. The Church needs institutions so as to be a community that can speak with authority in the name of Christ. The Spirit of truth is the Spirit of unity. But if it is the Church as a whole that is the bearer of authority then we cannot accept any simple and absolute division of the community into those who teach and those who listen. *Dei Verbum* made the first step of recognizing that the 'teaching office of the Church' must do both, but it did not take the second step of recognizing the sense in which the rest of the community must also be seen to have authority. Theologians and biblical scholars and other groups within the Church do have a certain authority as those who hear and interpret the Word of God. Until that is accepted then the authority of the Church will continue to be seen as something that stands over against the rest of the community, judging it from the outside, applauding the good theologians who agree with them and condemning the ones who get it wrong. The bishops are the final arbiters of truth as those that ultimately guarantee the unity of the community, the touchstone of our remaining in the community of Christ's Spirit.

Secondly, we must reconsider what is the nature of the Church's authority. Since the Gregorian reforms of the eleventh century this has been seen mainly in juridical terms, as the possession of a power over people, modelled on the power and authority which structure civil societies. But this contradicts the New Testament model of authority. 'It is not to be so among you' (Mk 10: 43). Christ is presented as having authority over men since he spoke the truth of their salvation. Robert Murray has written: 'Christ's authority is the authority of truth, which has an absolute claim on man, made as he is to know the truth; he *must* acknowledge the truth that he sees, or else be corrupted. But man is free, and the declaration of the truth must respect his freedom'[18]. Any exercise of authority in the Church which is not seen to spring from a concern for the truth of the Gospel undermines and discredits itself. In the end we can only say, like St Paul, 'By the open statement of the truth we would commend ourselves to every man's conscience in the sight of God' (2 Cor. 4: 2).

The Church, then, has the authority of truth as the community of faith. But we are still left with the problem with which we started: how is the Church to define itself as a community of faith, as it must do, by, in times of crisis and division, the exclusion of interpretations of the Gospel that it believes fall away from the fulness of the truth? Unless the Church can, in some way or other, discern the difference between truth and error then there would be no community of faith and no basis for authority. In recent years the Church has equated unity with uniformity. We believe the same thing because we say the same thing. And we have seen how this uniformity of belief was expressed in the only officially recognized theological language, neo-scholasticism. Much of the criticism of the Congregation for the Doctrine of Faith derives from the fact that it appears to demand that every theological position must be justified before the judgment seat of its own theological tradition. As Karl Rahner, perhaps the most respected theologian in the Church today, said: they regard 'their own mentality and their own intellectual and social milieu as the only one existing, and as accessible from the outset to all others'[19]. This demand for uniformity of belief was understandable in the nineteenth century since to most theologians it seemed the only alternative to relativism. Today we can no longer hide from the irreducible pluriformity of human discourse. We have come to see how even the New

Testament, the basis of our unity, consists of very diverse theologies which cannot be all reconciled in some single statement of our belief. Some theologians have replied that though we cannot all *say* the same thing we can all *mean* the same thing, and appeal to the distinction that John XXIII made between form and content in his opening address to the Council: 'For the substance of the deposit of faith or body of truths which are contained in our revealed doctrine is not identical with the manner in which these truths are expressed, though the same sense and meaning must be preserved'.[20] But this distinction between the words and the meaning is, to say the least, philosophically questionable. How can one identify this enduring truth that must be preserved if any and every expression of it is necessarily not identical with it? What one theologian will regard as a new expression of an old truth another will consider to be a betrayal. This distinction seems to provide us with a very uncertain route beyond the two unacceptable alternatives of a denial of pluralism and the fall into relativism.

'Faith is one in the sense that God's gift of himself, God's self-expression as healing and transforming presence, is one'.[21] The single self-gift of the one God, the God who is Father, Son and Spirit, is refracted through that diverse range of responses to our salvation that constitute the New Testament. The Church defined itself as a single community of faith by reference to this single canon. It discovered the unity of its faith in not just one theology, that of Paul or John or Matthew, but in a plurality of theologies that gave it a glimpse of a fulness of truth that no single theology could encapsulate. It arrived at the consensus that it was in this collection of documents that it could discern its single faith through a long drawn out process of discussion and debate, conflict and disagreement, that lasted for more than four centuries. We may not understand quite how the Church came to recognize in just these particular documents the expression of its faith and the foundation of its unity, but, if we accept the canon of Scripture, then we believe that somehow, in the Spirit, it happened. We may not be very clear how today we too can discern the difference between what is an inadequate interpretation of the Bible and what is a betrayal of the Gospel, but we can be sure that the process of discernment cannot occur through the suppression of debate and the avoidance of conflict.

The Church is maintained in the truth, to use Hans Küng's phrase, because the Word of God is heard from within many different situations, by Brazilian liberation theologians and German academics, by poets and peasants, by feminists and homosexuals, by blacks and whites. No single group within the Church can claim that the Gospel is heard by itself alone, not even the magisterium. It is through the conflict of different perceptions of God's Word that we are drawn towards a fulness of truth that none of us has finally appropriated. Our catholicity is the best guarantee of a certain objectivity. And this debate and dialogue must somehow include the Church of the past, the tradition. We must respect what Chesterton called 'the democracy of the dead'. They too received the Spirit. But if this tension between tradition and innovation, between a truth acquired and a truth sought, and this dialogue within a very diverse and pluralistic Church, is fruitful and leads to discernment, then we must believe that the valid nineteenth-century insight into the historical relativity of truth and meaning is not the last word. We may be strangers but we are not ultimately aliens to each other, even if the fulness of community will only be found in the Kingdom of God.

Of course there has been and is plenty of conflict in the Church, as Schillebeeckx, Rahner, Congar, Chenu, Küng and many other contemporary theologians have painfully experienced, but it has often been unfruitful and frustrating because the battles have been fought in terms of a model of the Church, as divided into the teachers and the taught, which is inadequate. Perhaps this gloomy history was an inevitable part of the process by which the Church hesitantly creeps towards a new understanding of itself. A magisterium that saw its authority as deriving from the difficult task of preserving the unity of the community in, through and beyond diversity would be less eager to declare its mind immediately on every controversial issue but, as Nicholas Lash says, 'perhaps only a faith that has lost its nerve feels obliged continually to insist that it is quite sure of itself, that it knows quite clearly what is to be said concerning the mystery of God'[22].

Notes

1. E. Schillebeeckx, O.P., *Jesus, An Experiment in Christology* (London, 1979).
2. F. Kerr, O.P., 'The Historicity of Theology', in *New Blackfriars,* 61, (1980), p.339.
3. quoted by B.M.G. Reardon, *Roman Catholic Modernism* (London, 1970), p.13.
4. quoted by N. Lash, *Theology on Dover Beach* (London 1979), p.36.
5. para. 113.
6. para. 107.
7. G. Daly, O.S.A., *Transcendence and Immanence, a Study in Catholic Modernism and Integralism* (Oxford 1980), p.20.
8. *Ibid.*, p.67.
9. *Ibid.*, p.80, from A. Loisy, *Autour d'un petit livre* (Paris, 1903), p.192.
10. Reardon, *op. cit.*, p.238.
11. Daly, *op. cit.*, from A. Fumagalli, 'Le inside di una nuova scienza', in *La Scuola Cattolica* 31 (1903), p.400.
12. F-M Braun, O.P., *The Work of Père Lagrange* (Milwaukee, 1962), p. 81.
13. para 45, from the Catholic Truth Society translation (1944).
14. From the Catholic Truth Society translation (1959).
15. B.C. Butler, *The Theology of Vatican II* (London, 1967), p.30.
16. The translations of *Dei Verbum* are all from *The Documents of Vatican II,* ed. W.M. Abbott, S.J., (New York & London, 1966).
17. quoted by N. Lash, *Voices of Authority* (London, 1976), p.106, from *Literature and Dogma* (London, 1887), p. 29.
18. R. Murray, S.J., 'Authority and the Spirit in the New Testament', in *Authority in a Changing World,* by John Dalrymple and others (London, 1968), p.34.
19. *Theological Investigations,* Vol 14 (London & New York, 1976), p.100.
20. quoted by M. Schoof, O.P., *Breakthrough* (Dublin, 1970), p.233.
21. N. Lash, *Voices of Authority* (London, 1976), p.38.
22. N. Lash, *Theology on Dover Beach* (London, 1979), p.31.

Literary categories and biblical images

HAMISH F. G. SWANSTON

Addressing the members of the Pontifical Academy of Sciences in the *Sala Regale* on the 1979 centenary of Einstein's birth, Pope John Paul II commended Galileo Galilei to them as a scriptural exegete. Galileo, said the pope, introduced 'a way of interpreting the Scriptures which goes beyond the literal sense, but which attends to the intentions of the author and the literary form in which they are couched'. Galileo was certainly not content with the literal sense of the scriptural text. In his *Letter to the Grand Duchess Christina,* having acknowledged that 'the holy Bible never speaks anything except the truth', he had gone on to say the text is 'often very obscure' and its meaning 'quite different from the plain sense of the words'; and, in an earlier note to his friend Castelli, had remarked that if the Bible were to be taken 'literally', we would have to consider God as having 'feet and hands and eyes, and no less corporeal and human feelings, like wrath, regret and hatred, or sometimes even forgetfulness'.

It was not for such anthropomorphic speculations, of course, that Galileo got into trouble. He offended by maintaining in public as in private conversation that the earth moves round the sun. Such a notion was thought by many to contradict the witness of the Bible at several places. At Ps. 19: 4-6, which celebrates the sun coming forth in the morning 'like a bridegroom leaving his chamber and, like a strong man, runs its course with joy', a course whose circuit is to the ends of the sky. Or at Eccles. 1: 5 where it is said that 'the earth abides for ever' while 'the sun rises and the sun goes down, hastening to the place whence he arose'. Or at the story of Joshua. As the Grand Duchess remarked when Galileo's thesis was first broached by Castelli in after-dinner talk, the sun's being made to stand still must surely imply that it had before been moving. That we can now suggest that Jos. 10: 12-13a is a fragment from the ballads of the 'Book of Yashar' (cf 2 Sam. 1: 18), and Jos. 10: 13b-14 is a prosaic chronicler's rendering of an imaginative prayer into a miracle narrative, is a fair instance of what has been happening in the exegetical discipline since Galileo's time. Scriptural studies have certainly proceeded in the general acknowledgement of Galileo's principle that 'nothing physical which sense-experience sets before our eyes, or which necessary demonstrations prove to us, ought to be called in question (much less condemned) upon the testimony of biblical passages which may have some different meaning beneath their words'. But they have proceeded also with rather greater curiosity about 'meaning' and 'words' than was manifested by any of those who were caught up in the Galileo affair.

Galileo had, evidently, his own reasons for putting aside what seemed to him 'the plain sense' of the texts. He wished simply to clear a space for his scientific exercise. Bellarmine was chiefly anxious about the authority not of Scripture but of Tradition. 'You are aware', he wrote to Foscarini, the Carmelite friend of Galileo, 'that the Council of Trent forbids the interpretation of the Scriptures in a way contrary to the common opinion of the holy Fathers'. Neither was much interested in those matters of literary form to which Pope John Paul II alluded. And we, too, may be a little suspicious of any enthusiasm for 'the Bible as literature'. Our suspicion, so far as it derives from a sense that the enthusiasm is for a comfortable translation, is in great part justified. Everything suffers in translation, except of course bishops, and the King James conversion of the prophet Isaiah into an Elizabethan tragedian is no more faithful a representation of the original than the Knox conversion of the feeding of the five thousand into an Edwardian picnic complete with hampers. But even with a translation on our laps we may properly make some literary judgments. We may distinguish poetry and prose, and several kinds of poetry, several kinds of prose, in the collection. And, whatever the translation, something of the original form should impress the reader. The vigorous old battle-song of Jael (Jgs 5: 24-31) contrasts immediately with a contemplative lyric like Ps. 23, 'The Lord is my shepherd', or a love poem like The Song of Solomon. We may learn how to distinguish a spy story, like that of Ehud and the secret weapon (Jgs 3: 15-30), from a cautionary tale, like that of Elisha the skinhead (2 Kgs 2: 23-4), and both from a novella like Jonah or a folk yarn like 'Samson and the foxes' (Jgs 15: 4-8) or an extract from an official file like 1 Kings 7: 15-44. And, if we attend to the Christian writings, we may learn to distinguish incidental snippets, those Aramaic remains of Jesus' own words, *talitha cumi* (Mk 5: 41), or *ephphata* (Mk 7: 34), from carefully-turned gnomic sayings like 'all who take by the sword shall perish by the sword' (Mt. 26: 52, cf. Gen. 9: 6), lively original parables like that of the Sower from allegorical elucidations of a later community (Mt. 13:1-9 and 19-23; Mk 4:3-9 and 10-20; Lk. 8:5-8 and 9-15), folk yarns about fishes and coins (cf Mt. 17: 27 with the tale of Polycrates' ring, Herodotus III, 42, and with rabbinic parallels) from eye-witness histories, exorcism rituals from sermons like James, personal letters like that to Philemon from tracts like Romans, surrealist dream memories in Revelation from liturgical formulae like 1 Cor. 11: 23-6).

It is not quite so quick a business to identify the cultural sources to which the scriptural writers have had resort. They certainly shopped around. The great environmentalist Ps. 104 derives elements of its poetic structure and a great deal of its imagery from an Egyptian hymn to the Aton sun-disk. More indirectly, Prov. 22: 17-23: 11 most probably depends from a Phoenician version of the Proverbs of Amenemope. The patriarchal narratives in Gen. exhibit the workings of a score or more case laws brought by the *apiru* donkey caravans from Nuzi in northern Mesopotamia in the fifteenth century. The suzerainty treaty between Yahweh and Abram (Gen. 15:9 ff), and, even more clearly, that between Yahweh and his people in Jos. 24, have, as Dr G. E. Mendenhall has shown, the forms of Anatolian treaties of the second millenium. The lives of the old donkey caravaneers had been governed by contracts with suppliers and buyers and solemn assurances of unmolested passage along the routes. The biblical writers have shaped their accounts of these treaties with Yahweh on the model of archaic forms preserved in the traders' tradition long after they had all ceased caravaning and sat down in Palestine. Memories of another kind are discernible in the story of the Golden Calf. Professor W. F.

Albright demonstrated that both the literary structure and the vocabulary of this episode in Ex. 32 derive from the destruction of Death in the Baal epic of Ugarit. And of another kind still at 1 Sam. 9 where the editor has found a place for a charming folk talk of the handsome youngster who sets out on a quest with one old retainer. Saul comes after three days to the house of a wise man where, after he has been greeted by maidens at the well and brought to the house on the hill in which a banquet is prepared for him as the chief guest, he is told the secret of his future. He will meet two men by the tomb, three men going to the shrine, and four musicians at the city gate and after seven days he will be king; a beautiful story, told with all the fun of Puss in Boots and all the magic of Cinderella. This is the kind of story that all sensible women and men enjoy.

From the nature of their material and the shortish time in which it came to be set down in writing, the evangelists were less likely to look for forms from any great range of literatures. The Hellenist culture offered divers letter forms as paradigms for various 'epistle' composers, and the author of Acts evidently found in the wanderings of Odysseus an epic model which he could employ in the presentation of Paul among the storms and islands of the Mediterranean, but in the main NT writers were content to accept the multifarious tradition of the Hebrews. Most elements of that tradition reappear. There is certainly various talk of the Covenant, (e.g. Mk 14: 22, Heb. 8: 13), of heroic struggles against Death, (e.g. Rom. 6: 9, 1 Cor. 15: 54 f), and there is clear evidence that Jesus was partial to folk tales. His most imaginatively effective parables are of this kind. The 'Prodigal Son', for example (Lk. 14: 11-32), begins just like the traditional quest story when the young hero goes off to seek his fortune, then seems to be turning into a tale of the mysterious foreign temptress, but settles into the structures of goose-girl and shepherd-boy tradition, rounding off with the epiphany of the despised lad as the hero come back from the land of the dead to feast among his people. The evangelists liked such stories too. When they told the story of Herod's massacre of the male children in Bethlehem (Mt. 2: 16 ff), there must have been quite a number of readers who bethought themselves of tales of tyrants and infanticides, of baby Sargon, baby Moses, even baby Nero.

There is a like catholicism in the scriptural writers' range of imagery. However nationalist their politicians, however intolerant their choir-masters, there were poets and chroniclers enough in Israel to appreciate the lively languages of Egypt, Babylonia, Ras Shamra and the old Palestinian culture. The historian's account of Solomon coming before Yahweh at the Gibeon shrine (1 Kgs 3: 4-15) has the form of Egyptian dream stories, the content of Egyptian incubation rites, and the image of an Egyptian king as 'but a little child', though it halts at the notion of Solomon sucking his thumb. The poetry of Amos' curse is replete with animal imagery of the lion, the bear and the snake from the Aton hymn (Amos 5: 19), and the lament of No-amon, the city sitting by the Nile, seems to have been transferred almost unaltered in Nah. 3: 8. The Babylonian delight in the image of the sky-god landing his chariot upon the flat roof of a ziggurat was evidently shared by the prophet Micah. He celebrated Yahweh who 'coming forth out of his place, will come down and tread upon the high places', (Mic. 1: 2). And, of course, the famous *tohu wabohu,* the waste and void of Gen. 1: 2 and Jer. 4: 23-6, though one element may derive from Bauu, the Phoenician nocturnal mother goddess, derived its mysterious imaginative power for the Hebrews from the Babylonian Tiamat, the old watery monster slain by the young god Marduk. He sliced her in two like a flat fish. He divided the waters, placing one half of her as a canopy above his head and the other beneath his feet as a dancing floor. Dividing waters, above and below at creation, left and right at the exodus, became the orthodox sign of Yahweh's power. Other images came from other gods. The old storm-god cult of Canaan provided an extended image for Yahweh at Nah. 1: 2-6. The Jebusite cult of El-'Elyon, from whose rocky house the streams flowed down to his people, has shaped Ps. 46. Ps. 74: 13 testifies to the continuing power of a Ras Shamra image of the seven-headed Leviathan and the divine hero who overcomes the monster. It is clear that the local cults, however distasteful to the military men, fascinated the Hebrew poets. The beautiful image of the priest Adapa before Anu in the Akkadian liturgy has been employed in the Zechariah vision of the priest Joshua 'standing before the angel, clothed with filthy garments', and then, as the ritual is performed, being brought out clothed by the divinity in rich apparel (Zech. 3: 1-5). And what had that psalmist in mind when he spoke of the sun in a way that provoked such lively discussion at intimate little Medici dinner-parties? The imagery of a hymn to the sun from a Canaanite astrological cult? Or perhaps he remembered a Babylonian sun-god who at evening entered his tent in the sea?

NT authors, though they were often content with the more domestic imagery of assaying (1 Cor. 3: 16 f), athletics (1 Cor. 9: 23 f), book-keeping (Phil. 3: 7-9), building (Eph. 2: 20), dice-throwing (Eph. 4: 14) and a whole range of other ordinarinesses, employed alien and exotic imagery at important moments in their talk of Jesus. They willingly entertained the Hellenist image of demonic commanders of the spheres as their image for Christ's cosmic servants at the ascension (1 Tim. 3: 16), the Roman imperial image of the citizen picking up an infant in acknowledgment of paternity as their image of God adopting the Christians as his sons (Eph. 1: 5, Gal. 4: 5), and the Mandaean liturgical image of the door through which the initiate may pass into a new world as their image for the Christian's entry through Christ into the Kingdom of God (Jn. 10: 9).

None of this is, perhaps, more strange to us than some Hebrew images which seemed entirely homely to the NT writers. We are likely to be amazed by the Jewish tale of the rock that rolled after their ancestors as they wandered in the desert, and to wonder how Paul came to express Christ's continuing presence with his pilgrim people in so bizarre an image (1 Cor. 10: 6). Those who would appreciate what is going on in the NT must be prepared to remythologize a little. We have to ready ourselves for the garden of Adam (Rom. 6: 12 ff, 1 Cor. 15: 22 and 45), and echoes of the voice of God at the beginning of things, the descent of the Spirit upon the waters, and the tempted man in the baptismal narrative of Mk 1:1-14; for the mystery of Moses, (Jn 3: 14, 6: 31 ff, 2 Cor. 3: 7-17), and that delightful reference to the Jewish story of the baby Moses in Egypt having to choose between gold and the burning incense coal of myrrh which arches from the Magi of Mt. 2: ll to the Maries at the end of the gospel when the body of Jesus is embalmed for burial; and for the Jerusalem ritual of King David, (cf the ubiquitous Ark imagery from 2 Sam. 6 in the visitation narrative Lk. 1: 39 ff, which declares that the Divine dwells again in a city of Judah, that there will be dancing and cakes and ale, and a new king upon the throne).

The NT is replete with such strangeness.

Those who read the Scriptures in hope of a more domestic revelation may be contented, however. The NT writers come engagingly close to us in their word-games, especially in their punning. Usually quite untranslatable, puns abound in the biblical literature, and commonly in that rudest form, the play on someone else's name. That hieratic Christian, the author of Hebrews, thought it proper to explain his pun on Melchizedek. It is perhaps the nicest proof that he did not write Hebrews that Paul moves on rather more quickly amid the groans that greet his play upon Onesimus, once Useless now Useful, (Phm. 11), or Syzygus, who will be a good Companion (Phil. 4: 3). Jesus liked such things too. The name of Baalzebul prompted him to tell a story about a 'lord of the house' (Mt. 12: 24, 27 and 29), and, most famously, he had a pun for Peter (Mt. 16: 18). Those who suppose that Jesus could not have said anything at once so dogmatic and funny must note that though, as Bultmann indicated, this saying deprives the Church of its radical eschatological character; it is, as Bultmann also remarked, unlikely to have been an invention of the evangelist, since the pun of *petros* and *petra* would demand an awkward change of gender in Greek. John Allegro, in his somewhat eccentric work, *The Sacred Mushroom and the Cross,* says that Peter's name is an obvious play on *pitrā*, a Semitic word for a mushroom, and that his being called 'stumbling block' (Mt. 16: 23), is another pun on *tiqlā*, the bolt-mushroom: 'The sacred fungus was the "bolt" or "key" that gave access to heaven and hell, a double-reference to its shape as a knobbed bolt for opening doors, and to its ability to open the way to new and exciting mystical experiences'. There may not be quite so much punning in the NT as Allegro suggests in his recreation of the secret cult of *amanita muscaria,* but certainly there is a great deal. It is an element in the great tradition that found it pleasing that Jacob was a 'heel' (Gen. 25: 26), and that Shaddai, an old divine name, promised 'destruction' for their enemies (cf Joel 1:15-18), and that when Amos saw a basket of fruit, *qaiṣ,* he thought at once of Israel's end, *qeṣ,* (Amos 8: 2). Paul sometimes put eschatology aside for scatology. His word games include a few blue jokes about circumcision (e.g. Phil 3: 2 and Gal. 5: 12), and a snigger at the genitals, (1 Cor. 12: 22b-24a).

Paul may have let himself go rather too far, but it is characteristic of the evangelists, as of literary craftsmen in any culture, to delight in the possibilities of language, to follow happily where the words lead. We may wonder whether, when the author of Luke was putting his scraps of information together as an infancy narrative, the name of Bethlehem conjured not only the famous prophecy in Mic. 5: 2 but also the associated images of the goddess and the clanging hooves, and thus led him to speak of Mary and the Manger. We may be almost certain that when the author of Matthew came on the Hosea image of the exodus it dawned on him just where Jesus had been hiding. He cheerfully turned 'Out of Egypt I called my son' into a story of the boy in Egypt. Then, Joseph and Egypt and tyranny and Moses and babies coming together in his mind, he knew just who had taken Jesus across the border and what infanticidal rage they had had to escape (Mt. 2: 13-5). In Mark there is some plain evidence of an image coming to direct the shape of the lengthy section of a gospel. Dr R.H. Lightfoot has shown that the four watches of Mk 13: 35 recur as literary markers in the passion narrative at 14: 17, 14: 32, 14: 72 and 15: 1. The structural importance of imagery may be more largely demonstrated, and in the passion narratives.

The carefully composed court history of David describes, in a famous passage, the time when the king, having so neglected the business of government, has given his handsome and ambitious son Absalom a chance to organize a coup against him. David is forced to flee Jerusalem with a few followers. He leaves the city by night, crossing the brook Kidron, resting first at the old shrine on the Mount of Olives where he prays barefoot, his head covered as a penitent (2 Sam. 15: 30). He then moves out further into the desert and is met by a member of the dispossessed family of Saul who jeers at David being unable to keep his throne. David's bodyguard wants to kill the taunting Shimei but David restrains them: 'It may be that the Lord will look upon my affliction and that the Lord will repay me with good for this cursing' (2 Sam. 16: 12). And so it proves. The old soldiers rally to their former commander, the chief traitor in the Jerusalem conspiracy commits suicide, the usurper flees, and the great hero returns in triumph to his kingdom. Yahweh has worked a total reversal for his servant.

This is a stupendous story. It is beautifully told. And it must have been the inspiration of a good number of camp-fire yarns and village festival songs. These are not preserved. It may well be that, like the deposition scene of *Richard II* at the time of the Essex rebellion, they offended the government and were suppressed. Solomon in all his glory had no wish to listen to songs of a king thrust from his throne. The story of David was, however, far too moving and mysterious for the Israelites to have put it quite aside. Old literary forms, turns of phrase, grammatical peculiarities, have strange ways of endurance, and may reappear in verse even if unused in ordinary speech for centuries. The archaic usages in the Song attributed to Solomon himself witness to this. And so it may have been that the folk songs of Yahweh's dealings with his servant David survived as an underground literature. They survived to provide, I think, the literary structure and imagery of those anonymous poems inserted at Is. 42: 1-7(?), 49: 1-6(?), 50: 4-9 (and 10 f?), and 52: 13-53: 12. After that they were no longer needed. They were superseded in the Hebrew imagination by these great poems. They celebrate a Servant of Yahweh who is rejected by his fellows, 'a man of sorrows, and acquainted with grief' (Is. 53: 3), and who in the midst of persecution 'opened not his mouth, like a lamb that is led to the slaughter (Is. 53: 7), and, developing further the old story of David, the poet says the Servant 'makes himself an offering for sin', he is 'stricken for the transgression of my people', for 'we like sheep have gone astray' (Is. 53: 10, 8 and 6), Yahweh himself declares '*Therefore* I will divide him a portion with the great' (Is. 53: 12). The Servant, like David, and yet like one who is greater than David, becomes the king designated by Yahweh. The earliest communities of Christians saw in the Servant a divinely-given image of Jesus.

When the evangelists came to set down their accounts of Jesus' passion it was already a commonplace in their communities that Jesus was the heir to David and the fulfilment of the Servant imagery. So they were ready to tell the story of Jesus' last days as the story of the true king who left Jerusalem by night with a few followers (Mk 4: 17 and parallels in the other gospels), crossed the brook Kidron (Jn 18: 1), and came to the Mount of Olives

(Mk 14: 26 *et al.*), to pray that the will of his Father be done (Mk 14: 36), and was mocked by his inveterate enemies (Mk 15: 29 *et al.*). And as the story of the Servant of God who, to point only to images from the fourth Servant Song used in the Matthew passion, gave himself willingly to death (Mt. 26: 28), kept silent before his judges (Mt. 26: 63 and 27: 14), was numbered with the wicked (Mt. 27: 38), and buried in the rich man's tomb (Mt. 27: 60), while his betrayer committed suicide (Acts 1: 18). And, as the resurrection of Jesus was at once seen as the fulfilment of a promise to a David (Acts 2: 24 ff), so the Suffering Servant song provided the soteriology of the early communities. Jesus was 'wounded for our transgressions' (cf Rom. 4: 25), he 'bore our sins' when we 'were straying like sheep' (1 Pet. 2: 24-5), so that 'many will be made righteous' (Rom. 5: 19, cf Is. 53: 11), he was 'the lamb of God who takes away the sin of the world' (Jn 1: 29, cf. Is. 53: 7, 11 and 12) and 'having been offered once to bear the sins of many' will come again in glory (Heb. 9: 28). It is a happiness that the great poet of the OT should have inspired one of the best poets of the NT. There is at Phil. 2: 5-11 an early song of Jesus who took the form of the Servant, became obedient unto death, even death on a cross, a song whose literary structure exactly reproduces that of Is. 53, the imagery of dereliction being supplanted by the imagery of glory precisely because of the theological conviction that God's own honour demands that he should justify his Servant: '*Therefore* God has highly exalted him and bestowed on him the name which is above every name' (Phil. 2: 9). It is thoroughly in the line of that scriptural tradition that these two songs should have been made by Handel into one of the most powerful numbers of his *Messiah*, whose eighteenth-century popularity was so delightful a sign of the collapse of Deism, and whose continued singing in our baths is a perfect tribute to the anonymous songsters of Israel.

Solomon may have suppressed the old songs of the despised king, but he was very well aware of the importance of tradition in the maintenance of monarchy. His first official appearance as crown prince was managed in a very old-fashioned manner. After his anointing at Gihon, the prince rode royally upon his father's mule into the city of Jerusalem as the people cheered (1 Kgs 1: 38-40). The mule was the old animal of the caravaneer. The accession ceremony showed the people that their most ancient tradition was newly centred in the king. The king proved disappointing but the image proved powerful enough for the prophet Zechariah to celebrate a coming king who would enter his city 'riding on an ass, on a colt the foal of an ass', (Zech. 9: 9), and for the Matthew account of Jesus' entry into Jerusalem, to present him as being acclaimed as the king 'who comes mounted on an ass' (Mt. 21: 2-8). Indeed, the evangelist was so impressed by the language of the prophet that he felt compelled to say that Jesus rode two animals at once, an ass and a colt, (Mt. 21: 7).

It is doubtful whether the evangelist would have been greatly disturbed if the oddity of bestriding two beasts had been pointed out to him. We have to recognize that once, with the help of Galileo, we have reached behind 'the plain sense of the words', and, with the help of so many Jewish and Christian scholars, we have become aware of 'the literary forms' of the scriptural writings, we have yet to attend carefully to that third element which Pope John Paul II identified in the exegetical task, 'the author's intention'. When the evangelist placed Jesus on ass and colt at the Jerusalem gate he was working in a tradition which was less careful for historical or practical detail of that sort than for the imaginative structure of revelation, for, though not quite in Coleridge's sense, 'a translucence of the Eternal through and in the Temporal'.

That 'author's intention' may be discerned only through and in literary forms and images that the author puts to use: an harmonious verse, an elegant narrative, an entrancing fairy tale, a quickening image, witnesses to the possibility that our experience, since it can be so precisely phrased, may not be as higgledy-piggledy as it seems when we ourselves are fumbling for words. Through and in the fairy-tale sequence of young Saul's journey to the land of Zuph, the strange portents of the coming king, we are made aware of Yahweh's being before us in his care. Through and in the elements of the parable of the Good Samaritan, from the ineffectiveness of priest and levite to the rescuer's promise to return, we are made aware of the gracious power of the Lord who will come again. Through and in the fourth evangelist's subtle summonings of 'the fountain of living water', 'the true vine', 'the good shepherd' and 'the light of the world', we are made aware that the revelation which has its ground in the events of Hebrew history opens up into universally recognizable signs and is for us.

A work of literature expresses what Wallace Stevens called a 'blessed rage for order'. The range of forms and images in the scriptural writings is both an acknowledgment that the divine cannot be adequately expressed unless the literary devices of many peoples are brought into service, and an announcement that the order insinuated by such literatures is finally discoverable in Jesus. It is ever the authors' intention that their readers should make that discovery.

For the psalmist's great-aunts, talk of the sun coming out at his morning gate may have been a literal commonplace. For his great-nephews, the image of the sky god's progress may already have been a quaint survival in a disbelieving age. For Bellarmine, it seemed very like a geocentric proposition. For Galileo, it was, perhaps, the unfortunate slip of a fanciful poetaster. Rejoicing that we inherit such a diversity of response, reverencing the saint and the scientist, yet having about us something of the great-aunt and the great-nephew, we must attend to the psalmist's words if we would find a meaning for ourselves.

Bellarmine was so far right: the psalmist did think of himself as at the centre of an universe. Galileo was so far right: the psalmist was not greatly interested in astronomy. The psalmist was happy to have found a celebratory image for that shining Law which protected him and his fellows from end to end of the world. If we read his verses according to his manifest intent then we may be quickened into an appreciation of what it means for us that the Law is fulfilled in one whose face shone like the sun, (Mt. 17: 2). Through an obedient reading of this literature we may come ourselves, in the exciting language Paul was as ready as the psalmist to enlist from an alien cult (1 Cor. 15: 49), to bear the image of the man of heaven.

The spirituality of the Bible

N. D. O'DONOGHUE

This essay will be concerned with the spirituality of the Bible *from a Christian standpoint*. It is concerned, then, with the whole Bible, but from a perspective which focusses on the death and resurrection of Jesus of Nazareth. This is 'the end which is also the beginning', inasmuch as it is seen as the source of all meaning and power for the spirit of man.

1. The cross

The New Testament may be read, for the most part, as a gathering together of various meditations on the death of Christ. It is this, rather than the presence of myth, that prevents us from reading the gospels as history in the usual sense, where what counts as central is what happened in life, in the life of a man or a nation, or across some wider canvas. The gospel story is primarily the story of the death of a man, a man whose death is uniquely important to all men, for, through it, all men are released from the bondage of sin and Satan. So this death is 'good news' to all who receive it in faith. It is the way to true life.

But this life is life *through* death; and a Christian is called through death to life. In the large view he is given to share in life, but in the present, and in the immediate future, he is asked to share in the death of Christ, and in the sufferings that, as it were, mark the stages of life lived in the direction of death. So we find that the first Christians are faced with a formidable challenge to suffer and to die in the way of Christ's suffering and death. They are co-heirs with Christ, sharing his sufferings. The shadow of the cross lies over the Church of the NT as it has lain over the Christian centuruies. The acceptance of the cross in its various forms of voluntary asceticism, self-denial and martyrdom is one of the marks of the true disciple.

However, this spirituality of the cross is of itself a lamp without light. The light is love. What is shown forth on the cross is love, and it is to this love that the disciple is called. The four gospels are four faces of love as revealed in four faces of death. Already the disciple is asked to meditate on an immeasurable mystery of love. Later Christian spirituality echoed this meditation in a million hearts, but it could not really deepen it. Yet its greatest statement, as meditation, is not to be found in the NT, but in the OT, in the psalms and in the prophets, above all in Isaiah. The NT writers bear witness in clear, objective statements to the fact and the fulfilment. It is in the Old Testament – in Isaiah especially – that we find the heart-beat of Calvary. The writers have been as it were shocked out of all expression of feeling. So it is that, from the beginning, the Christian liturgies of the passion found their keynote in the OT: indeed the passion witnesses themselves use the OT as a kind of chorus or liturgical commentary on the event. It must be remembered that for the first Christians 'Scripture' meant the OT. This was the linguistic heritage in which they could express their shattering experience of Christ's death-for-love.

But this death-for-love and this suffering-for-love called for a response from the disciple; and this is expressed and commended many times in the Acts of the Apostles and in the epistles. It is perfectly summed up in the passage in the Acts where the apostles, after being flogged, go forth rejoicing because 'they have had the honour of suffering humiliation for the sake of the name (of Jesus)' (Acts 5: 41). This has become so much the authentic accent of the true disciple of Christ over the centuries that we easily miss its strangeness, the kind of entirely new 'language-event' which it affirms: a testimony written in pain, humiliation and the flowing of blood.

2. The new commandment

'I give you a new commandment: love one another; just as I have loved you, you also must love one another . . . A man can have no greater love than to lay down his life for his friends.' Here the death-for-love as foreseen illuminates the whole of human life, all human relationships. The washing of the feet has set the disciples in the same way as Jesus is going: it is a sign of sharing in the one service, a service that goes the whole way for love, the whole way to Calvary. The commandment is new because the sacrificial death which defines it is new. It encloses, extends and transforms the OT commandment of loving the neighbour as oneself, which is elsewhere accepted and commended by Christ. The parable of the Good Samaritan at once affirms this ancient commandment and transcends it.[2]

What is clear also, both from the parable of the Good Samaritan in Luke and the tableau of the last judgment in Matthew, is that this new force of love-unto-death breaks through and relativizes all actual and possible systems of belief. It is not orthodoxy but love that recommends the Samaritan: it is not discipleship in word but discipleship in the truth of love that opens the way to blessedness. This primacy of love is expressed most eloquently in the famous eulogy of charity in St Paul's first epistle to the Corinthians (1 Cor. 13).

This charity flows directly from the sacrificial death of Jesus on Calvary and so contact with this stream of life, this 'living water' is all-important. This contact is made through faith; so, in a sense, it is faith that animates the true disciple. It is through faith in the redemptive, all-sanctifying death of Christ that the disciple has hope of eternal life. 'In short, there are three things that last: faith, hope and love.' But hope rests on faith, and faith lives only by contact with the source, so 'the greatest of these is love' (1 Cor. 13: 13).

The most delicate and important question here is the relation of this new force, this love that flows from Calvary, with ordinary love and that human goodwill and rectitude which we find in small or large measure in all human societies. Do we with St Augustine, Luther, Kierkegaard and Barth dismiss all that is outside this source as evil or, at best, vitiated? Or, with Karl Rahner, do we affirm an anonymous flowing of these saving waters wherever there is human goodwill? Or do we, with St Thomas Aquinas and the scholastics, say that all reality is good, however it may fall short of perfection? In this last viewpoint there is still a large chasm between the natural and the supernatural (which flows from Calvary), but they are ultimately one in the analogy of being and the analogy of love. The new life does not take the place of the old or destroy it but rather fulfils it. This is, ultimately, the typical approach of the philosopher who is a Christian, of Maritain and Marcel, for example.

From this latter, more humanistic, standpoint the new commandment encloses a moral system which it transcends and transforms without, however, contradicting it. Indeed there is a sense in which the 'good news' makes its primary appeal to man's ethical sense, calling him to look at his life and that of the world around him in the light of his own conscience: this is how St Paul writes in the first chapter of Romans, and the words of Jesus in the gospel are constantly appealing to his hearers' natural sense of right and wrong. It is true that the OT provides instances of unethical behaviour which seems to be commended, as when Jacob deceives his father, but these are shadows which the New Commandment dissipates by the very force of the ethical clarity at its centre. This is clear from the great restatements of the Sermon on the Mount concerning human behaviour: 'It has been said . . . but I say to you' (Mt. 5). The new teaching clarifies the ethical, and immediately takes us beyond it into the atmosphere of death-for-love and love-unto-death.

We have here a spiritual ideal and a spirituality which has its roots in the ethical, in everyday justice and decency, but which goes far beyond it. Yet it goes beyond it *in its own direction*. Indeed it completes it for any concept of man, such as that of Aquinas, which sees him as *capax Dei*, open to the infinite. It is only by making his own, according to his measure and circumstances, of the love that reveals itself on Calvary, that man truly fulfils himself as man. The whole meaning of the story of the rich young man is that by refusing the invitation to go the way of the New Commandment he fails precisely as a *man*. We are dealing with spiritual vision that challenges every man in his manhood, and every woman in her womanhood (for the women who followed Christ were spared nothing of this challenge).

3. The call to discipleship

It might be well at this point to ground our study of the spirituality of the Bible in a particular passage. I have chosen the tenth chapter of Mark as at once representative and compendious: it names or hints at most of the central themes.[3] But it also reminds us that in talking of the spirituality of the NT we are dealing with a person, a living, breathing, loving, suffering human being. We do not understand this man at all unless we linger over the picture of a man with his arms round those children who were brought to him. We must also try to catch that glance, or rather that gaze, which was directed to the rich man, a gaze of love, *agapé*, the expression in human eyes of that deepest mystery of all, the same that unites the Son with the Father, the same that Paul eulogizes as the 'better way' far beyond all spiritual 'gifts' (1 Cor. 13).

Yet this love, for all its tenderness, makes absolute demands. The rich man is faced with a shattering and decisive option. It is a situation that repeats itself again and again in the NT. What is particularly interesting about it here is that it is not an option concerned with salvation, with eternal life (vv. 18 to 21). By obeying the 'commandments', the ethical code of the OT, and basically, of the NT, the rich man is safe. He can stay with his riches, administering his estate honestly, no doubt with due concern for the poor, as recommended by the ethical code according to which he lives. Jesus does not try to activate further the man's social conscience: the request to give everything to the poor shows concern for the poor, certainly, but is directly concerned with the giving rather than with the relief of poverty. Or, rather, it is concerned with another kind of poverty and another kind of relief of poverty.

For when Jesus says 'Come, follow me', here or elsewhere, he is not merely calling his followers to accept salvation but to share in the work of salvation, to become not only saved but saviours, to share in his own death-in-love and love-unto-death. This is the 'cup' placed before the Sons of Zebedee; this is the 'baptism' that is offered them, the baptism of blood towards which he himself is travelling (vv. 38 to 40). This is the way of *imitatio Christi,* of the following of Christ, the way of Christian monasticism throughout the ages. It was the way chosen at first by Martin Luther, who, like many another, could not, in his particular circumstances, rise to its full dimensions, and chose rather the way of being saved by the living contact of faith in Christ. Since Christ had accomplished it all, why should the disciple presume to add his 'works' to the great work of salvation? Luther has his texts to support his 'salvation by faith alone', though our present chapter and other texts seem to go against him. It can scarcely be argued against Luther that the saving work of Christ is in any way inadequate or needs supplementation (unless we lean far too heavily on Col. 1: 24). What can be argued is that the Christian is called not so much to salvation as to a participation in the mystery of love, *agapé*, that manifests itself and realizes itself historically on Calvary. In the last analysis this love cannot be given to man as a 'saving grace' merely, an extrinsic gift, a kind of merchandise of salvation. It must be encountered within, in 'the deep heart's core'; and this intrinsic presence of *agapé* is possible only by 'drinking the cup' of the passion and death of Jesus. It is only thus that the rite of the Eucharist comes fully alive, that the disciple truly meets the gaze of Christ in the breaking of bread.

This encounter in love is intensely personal, but it is by no means private. Rather does it open out to a world in desperate need, a world held bound by the dark lord of ultimate death. Those whose hearts this lord possesses through riches are poor indeed. Jesus, and those who follow him, attack this possessive power directly, and they must begin by disengaging themselves from its grasp; only then are they in a position to bring justice to earth. Jesus, and Paul following him, were concerned almost exclusively with this tremendous battle for the hearts of men, fighting against 'principalities and powers.' We who follow this same path must be primarily concerned with this same conflict and with the armour of God (Eph. 6: 11) by which we engage bodily in it. But as the blind man called out to Jesus (v. 47), so the poor call out to us today. That same gaze of *agapé* which called to the rich man pierced the blindnes of Bartimaeus. It is the gaze of a man walking steadily towards torture and death (v. 34). Only those who *really* follow can hope to liberate men from their blindness and their poverty. Such a man may be a Camilo Torres. The Marxist hero walks beside him to torture and death, drawing from the same source in the bosom of the Father, who alone is good of and from himself (v. 18). Yet in many of the Marxist revolutionary movements the source of the movement itself is vitiated by hatred and deceit: the social-spiritual ideal did not from the start ground itself in the ethical. Jesus will have his followers look always to the ultimate source of all goodness: 'Why do you call me good? No one is good, but God alone'. So, touching this source in the valley of the incarnation, he puts his arms round the little children whose angels see the face of the Father continually (Mt. 18: 10).

4. Prayer

The death of Jesus is a death completely lived in the dying. Externally it is something done to Jesus; internally and in truth, it is not only fully accepted but fully activated. Jesus prayed his dying and his death. This is clear from all four accounts of it, though each different account has its own angle of vision. Again, the language of this prayer is largely provided by the OT.

The sacrificial prayer of Calvary has emerged from the anguish-prayer of Gethsemane. Here we meet again the 'cup' presented to the Sons of Zebedee. As we looked at this incident it might seem that the acceptance of the 'cup' would be almost unbearable for them but not for him. But the whole point in the humanness of Jesus, of God *become* man, is that as man he is without any privileges. So we see that in Gethsemane 'sudden fear came over him and great distress'. 'He threw himself on the ground and he prayed: Father everything is possible for you. Take this cup away from me. But let it be as you not I would have it' (Mk. 14: 32 ff).

Jesus prayed his life as he prayed his death. This is especially clear in the Gospel according to Luke. It is quite illuminating to go through the third gospel with an eye on this theme. We find that it is the story of a man of prayer, the prayer that surrounds him from his conception and before, the prayer of Mary his mother who 'treasured these things and pondered them in her heart', the prayer of Simeon and Anna that draws on ancient fountains. But, above all, it is the story of the prayer of Jesus himself: he spends whole nights in prayer; he is presented as at prayer at the great crucial moments of his life, especially at the theophanies of the baptism and the transfiguration; one of these nights of payer precedes the choice of the twelve, one of whom will betray him. One of the strangest of these Lukan prayer-texts is that in chapter 22 which reads: 'Simon, Simon, Satan, you must know has got his wish to sift you all like wheat; but I have prayed for you Simon, that your faith may not fail'. Here Satan, the adversary, has, as it were, his rightful place (through man's connivance?), and all that stands against him is the prayer of Jesus, the same prayer that reaches its full dimensions on Calvary. It is the prayer of Jesus that liberates mankind from bondage.

We are here in full view of the externals of the mystery of mysteries: the relation of Jesus with his Father; perhaps the single passage that best resonates this mystery is John, chapter

17, with its many nuances in the vocative, and its calling forth of the 'glory which I had with you before ever the world was' (v. 5). When the disciples asked for initiation into this mystery they were given the Abba-prayer, what we know as the Lord's Prayer in its longer, Matthean, version. The power of this prayer is constantly passing away into its multitudinous echoes – like every mantra it tends to become mere sound – yet it is in itself always fresh and powerful, revealing ever new depths of meaning as we enter more fully into the atmosphere of those lonely nights of prayer in the hills of Galilee. It is forever human, and forever divine.

5. The Holy Spirit

The world of the prayer of Jesus is, at first sight, a very masculine world, and this is accentuated by the fact that it is a group of *men* that is first initiated into this world. Yet in the fulness of the act of prayer, which is the Act of Calvary, the Act of love-unto-death, the women-followers of Jesus come forward into the light: in the synoptic gospels they are focussed at a distance from the cross, with the men disciples (in Matthew and Mark we are told that they were a *large* group of women); in John the focus is sharper, and it centres on the giving of *the* woman (who is also named as 'the mother of Jesus') to the 'disciple whom Jesus loved', and the giving of the same disciple to the woman. For John this was the act which completed the prayer-unto-death of Jesus (19: 28), and so, as in Luke the woman enclosed the beginnings of the mystery of Jesus-salvation, so here, the woman encloses the fulfilment of that same mystery. He who had become man in a woman through the Holy Spirit (Lk. 1: 35), now gives back the Spirit to the Father. The prayer of Jesus is fulfilled in the glory that was before the creation of man and woman, the glory that is the breath of God issuing from the Father and the Son (Jn 16: 13-6).

The Spirit that goes forth to the Father in the final act of the prayer of Jesus is seen from the Christian standpoint as the *Ruach* of the OT, which can mean a man's extreme anguish as well as the inner life of God.[4] For St Paul it becomes the inner Spirit of God within the spirit of man (Rom. 8: 26): it is the deeps, the well-springs, the feminine, without which the spirituality of the NT is a head without a heart, an asceticism without a mysticism. Without it man cannot become a child, cannot enter the kingdom of heaven, and the gesture of Jesus as he puts his arms around the children before he walks firmly to his death, becomes a mere triviality (Mk 10: 16).

But of course, the outpouring of the Spirit had to await the resurrection, that other part of the Christian affirmation, the resurrection with its fulfilment in Pentecost. The death of Jesus has, in fact, made an end to death for man, because the prayer of Jesus has absorbed death through the power of love. Love-unto-death is love-stronger-than-death. As a man receives this love he receives life. The man who came to pray and prayer-unto-death was the man who said: *I am the life;* and it is life that is, finally and definitively, offered to the disciple. This new life in Christ, here and hereafter, is a constant theme in St Paul; but it is important to note that the sharing in the new life of Christ, in the light of the resurrection, comes only by way of a sharing in the death of Christ. There is no way *round* the cross; the only way is *through* the cross (Rom. 6).

It is through the Holy Spirit, issuing from the risen Christ who has been taken up into the glory of the Father, that the disciple can enter into the mystery of the prayer of Jesus. Here again, St Paul brings the teaching of the NT into focus for us. 'The Spirit comes to help us in our weakness. For when we cannot choose words in order to pray properly, the Spirit himself expresses our plea in a way that could never be put into words, and God who knows everything in our hearts knows perfectly well what he means' (Rom. 8: 26). As the disciple reaches upwards towards Thabor and Gethsemane, towards Calvary and the resurrection, the Holy Spirit that overshadowed the Virgin Mary is within and around and everywhere. So prayer is all; and all is prayer.

6. Transcendence and permeation

Like most spiritual theories and *praxeis,* Christian spirituality looks upwards; it affirms transcendence. Jesus tells the rich young man that if he follows him, he will have treasure in heaven. The theme that we have not here a lasting city, but seek one that is to come, is a recurring one; in some of the NT writings it is accentuated by the conviction of the nearness of the day of the Lord, the *parousia* in which the world as we know it will pass away to make room for a new heaven and a new earth. We have, then a spirituality of transcendence.

But this transcendence, once we examine it closely in the light of Christ's love-unto-death, has a special quality: it is a transcendence through *permeation*. The disciple who follows Jesus does not forsake his fellow man; what he forsakes is the world as possessed and possessive, the kingdom of the prince of this world. He has freed himself from the world in order to save the world; he has left it in order to enter into its depths. The disciple is called to take upon his shoulders the cross of the world's pain and grief and hopelessness; he is intolerably stretched to bridge the rupture between God and man, the creative will and the destructive will: he is drawn into the Abba-prayer of Jesus.

It is true that Christian spirituality as transcendent received into itself, and was enormously enriched by, the Platonic and neo-Platonic philosophies of transcendence; and this enrichment of Christianity by philosophies and spiritualities of transcendence is always being renewed, today as much as ever before. But Christian spirituality has never stopped there; it has had always to return to the incarnation and to the *terribili quotidiano* of permeation. The young Augustine could be happy in his philosophical retreat at Cassiciacum, but the same Christian impulse that led him there forced him not only to open to the woe of the world (as every Christian contemplative has to do) but to face forward into all its controversies, ambiguities and terrors. The Christian does not escape the dark shadows of earth nor the darkest shadow of the cross. Only in this direction lies the kingdom of heaven which is, nevertheless, the kingdom of childhood.

The incarnational quality of Christian spirituality has ensured that a doctrine of *spiritual* liberation must permeate all human life. And whatever one may say about the claims of some 'liberation' theologies there is no doubt but that Christian love must issue in action, and may well issue in political action.[5] But here again the road cannot be the road to utopia but the road to Calvary: for the Christian there is no way *round* the cross. That is why the Christian revolutionary is the true realist: he knows where he is going.

7. The Old Testament

It has been noted already how the OT supplied the gospel-writers with an available commentary on the central fact of the death of Jesus. It is natural that people saturated by a certain literature should express any new fact in terms of this literature, and this is a partial explanation of the presence of the OT in the NT. But the deeper explanation, of course, is that the NT writers saw the Christ-event as the fulfilment of all that had been 'written'. Thus we see the author of the Epistle to the Hebrews calmly appropriating the OT and refusing it any validity apart from Christianity. This has been the attitude of many Christians, some of whom have been even less successful than the author of Hebrews in actually reading what was written. It does not seem to have occurred to these writers, nor does it occur sometimes to modern scholars, that there may be several approaches to the one body of literature, that there is enough and to spare in the OT, both for Christian purposes and for Jewish or other purposes.

Certainly it is not by any means necessary for Christian spirituality to *appropriate* the OT; indeed a certain openness and flexibility of approach make it all the richer as a spiritual resource-book. One need only look at the history of Christian spirituality to see how this has worked in practice. To take the Carmelite spiritual tradition as an example, we find the three greatest Carmelite writers making as much use of the OT as the NT. A look at a biblical index of the writings of St Teresa of Avila shows that there are approximately the same number of references to both testaments. St John of the Cross articulates his deepest doctrine, that of the dark night of the spirit, in terms of the second chapter of the Book of Jonah. St Thérèse of Lisieux finds almost all her key texts in the Old Testament, in Isaiah 66, for example. It is as if these great companions of Mary and the beloved disciple in the prayer of Jesus were sharing the same expressive heart-beat of Calvary.

One final word. If Christian spirituality has at its centre the expressive heart-beat of Calvary as it pulses through the whole Bible from Genesis to Revelation, it must be said that this heart-beat constantly passes over into joy and into the glory which united the Father and the Son before the world was made. For the spirit of man, the Bible ultimately is the good tidings of great joy.

Notes

1. 'If we are children we are heirs as well: heirs of God and co-heirs with Christ, sharing his sufferings so as to share his glory' (Rom. 8:17). (All biblical quotations in this chapter are from *The Jerusalem Bible.*) Perhaps this is the place to remark that in what follows the names 'Jesus', 'Jesus of Nazareth', 'Jesus Christ' and 'Christ' are used interchangeably.

2. The text of the NT as given here is a putting together of Jn 13: 34 and Jn 15: 13. The washing of the feet (13: 8) is for John the central rite in which the relationship of the disciples to Christ and to one another is expressed; it opens up to feminine discipleship in Jn 12: 1 to 8 where we find one of the two beloved women disciples (11: 5) anointing the feet of Jesus as he goes on his way to Calvary. A shaft of light issuing directly from Calvary links these events together: it is a light not usually visible to commentators, though linguistic and structural analysis is groping in the direction of this kind of light. See, for example, R. W. Funk's analysis of the parable of the Good Samaritan in *Language, Hermeneutic and the Word of God* (New York, 1966), pp. 219-22, where Lk. 10:25 ff. is related backward to the OT and forward to Calvary.

3. The reader is referred to this chapter here, as if it were inserted in the text. Reading this chapter in the light of Calvary illuminates the passage on divorce as not only establishing a moral precept of loyalty and commitment between man and woman, but as referring (primarily?) to the new Adam who leaves his Father to espouse the new Eve, the Church born from his side (see Gen. 2: 18-24). As commentary on discipleship this chapter is quite shattering since it shows the first disciples as more than half deluded, *all of them*, as to what discipleship meant, and enumerates moreover, three separate but conjoined principles of purification: the drinking of the 'cup', the first-last principle, and – most demanding of all – the becoming as little children. It may be noted that the rich *young* man of Matthew is here simply a 'rich man'; in Luke he is a 'ruler'. Each evangelist tells the story of the death of Jesus in his own way, and arranges his facts accordingly.

4. See A. Heschel, *The Prophets* (New York, 1962), vol. II, ch.7.

5. See O'Donoghue, 'Liberation Theology and the Irish Experience' in *The Irish Theological Quarterly*, January 1979. Spiritual liberation articulated itself through the sacramental system as it gradually emerged in the Church, and this system opens out to the social and political orders.

The Old Testament in the history of Israel

LIONEL SWAIN

The OT is not just one book. It is a collection of books, indeed, the extant literature of a people with a long history, beginning with Abraham in the nineteenth century BC and ending (as far as this literature is concerned) in the first century BC. The order in which this literature now appears in our bibles is the result of long and complicated editing processes. It bears no resemblance to the order in which the different books and their parts originated. Nor does it pay any respect to the wide variety of factors which have influenced their development. In its present form, the OT is the written witness to Israel's faith, as this has been interpreted by innumerable storytellers, lyricists, annalists, chroniclers, legislators, lawyers, liturgists, historians, sages and scribes throughout the course of Israel's long history and in the many vicissitudes in which this people has found itself. Once the OT is viewed in this light, it becomes obvious that if its various parts are to be understood adequately they must be situated in the different contexts in which they originated and by which they have been affected during what may turn out to be a long and tortuous journey towards their final setting in the Bible in its present form. The disentanglement and analysis of the Bible's component parts, leading to their assignment to different historical settings, is the task of historical criticism. The results of the continuing researches in this field will be found in the latest and best commentaries on the individual books of the Bible. And the person who wishes to mine the spiritual treasures of the Bible has no alternative but to study these commentaries. The aim of the present chapter is to give the reader a very general idea of the historical origin and development of the different parts of the OT and, it is hoped, to whet his appetite for weightier essays on this topic. The very length of this present study is a sufficient indication that it has not the slightest pretention to be definitive. Nor does it claim to be a *status quaestionis* of all contemporary writing on the subject. Such an enterprise would not be possible in the space available — if at all. What the reader will find here is a pointer to the Bible's historical dimension and a broad outline of the origin and development of the OT which he is invited to fill in for himself.

The Chronology of the Old Testament

There is little or no unaminity among scholars with regard to the chronology of the OT period. And there is hardly a single date alleged for an event or a personage which is not contested by some specialist. For our present purposes, however, it is taken for granted that Israel's long history can be divided into the following eight phases or periods (the dates given being necessarily approximate and provisional):

1.	The period of the Patriarchs:	1850-1240
2.	The period of the exodus:	1250-1200
3.	The period of the Judges:	1200-1040
4.	The period of the monarchy:	1040- 586
	United: 1040-931	
	Divided: 931-586	
5.	The period of the exile:	586- 538
6.	The Persian period:	538- 333
7.	The Hellenistic period:	333- 63
8.	The Roman period:	63 BC-135 AD

Clearly this outline adopts the Bible's own version of history, with the exception of the 'early history' presented in the first eleven chapters of Genesis. The material of these chapters does not belong to the history of Israel proper. The latter begins only with Abraham, although this assumption is made here in full cognizance of the fact that a not inconsiderable number of scholars would contest Abraham's existence as a historical personage and maintain that Israel enters the historical stage only with the monarchy. Avoiding the challenging and intriguing questions which such divergent views may pose, our task is simply to follow the outline of Israel's history as given and attempt to answer the question: which literature saw the light of day or was elaborated in each of the different periods of this history? As we shall see, the prophets are privileged in this regard, since many of their oracles are related explicitly with contemporary events. Nevertheless, even in this case there is need for considerable caution, since a careful distinction has to be made between the time at which an oracle is uttered and the historical context in which it is recorded. In the final analysis, in this case, as in all others, the critic is impelled to decide which historical setting provides the best context for the passage in question.

1. The period of the Patriarchs

The art of literacy was such a rare luxury in the nomadic or semi-nomadic society conjured up by the stories in Genesis concerning Abraham and the Patriarchs that it is unlikely that the ancestors of Israel were literate. Thus there was no literature in the strict sence of written communication in the patriarchal age. On the assumption, however, that much of the material in Genesis hails from the supposed time of the Patriarchs, it is reasonable to hold that there was literature in the wide sense of oral communication. This would have been in the form of brief sayings or stories told to explain the origin of the family, to extol the prowess or cunning of an ancestor, to highlight the importance of a sanctuary. This literature would have been of an essentially tribal nature, centred on the family, the clan or the tribe. It would have originated by the camp fire or in the tribal sanctuary. Initially it would have been extemporary, improvised by the father of the family. But eventually it would have become part of the family inheritance and transmitted within the family from one generation to another. Finally, when the tribes were amalgamated to form the people, this vast body of oral tradition would become part of the patrimony of the whole people and, as such, it would be consigned to writing.

The remarkable archaic character of this literature, even when it was transcribed centuries after its inception, is an eloquent testimony to the tenacity of those early traditions and to the retentiveness of the non-literate memory. Not unreasonably, the ancients considered that the spoken word was more effective than the 'dead', written word and that the living memory was more reliable than inanimate materials when it came to the transmission and the recording of information. This is a point to be kept constantly in mind when we move on to consider Israel in a more literate setting. Even with the eventual advent of writing, oral communication does not go into demise. It continues alongside the written word and acts as a powerful interpretative and actualizing influence on the text. The written and spoken word go hand in hand. The peculiarity of the Bible is that so much of it is written oral tradition, that is, literature which originated as the spoken word. This does not apply to the whole of the OT but it certainly does apply to the patriarchal material.

2. The period of the exodus

The social condition of the children of Israel in Egypt at the time of the exodus was no more conducive to literary production than that of their ancestors. It is improbable, therefore, that they recorded their religious experiences during this period in writing. Granted the ancient character of at least some of the material in Exodus, it is more likely that this material originated as oral narration and was transmitted orally. Nevertheless, it is very possible — if not even probable — that the thirteenth century saw the first examples of Israelite written literature. If there is any historical substance in the tradition concerning Moses' education in Pharaoh's family, he would probably have been literate. Moreover, the Sinai desert has provided some of the earliest samples of Semitic writing (from about the time of the alleged exodus). The Decalogue (Ex. 20:1-17), while it has obviously undergone elaborations, bears the stamp of an early written document. It is not unreasonable to see in it, therefore, a literary production from the time of the exodus. The case of the Code of the Covenant (Ex. 20: 20 — 23: 33) demands more hesitation. This code very probably contains ancient written material, but it reflects a period later than the exodus itself. It could be placed either at the very end of the Mosaic era or in the period of Judges. Suffice it to say that, as we follow Israel's career, the conditions for the emergence of written literature begin to appear and we are able to assert, however tentatively at first, that such literature was produced.

3. The period of the Judges

With the entry of the Israelites into Canaan the possibility of literary production was heightened by the impact upon them of a literate civilization. True, Egypt was a literate civilization. But there the Israelites had been in a state of servility. Now, in Canaan (however the settlement is interpreted: as a conquest or as an infiltration), they were on the crest of a wave. This was their first effective contact with a literate culture. They entered Canaan not merely as nomads or semi-nomads but as tribes about to be civilized. As such they were profoundly influenced by the very peoples whose land they came to possess. And archaeology has unearthed some magnificent examples of the literature of those peoples, especially of the inhabitants of Rash Shamra or Ugarit. Myths, prophetic oracles, psalms, proverbs — these are but a few of the literary genres which the incoming Israelites inherited from the inhabitants of Canaan. It is not easy, however, to assign specific parts of Israel's literature to this period. Possible candidates are the refrains which concern the ark of the covenant, the oracles of Jacob and Balaam. More probable is the song of Deborah (Jg. 5: 1-31). This smacks of a work which was written if not for the occasion at least very soon afterwards. For all this, however, the spoken word continued to be the predominant means of communication during the period of the Judges (which, for our purposes, includes that of Joshua and the conquest). The contemporary or near contemporary material, presently situated in Joshua and Judges, would have been transmitted initially by word of mouth and, not unlike the previous patriarchal traditions, within the confines of the individual tribes or in association with particularly local sanctuaries. It was only generations later that these traditions were welded together to form a national saga.

4. The period of the monarchy

The institution of the monarchy in Israel signalled a tremendous leap forward as far as literature was concerned. The first king, Saul, was more like the previous judges and ruled charismatically. It was with David that the dynastic principle was introduced, witness the oracle of the prophet Nathan (2 Sam. 7). David also made Jerusalem the political, cultural and cultic centre of his nation. This move itself necessitated the creation of a considerable personnel to staff the state agencies: priests, scribes, musicians. David did not manufacture all these *ex nihilo*. Nor had he brought them with him. He took them from the indigenous culture. Most of the institutions of David's reign – institutions which were to become the organs of Israel's literature – were assimilations of Canaanite or Jebusite civilization. The books of Samuel and Kings contain elements from the archives of this early period of the monarchy. It is probable, too, that some psalms or, more precisely, some parts of some psalms originated at this time. As we shall see, the Psalter, in its present form, first appeared after the exile. But it does undoubtedly contain elements which are much older. Without endorsing the Jewish tradition that David actually wrote psalms, it may be reasonably maintained that some parts of the Psalter come from this time.

Nevertheless, even David was more of a warrior than a statesman or politician, and it was left for his son, Solomon, to undertake a thorough organization of the Israelite state. This he did with considerable gusto and verve, casting his net far and wide for the personnel for his administration. The building of the temple in Jerusalem gave considerable impetus to the composition and singing of psalms, as well as to the elaboration and establishment of ritual. And Solomon's international policy facilitated the publication of a wisdom literature, particularly in the form of proverbs. As Moses in the case of the law and David in the case of the psalms, Solomon is especially connected with the wisdom literature in Jewish tradition. But as in these other cases the association of Solomon with the whole of this literature is largely fictitious. It is probable, however, that some elements of this literature did originate in his day, indeed with himself. These elements would have circulated, either orally or in written form, among the sages and their pupils until the day when they would have been incorporated into large collections, eventually to appear in the wisdom books, notably the book of Proverbs, in their present form.

We have seen that, from their earliest times, the ancestors of Israel could boast of story-tellers, men who were skilled at recounting the past. It was during the early monarchy that this art reached its apogee with the creation of historiography. This was not the cold, clinical re-telling of past events, but the committed interpretation of events and personages in the light of faith in the God of Israel. In other words, these first histories, as indeed the oral accounts of the exploits of the patriarchs, Moses, Joshua and the Judges which preceded them, were essentially theologies. It is possible that the reign of David saw the publication of the first of such histories (which clearly transcended mere annals), namely, an account of the origins of the Israelite monarchy from the anointing of Saul to the taking of Jerusalem. But the undoubted masterpiece of this genre is the history of the David succession (2 Sam. 10-20, 1 Kgs 12). This was probably during Solomon's reign. Comparable with this is the history of Solomon's reign (1 Kgs 3-11). It is likely that the eventual authors of Samuel and Kings found these, and similar, accounts already in their written form.

The reign of Solomon very probably also witnessed the first attempts on the part of these historiographer-theologians to transcend the immediate past and provide a synthesis of history stretching from the beginning to their present, that is to say, the point which they considered to be the climax and culmination of God's saving plan, not only for Israel but also for humanity. It is to this atmosphere that we owe the first sustained theological work in the literature of Israel, that of the Jahwist. It is disputable whether it first saw the light of day as a written document or as an oral account, although the former is more probable. What is certain is that it incorporates a vast amount of previous material (including written, but largely oral) which was gathered from many different sources. It is also apparent that its author or (more probably) authors were very familiar with non-Israelite literature and traditions. This history begins with Gen. 2 and concludes with the book of Exodus. It was to be one of the four main documents or traditions which the eventual editors of the Pentateuch used in their own composition.

After the death of Solomon (931), the separated kingdoms of Judah in the south and Israel in the north had their own chequered histories. These were chronicled by the annalists of the respective kings in their capitals of Jerusalem and Samaria. When the latter fell to the Assyrians in 722/721 many of the pious inhabitants of the northern kingdom fled to the south and sought refuge in Jerusalem. It is assumed that they brought with them the northern theologians' version of Israel's history, beginning with Abraham and terminating, like J (Jahwist), with the exodus. This document or tradition was probably produced towards the end of the ninth century BC (about a century after J). It is usually designated the Elohist (E) and is chronologically the second major source of the Pentateuch. It is reasonable to assume that, soon after 722/721, there was an amalgamation in the south of J and E providing JE.

The eighth century BC also provided the setting for yet another phenomenon of great importance for the literature of Israel: prophetism. The prophetic tradition in Israel has quite a long history. As we have seen, it derives mainly from the Canaanite culture. But it is only in the eighth century BC that we meet literary prophets for the first time. These are often so called not because they wrote books but because they have books associated with their names. In this regard, it is important to distinguish between the prophet as a historical figure, together with his teaching, and the author or authors of the books in which the life and teaching of the prophet are presently conveyed. It is obvious that the prophetical books give us direct access only to the teaching of their authors and not to that of the prophets themselves. In their present form the prophetical books are the product of considerable editing, adaptations and additions, a complex of processes which does not exclude the ascription to a prophet of a saying, an action, a teaching for which he was in no way responsible. Such a procedure need surprise no one who knows how Jewish tradition has attributed the whole of the Torah to Moses, the whole of the Psalter to David and all the wisdom literature to Solomon.

This stress on the necessary distinction between the prophets and the prophetical books does not entail, however, that the former evaporate into thin air under our critical gaze. Some prophets (Jonah, for example) may be purely fictional characters, but the majority are real flesh-and-blood invididuals whom we are able to situate historically. Hence the first 'literary' prophets were Amos and Hosea who preached in the northern kingdom for a very short time about 750 BC. These were followed in the south by Isaiah who had a very long career (740-700 BC) and Micah (740-736). The teaching of these prophets would have been transmitted orally (if not already partially in writing) by their disciples and by pious groups of Israelites. It is also possible that their theologies affected the edition of JE. In any case, as I have already intimated, it was only generations after the prophets themselves that the books with which their names are associated were finally edited. And by that time they had already acquired larger or smaller accretions.

After Isaiah the prophetic voice seems to have been silenced in Judah until the last third of the seventh century. Evidently the annalists and chroniclers were still working at the court of the kings of Judah, since we have traces of their writing in the present book of Kings. But we have to wait until the reign of Josiah (640-609) for the inevitable renaissance of Israelite religion and, therefore, religious literature. The prophet Zephaniah preached briefly in about 630 and Nahum in about 612. But the two great phenomena of this time were the reform by king Josiah and the preaching of Jeremiah. The stimulus for Josiah's religious reform was the discovery in the Jerusalem temple of the 'book of the law' (2 Kgs 22: 8). This 'book of the law' is generally identified with Deuteronomy or at least the Deuteronomic Code (Dt. 12-16), a work which evinces many associations with the thought of the northern theologians. It is supposed that the reform of Josiah (622) was the setting for the production of a new version of Israel's history by the Deuteronomic theologians (D). This history is contained not only in the book of Deuteronomy but also in a first edition of the whole corpus: Joshua-Judges-Samuel-Kings. As we have seen, previous generations had provided the sources for such an enterprise, but it was left for the Deuteronomic theologians to sift this material and to weld together what they considered relevant into a comprehensible whole. Consequently, Joshua-Kings is a composite work or collection of works which contains many different genres but which still exudes a unified set of interests and preoccupations, expressed in an unmistakable language and style: that of Deuteronomy.

Jeremiah preached in Jerusalem between 627 and 587. The prophet Habakkuk entered the scene very briefly in about 600. Jeremiah witnessed the downfall of the kingdom of Judah and saw his people go into exile. A large part of his teaching bears resemblances to Deuteronomy, which raises the question of his role in the reform of Josiah: did he merely draw from it or did he even instigate it? Whatever the answer to this question, Jeremiah's name is as inseparable from the third main source of the Pentateuch (which, subsequently, 'pours over' into Joshua-Kings) as Ezekiel's name is from the fourth main source, that is, the Priestly tradition or document.

5. The period of the exile

From the viewpoint of Israel's literary history, the Babylonian exile represents a veritable watershed. The exiles must have arrived at their destination with an immense amount of literary luggage, made up mostly still of oral traditions stretching back to their distant ancestors, but also containing considerable written documents: notably J, E, JE, D (at least in a first edition). They would also have, if not yet in writing, the preaching of the prophets, beginning with Amos. In particular, the voice of Jeremiah would still be ringing in their ears. The exile would be a time when the children of Israel would unpack, examine and re-arrange this luggage. It was a time of editing, the literary counterpart of profound heart-searching and meditation. But even during this period there was literary creation. Ezekiel preached from 597 until well into the period of the exile. It is from that period that we obviously have the Lamentations. The fourth major source of the Pentateuch: the priestly history (and legislation) doubtless originated (at least in a first edition) during the exile among the priests who were associated with or influenced by Ezekiel. The priestly history (P) begins, like J, with the creation of the world. It also incorporates the legislative material of Leviticus and Numbers. Towards the end of the exile (550) an anonymous prophet announced his message of consolation to the exiles. This is contained in Isaiah 40-55. We have seen that the prophetical books include not a few passages which emanate from times other than that of the prophet associated with the book. Isaiah 40-55 is the most striking example of this.

6. The Persian period

Soon after the exiles returned home they were encouraged in their work of restoration by two prophets who preached at about the same time: Haggai (520) and Zechariah (520-518). From this point on, however, it becomes increasingly difficult to situate Israel's literature historically with any real precision, with one or two exceptions. Three obvious major additions to the book of

Isaiah: chapters 24-7, 34-5, 56-66 are generally placed at the beginning of the fifth century, as is the prophet Obadiah. Both Malachi and the book of Ruth are usually situated in the middle of the fifth century. The book of Job is assignable to the end of the fifth century. The next half of a century probably saw the publication of the Song of Solomon and chapters 9-14 of the book of Zechariah. All this hesitation with regard to the precise dating of the literature during this period is due to the lack of real historical context. But this is not missing in the case of one major work: the Pentateuch, that is, the five books of the Torah: Genesis, Exodus, Leviticus, Numbers and Deuteronomy received their definitive form in the context of the mission of Ezra (398). This was obviously a time of considerable editing and consolidation. It could have also provided a favourable setting for the final edition of both Proverbs and the Psalter, both of which, in any event, are to be situated in the Persian period. The prophet Joel and the Chronicler, who was responsible for the books of Chronicles and Ezra-Nehemiah, may be placed right at the end of this period (350). The books of Tobit* and Jonah hail from either the end of the Persian period or the beginning of the Hellenistic period.

7 & 8. The Hellenistic and Roman periods

The mid-third century provides a reasonable setting for the books of Ecclesiastes and Esther. About seventy years later there appeared the book of Ecclesiasticus* (Ben Sirach). It is difficult to give anything like precise dates to these books (as to many others during the Persian and Hellenistic periods), but when scholars come to the book of Daniel they are on surer ground. This work clearly reflects the great persecution of the Jews by Antiochus Epiphanes (167-164) and is to be situated in that mid-second century context. 1 and 2 Maccabees* were published towards the end of the second century. The book of Baruch* could be at home any time between 150 and 60 BC, the book of Judith* between 100 and 50 BC. The book of Wisdom,* the last book of the Old Testament, appeared about 50 BC.

* These books are not recognized by the Protestant Churches as belonging to the OT canon. They are usually referred to as the Apocrypha. This also applies to some additions to the books of Daniel and Esther.

Summary

My already very rapid survey of the origin and development of the OT literature might be presented schematically as follows:

1. *The period of the Patriarchs*
   oral tradition alone

2. *The period of the exodus*
   oral tradition + the first written documents

3. *The period of the Judges*
   oral tradition + further written documents

4. *The period of the monarchy*
   oral tradition + historiography: Davidic Succession, etc.
   J, E, D
   Joshua-Kings
   Psalms
   Proverbs
   Prophets: Amos, Hosea, Isaiah, Micah, Zephaniah, Nahum, Jeremiah, Habakkuk, Ezekiel

5. *The period of the exile*
   oral tradition + Prophets: Ezekiel, Isaiah 40-55
   Psalms
   Lamentations
   P

6. *The Persian period*
   oral tradition + Prophets: Haggai, Zechariah, Obadiah, Isaiah 24-7, 34-5, 56-66, Malachi, Zechariah 9-14, Joel, Jonah
   Ruth
   Job
   Song of Solomon
   Pentateuch
   Proverbs
   Psalter
   Chronicles
   Ezra-Nehemiah

7 & 8. *The Hellenistic and Roman periods*

oral tradition + Ecclesiastes
Esther
Ecclesiasticus*
Daniel
1 and 2 Maccabees*
Baruch*
Judith*
Wisdom*

Conclusion

It is obvious that the order in which our bibles present the biblical literature is quite different from that in which it appeared. It is just as obvious that if we wish to re-capture and trace the religious experience which is expressed in this literature we must attempt to read it in its correct order. Scholarly opinion may vary widely on the particular date to which a particular passage may be assigned. But that there is such a date nobody doubts. And few would question that the time and the circumstances in which a given passage was written are important for its comprehension. It is only when this anchorage of God's word in time, space and behaviour of real men and women is appreciated that the full significance of 'the Word became flesh' (Jn 1: 18) can begin to be seen.

The ethics of the Old Testament

JOHN L. McKENZIE

In discussing the ethics of the OT one must first remove the implication of the title of this essay that there is 'an' ethics of the OT. The books of the OT come from at least a thousand years of Israelite and Jewish history and from a large number of authors who do not represent a single uniform moral code. The books of the OT present us with a number of ethical practices, none of which can be dignified by the name of moral code. These practices are presented without any systematic organization or any basis in moral theory. The modern interpreter often attempts to furnish the systematic organization and theological basis which are missing in the OT literature; but these elements are intruded from his or her own theology and ethics.

The modern interpreter usually attempts to harmonize the OT ethical materials with his or her own ethics. The position of the OT in Judaism and Christianity as a canonical source of revelation compels the interpreter to an apologetic attitude towards the ethics of the OT even if the interpreter personally does not share the belief in a canonical source of revelation. That belief has had such a massive influence on historical Judaism and Christianity that it could be dismissed as trivial only by one who attaches no value to historic Judaism or Christianity. Few interpreters of the OT have adopted this position. This has meant that they have found it difficult to study the ethics of the OT with objective critical detachment, to say the least. One rarely achieves such detachment about something to which one has a personal commitment. Yet it should be unnecessary to explain why the ethics of the OT must be submitted to a historical and critical examination. This essay presupposes such an examination; it is impossible within the allotted space to present such an examination in sufficient detail.

It is necessary first of all to separate the various ethical streams which appear in the books of the OT. These will furnish headings for the discussion which follows. In addition, some special questions arise which do not easily fall into this classification. The three main streams are obviously the ethics of the codes of law, the ethics of the prophets, and the ethics of the wisdom literature. I do not imply that these are three homogeneous streams; the variations within each of the three are striking. But each of the three groups has a certain community of approach and a certain community of ethical values which may be more easily recognized than synthesized. It is impossible to give due attention to critical problems within each of the three streams. The three ethical traditions represent centuries of development. They are not the products of a culture which had come to a halt. It is beyond our powers to trace the developments with precision, and even the developments we can trace are more often than not discerned by educated guesswork. In this essay I can give this important aspect of the study of OT ethics no more than a few glances.

What I have called the legal stream of ethics is found in the legal collections of the OT. For practical purposes these are all found in the books of Exodus, Leviticus, Numbers and Deuteronomy. Again for practical purposes it can be said that these materials range from the tenth to the fifth centuries BC, that is, from the early monarchy to the post-exilic Jerusalem community. A few of the laws may be earlier than the monarchy. By far the greater part of the latest laws are ceremonial and without ethical interest. The civil and criminal laws are manifestly the laws of an agricultural and mercantile society which exists in a culture of villages and a few small towns. Modern discoveries of laws of other ancient near eastern societies have shown that very little Israelite law is original or peculiarly Israelite. Israel borrowed its laws without substantial modification from the common culture of the ancient near east. In the ethics implicit in a collection of laws, Israel shows nothing distinctive.

This is a point of some importance in the evaluation of the Law mentioned so often in the NT. In later Judaism the Law, which was identified with the five books of Moses, and not only with the laws in the proper sense, was regarded in Pharisaic

Judaism as a complete revelation of the moral will of God and a complete guide of human conduct. At the risk of some oversimplification it can be said that both Jesus and Paul rejected the Law as a complete moral guide revealed by God. One would hardly expect the ethics of an agricultural village society to become the absolute standard of human behaviour, especially when some of its limitations are considered. To these we must now turn.

The first of these limitations we may discuss is the ethics of the holy war. This ethic is found in the narratives of the book of Joshua and in some of the laws of Deuteronomy. The holy war was fought to acquire or defend the land which Yahweh had given Israel. It was believed that Yahweh assured victory. No booty was taken in the holy war; all prisoners of either sex or any age were killed, and all property was destroyed. Since ancient war was candidly recognized as brigandage — has it ever been anything else? — and since slaves were the most valuable form of booty, one must say of the holy war that it was not robbery. And that is about all one can say for it. Christians have too often taken it as a model for war against unbelievers or heretics. It is unnecessary to explain that the holy war is entirely repugnant to the ethics attributed to Jesus in the Gospels — or impossible for me, if anyone finds it necessary.

It must be remarked that the consensus of modern interpreters is that the book of Joshua is almost totally unhistorical, and so therefore are most of the episodes of the holy war. Some bible readers are more shocked by this consensus than they are by the ethic of holy war. There could never have been more than a few isolated instances of the practice of the holy war. The problem is not one of history but of the proposal of an ethical ideal, usually attributed to the literary school of Deuteronomy. Certainly this ideal cannot be reconciled with the Christian ethic, and perhaps no more can be said about it. Jesus is quoted once as distinguishing between what was said to the men of old and what he said. We may conclude that a critical reading of OT ethics is not only permissible but necessary.

A second limitation can be put only in general terms, but not so general as to be meaningless. The ethics of the laws of the OT is the ethics of a people, however one defines that people. Other peoples and individual members of other peoples are not the concern of Israelite laws or Israelite legal ethics. Strictly speaking, neither the Israelite people as a whole nor individual Israelites were the subjects of ethical obligations towards other peoples or individual foreigners. Compassion is recommended in Deuteronomy towards the resident alien, but nothing is owed him. The foreigner was by definition an enemy; this does not mean that active hostility was perpetual. It did mean that foreigners were not included within the circle of those called in the laws 'neighbours'. The laws recognized and enforced certain social duties towards the neighbour; these were not owed to others. The saying attributed to Jesus as a quotation from the Law, 'You shall love your neighbour and hate your enemy', is not a quotation from the Law; but it is an accurate summary of the social attitude incorporated in the Law – with the reminder that 'hate' in such messages strictly means to love less. The human experience of xenophobia shows that this reservation really means very little. The ethics of the laws of the OT lacks a broad human perspective and is as narrowly clannish as any other ethics.

Modern readers of the OT are more troubled by two further limitations than any earlier interpreters were. The third limitation is slavery, which the OT laws (and indeed the other two streams) accept without question or reservation. Before we addres the OT ethical position on this topic several points should be brought to attention. First of all, not only the ancient world but also almost the entire world of mankind accepted slavery until little more than a century ago. Secondly, the NT as well accepts slavery without question. Thirdly, there are a number of social problems for which slavery often made provision as well as contemporary social systems do. These points indicate that the OT ethics of slavery cannot be addressed as if it were singular. One must address the general human attitude towards slavery; and I do not conceive this to be the task of one who is assigned an essay on OT ethics.

It has often been said or hinted by interpreters that Israelite laws of slavery exhibit a higher degree of humanity than other ancient laws. As far as I know, this cannot be supported. Israelites obtained slaves by war and they engaged in the slave trade; a humane way to conduct these enterprises has never been found. There is no reason to think that the Israelites did not engage in the universal practice of raids to capture slaves. There have always been times and places in which slavery was more humane or less humane. In Israelite law the killing of a slave was not murder. I find it impossible to rationalize the humanity or inhumanity of the treatment of slaves at different times and places. Where it was left to the moral judgment of the individual slave owner, anything could happen. It is difficult to believe that the landlords of whom Amos and Isaiah spoke were humane slave owners. I believe that the only expression of genuine humanity towards slaves in the entire OT is found in Job 31: 13-15.

A fourth limitation has become of profound concern to many in the contemporary world, although members of the Jewish and Christian communities lived without this concern for many centuries. It should be said at once that one may not conclude that because the concern is new, it is not valid. This limitation is the social position of women. It should be admitted without dispute that in Israelite society and law woman was a depressed class. From birth to death every Israelite woman belonged to some man; in widowhood to her eldest son. 'Belonged' seems the proper word here. She was not a slave, but she was not a free agent. It seems that Israelite society had no place for the unattached woman of any age. In Mesopotamia in the second millennium BC women appear as independent economic agents. Nothing like this appears in Israel or Judaism until the late fifth century BC in a Jewish community resident in Egypt.

Polygamy appears as acceptable throughout all of Israelite and Jewish culture and law. In fact the practice seems to have become less and less common from the earliest period to the latest; but ethical considerations seem to have had nothing to do with this modification. Polygamy became less common as it became more expensive; and even as a luxury of the rich it seems to have disappeared in Judaism before the beginning of the Christian era. The legend of the thousand wives of Solomon seems to have been told with some relish and some envy; it is very doubtfully historical. Most OT heroes in the early books were polygamous. It should be observed that in a culture which had no place for the unattched woman polygamy did provide for what seems to have been an excess of women in the population.

The Israelite laws of divorce are not found explicitly in the legal codes. Allusions to divorce both in the laws and in other books show that the OT ethics did not differ here from the ethics of their neighbours in the ancient world. Any difference was not in favour of the position of women. Divorce was one-sided; as the husband took a wife, so he could reject her. She was passive in the entire process, protected against arbitrary divorce only by the power of the men in her family. Ancient marriage contracts often contained a clause protecting the wife from divorce. The causes of divorce are not specified. In a celebrated rabbinical dispute which left echoes in the gospels it was maintained by one school that the husband might divorce his wife simply at choice, by another that he might divorce her only for adultery (a capital offence in the earliest Israelite law, no longer enforced in NT times). Jesus took a stand on divorce so rigorous that it was rejected not only by the rabbis but by most Christians.

The second stream of ethics is found in the prophetic books, and not equally in all of them..Most interest has long fallen on the pre-prophetic books, especially Amos, Isaiah, and Micah; these books have an obvious thrust towards social justice, but the same thrust is found, if less prominently, in the books of Hosea and Jeremiah. This thrust for social justice will be the concern of this portion of this essay, for it is here that the creative moral utterances of the prophets are heard, utterances which have echoes in the psalms and in the gospels, and which are often quoted by modern spokesmen for social justice. A brief review of the social background of the prophetic utterances should be helpful, but a more detailed study of this material is necessary for anyone who wishes to read the prophets with genuine understanding.

Earliest Israel appears to have been a community of small land-holders; each piece of property was possessed by a family. There are numerous indications that earliest Israelite law and custom prevented the alienation of land outside the family. Almost all Israel lived in agricultural villages; towns were really no more than larger villages where there were craftsmen and markets. Justice was administered locally by the adult heads of families. In such a society the Israelite rarely dealt with strangers in law or trade; his business was done with his 'neighbours', those whom he knew and to most of whom he was related. In such a society there were no wealthy and no really poor. the tradition of family land ownership effectively prevented the agglomeration of large estates and the growth of a class of landless casual labourers. It probably meant also that few Israelites could afford to own many slaves. One does not wish to paint too idyllic a picture of early Israelite society. Certainly it was unable to sustain itself against the growth of wealth and large estates. This reconstuction would be substantially accepted by most contemporary interpreters.

Whether early Israelite society was idyllic or not, it seems certain that it was destroyed by the political and social changes introduced under the monarchy founded by David and Solomon. These changes can be briefly enumerated. The monarchy introduced a class of professional soldiers who had to be supported by the Israelite economy. It introduced wealth produced by trade. In Israel as elsewhere in the ancient near East trade was a royal monopoly and merchants were the agents of the monarch. It introduced a class of professional administrators. This meant that justice and local affairs were no longer administered by elders, one's 'neighbours', but by royal officers. This royal system was supported by taxation. Royal officers were rewarded by gifts of land. Royal merchants and royal taxes created an economy of debt in which the Israelite peasant lived, often at the cost not only of his land but of himself and his family; for oppressive taxes and interest rates — we have some information about both — could sometimes be redeemed only by the sale first of land, then of the members of one's family, finally of oneself. A small clas of extremely wealthy merchants, landlords and royal officers was supported in luxury by the progressive impoverishment of the Israelite peasantry. It is not surprising to learn that for its maintenance such a system demanded adventures in foreign trade and foreign war which the system was unable to support.

Any idyllic past of early Israel cannot be reconstructed from the sayings of the prophets; they show no awareness of the vanished golden social age. Their criticisms of their contemporary society are not based upon its violations of Israelite law. They are based upon a presupposition that the society is contrary to the known character of Yahweh the God of Israel. The prophets do not appeal explicitly to any source which we can identify on which this knowledge is based. Yet it cannot be doubted that by the eighth century, the time of Amos, Hosea, Isaiah, and Micah, Yahweh was known as the God of the exodus. In this character he was saluted as the liberator of the oppressed. The background of the exodus narratives is extremely complex; but the solution of this problem is not essential to establish the moral character of the God of the exodus.

There is no doubt that the social ethics of the Israelite prophets has no echo in the world of the ancient near East. On the other hand, there is no reason to think that Israelite society was singular in its exploitative character. Recent studies indicate that pre-Israelite Canaan was an oligarchy of wealthy landlords and merchants supported by a politics and a religion which were also supported by the oligarchy. Many now think that earliest Israel arose in revolt against the oligarchy. Whether this be the origin of Israel or not, there can be little doubt that David and Solomon instituted a polity and economy modelled after the Canaanite system, represented in the period of the monarchy by the Aramean kingdoms and the city-states of Phoenicia.

The prophets were not lawmakers or judges, and their ethical sayings are not couched in legal language, even the legal language of the eighth century BC. They were preachers, and they spoke to arouse feelings. They did not have a programme of reform or of any action which could be done by any social or political agent. What they proclaim is the political and social collapse of a community; the agents of this collapse will be foreign conquerors who have no special reforms in mind. The prophets do not announce or proclaim or recommend a better society; they announce the end of a society. One can deduce from their preaching an ethical analysis of the collapse of the society, but not a programme for its reform. Nor is the collapse of the society seen as a step towards a return to an idyllic past. Hosea spoke of a return to the desert; but in the Exodus traditions the desert was the place from which Yahweh had delivered the Israelites from the perils of death to the good life in the promised land.

The ethical complaints of the prophets, when summarized, seem few and obvious. They are, as I said, preachers; they do not engage in theoretical analysis of the ills of their society. The major complaint is the oppression of the poor by the rich. It is necessary for the modern interpreter to fill out concrete details of this complaint from the background sketched above, and to see that the acquisition of wealth and large estates was accomplished through the improverishment of peasants and craftsmen. The prophets speak often of the corruption of legal processes by bribery; and students of the Bible believe that the story of the extortion of Naboth's property by the bribery of judges and witnesses was not a solitary instance of this abuse (2 Kgs 21). I have already mentioned the economy of debt and royal taxes under which the Israelite tenant farmer lived without any hope of escape or even of alleviation. The prophets also speak often of a lack of compassion for the weak and the helpless members of society. It does not seem too much to say that the monarchies of Israel and Judah had come into the total control of the land-owning oligarchy, and that the Israelite who was not a member of the establishment could expect nothing from his rulers. Jeremiah went so far as to describe a community in which mutual trust had perished completely; one could not count on one's neighbour to tell the truth even in simple matters. If the passages of the prophetic books which express a hope for a kingdom of righteousness in the future come from the prophets of judgment – and many think they do not – they certainly express no hope that this kingdom will be achieved by ethical reform.

The third stream of ethical tradition I have identified with the wisdom literature. Here again some preliminary remarks. Unlike the ethics of the laws and the prophets, which are social in the sense that they are addressed directly to society, the wisdom ethics are individual and personal in the sense that they propose the good life as the happy life for the individual person. This good life is presented as within the reach of the individual person and is not dependent on the society for its achievement. This independence is subject to certain reservations. The wisdom ethics presupposes an enduring stable social structure within which one can plan one's life. The individual person does not create this structure nor can he alter it. The wise men have no ethics for catastrophe, nor even for a rapidly changing society such as that of modern times. This is not to imply that modern man has found an ethics for his own times either. Furthermore, the wisdom ethics not only presupposes a stable society, it also presupposes a certain level of prestige in that society. The wisdom ethics, like the Stoic ethics, was an ethics of the ruling class.

Modern studies have shown that there was an international ethical wisdom which was shared by most peoples of the ancient near East. There certainly must have been an exchange of ideas in this area, and in a few places the exchange can be traced. The international wisdom ethics is dominantly secular, meaning that it does not use religion as a source nor as a motive. It is not anti-religious, simply non-religious. This can be seen in Israelite wisdom; the religious element is a superficial veneer laid over the ethics proper, which could stand without it. Here the wisdom ethics is in sharp contrast to the ethics of the prophets, in which the sole motivation and sanction of ethics is the will of God.

It is generally thought by scholars that the source of the ethics of wisdom was the scribal schools of ancient temples and palaces; that the manuals of conduct were the exercise-books of student scribes; and that the maxims were addressed to ambitious young men who could hope by combining their scribal skills with prudent conduct to rise to the highest positions in the bureaucracies of ancient temples and palaces. One must say that the system of wisdom ethics seems well adapted as counsel for advancement in such a career. This view also helps to explain the candidly eudaimonistic, even utilitarian character of much of the wisdom ethics. Good conduct leads to worldly success, and bad conduct destroys success. Perhaps interpreters of the wisdom ethics have found fault with it for not being what it never pretended to be.

If, however, the ethics of the ambitious young scribe combined with a collection of maxims of traditional popular wisdom became a general form of ethics, they deserve some examination. It is obvious at first glance that the wisdom ethics deals entirely with personal relations: the relations of husband and wife, of parents and children, of neighbour to neighbour, of superior to inferior and inferior to superior. It is not purely the ethics of the Israelite village; but the maxims of folk wisdom often reflect the life of the village. But the life of the scribe was lived in the palaces, the temples and the market places of the larger cities. I have said that the ethics of the wisdom books would seem to be directed to the production of a courtly gentleman, and their principles might be summed up as: Give offence to no man. This may not be profound morality, but it rises above the combative behaviour which seems to have become characteristic of modern cities. The reflective reader may be reminded of Machiavelli; but he should remember that the courts of the ancient Near East were not the courts of renaissance Italy.

In more detail, the relations of husband and wife are seen entirely from the husband's point of view. The world of the wise men, like the world of Israelite law, was a man's world. Within this framework, which many of our contemporaries do not accept, the husband is told to accept the responsibility for his wife and to recognize her value in the home and family. Divorce is discouraged, and infidelity sharply rebuked. Other ancient wisdom writings recognize that a man's career can be helped or ruined by a wife. The modern reader will miss references to marital affection; these references are not frequent but they are not entirely missing. If for no other reason than self-interest and the desire to preserve a happy family life, the student of wisdom is warmly advised to love and cherish his wife.

The rearing of children is a responsibility laid upon both parents, and almost to the point that little seems to be left to the determination of the children. The wise men, like modern educational theorists, were ambiguous about just how much could be achieved by rearing. They were sure that there was no way to rear the young properly except by a discipline which was harsh by modern standards. 'Spare the rod and spoil the child' is not an exact biblical quotation, but it catches the spirit of the wise men. On the other hand, the wise men sought to foster in the children an enduring love and respect for their parents which would lead them to accept gladly the care of their parents in their old age, which society laid upon them.

If the ambitious young scribe were successful in his career, he would sit with kings and princes. It was of literally vital importance that he never forget that he was a man of lower station than those who employed him. In all probability, the scribe who wrote the records and who alone could read them possessed that knowledge which is power. This knowledge he must never flaunt. To his superiors submission was due;

obsequiousness is not expressly recommended, but it is in other wisdom documents of the ancient near East. The documents do not tell us, but we can conjecture that the world of scribes was a highly competitive world like the modern business and professional world. One's equal or inferior today might be elevated in the court of an absolute monarch tomorrow above one. Courtesy, kindness and friendliness were the rule of the scribe's behaviour to all; the wise man did not make enemies. Excess in food and drink might be offensive; the young man is earnestly advised to abstemiousness. The wife of one's employer or of one's associate might be a temptation; this temptation should be recognized as a deadly peril.

One may paraphrase G.B. Shaw and say that the middle-class morality of the wisdom books is good for those who can afford it. If scholars are right about the origin and source of wisdom morality, it was intended for a small group who served the ruling classes. As such it does not speak directly to those who do not belong to this group, however well it may speak directly to those for whom it is intended. And this leads us to some summary remarks about ethics. My decision suggests that none of the three streams speaks to all of Israelite society, and only the wisdom stream speaks to the individual members of any particular group of that society. Like most societies of the ancient world, the Israelite society had no ethics for most of its members. The ethical decisions in the lives of most Israelites were made by someone who had power over their lives and destinies. The laws, the prophets and the wise men address these ruling classes, or some portion of them; but to the ruled there was really nothing to say. Morality presupposes the responsible freedom of the individual person. This freedom was denied by Israelite society to most of its members.

The moral revolution proclaimed today is less a statement of new standards than a declaration of the freedom of the individual person to achieve moral responsibility no matter what his or her state or condition in society. A Christian believes or should believe that the moral quality of his or her life is not decided for him or for her by others, or by society.

Prophecy in the Bible

GEOFFREY TURNER

There is a common opinion which is close to the truth that prophecy disappeared soon after 400 BC when the priest Ezra moulded Judaism into an inward-looking religion, based on a strict view of race and law. Yet we know from Josephus that there were a number of Jewish prophets active in the first century AD, and without reckoning Jesus and John the Baptist, the prophets of the early Church ranked first after the apostles (1 Cor. 12: 28; Eph 2: 20). These prophets did not write anything, however, and we know little or nothing of what they said and did. They functioned chiefly in worship (1 Cor. 12: 23-33), they possessed knowledge of 'mysteries' (1 Cor. 13: 2) and sometimes predicted the future (Acts 11: 27-8; 21: 10-2), but prophecy as an integral part of Christian worship did not long outlive the close of the first century.

Classical Jewish prophecy had its roots in a series of political crises which took place between 850 and 500 BC in the kingdoms of Israel and Judah, divided since the death of Solomon in 922 BC. Yet the Jews could already look back on a long religious tradition before the appearance of the first prophets, a tradition based on Yahweh's convenant with his adopted people. After the Jews had settled in their so-called 'promised land' the first threat to their existence came from the Philistines but this had been resisted by David in the tenth century. Despite their good fortune, Elijah (850 BC) later demonstrated that they had proved unworthy of their covenant with Yahweh, but the real problems came in the middle of the eighth century with the menace of the Assyrian empire. The earliest warnings were given by Amos and Hosea, then Micah and Isaiah (750 BC). Tiglath Pileser seized the northern provinces of the kingdom of Israel around 733 BC and when the capital city Samaria fell in 721, that was the end of the northern kingdom. Jerusalem capitulated to Sennacherib in 701 and Asshurbanipal reached

Thebes in Upper Egypt in 664. This was, then, a time of enormous political tensions, as can be seen in the books attributed to Zephaniah and Habakkuk. But the decline and eventual collapse of the Assyrian empire (612 BC) brought no relief, for after the death of the religious reformer King Josiah the southern kingdom of Judah was conquered by the Babylonian Nebuchadnezzar and virtually all the influential members of Jewish society were deported to Babylon in 597 and 587 BC. Jeremiah tells how the state of Judah was virtually demolished at the time. For the next seventy years Yahwism was sustained by the exiles in Babylon who included Ezekiel and the prophet known as Second Isaiah. After the release of the exiles in 538 BC with the fall of the Babylonian empire to Cyprus the Persian, Haggai and Zechariah presided over the faltering attempts of those who had returned to Jerusalem to rebuild their temple and their nation. So prophecy from the ninth to the sixth century was a response to a variety of political crises.

The books of the OT as we have them now were written at a surprisingly late date, probably soon after 400 BC. The books which concern us here were at one time known as the Latter Prophets; the Former Prophets comprised the successive history books compiled by the Deuteronomist: Joshua, Judges, 1 and 2 Samuel, 1 and 2 Kings. The prophecies of the Latter Prophets were originally recorded on four long scrolls: Isaiah, Jeremiah, Ezekiel and the so-called Minor Prophets. However, the prophecies of the original Isaiah (chapters 1-39, eighth century, Jerusalem) did not fill the first scroll, and sixteen further chapters by an anonymous prophet now known as Second Isaiah were added (chapters 40-55, sixth century, Babylon), together with a miscellany of prophecies related to the rebuilding of the temple (chapters 56-66, late sixth century, Jerusalem) sometimes known as Third Isaiah.

These prophetic books are shapeless collections of traditional material, little of which was written by the original prophets, and a few scholars have even gone so far as to say that it is impossible to reconstruct the authentic words of the prophets. This is surely an exaggeration. But it is true that the prophets were men of their own time responding to particular circumstances, and they spoke an urgent message which was not meant to survive the crisis to which it was addressed. Yet their words were remembered, for they sometimes had personal companions, they acquired disciples, and prophetic schools developed round them, some of which no doubt lasted several generations – like, it would seem, the Isaiah school of prophets. Although we call them the writing prophets, they rarely wrote anything, though there were some exceptions when a warning had to be preserved to await fulfilment at a later time (Is. 8: 16; 30: 8; Jer. 30: 1; 36; Hab. 2: 2). Generally the original prophetic oracles were remembered orally and preserved in written form by the disciples of the prophets. Only at a much later date were they edited into the long compilations with which we are familiar. The oracles we now read are by no means in historical order and the arbitrary chapter headings give no indication of where one speech ends and another begins. The oracles became detached from their historical context at an early stage and very often it is only the inclusion of a later editorial passage that relates the original oracle to a specific historical incident. This leads to a further difficulty in reading these books: we cannot always be sure what is original prophecy, what is later development and what is editorial comment. As a rough generalization, we may say that editorial matter and stories about the prophets are in prose, and the words of the prophets are in poetry – Hebrew poetry is marked by rhythm and parallelisms. But our first impression is likely to be similar to that of Luther who said: 'They have a queer way of talking, like people who, instead of proceeding in an orderly manner, ramble off from one thing to the next, so that you cannot make head or tail of them or see what they are getting at'.

A glance at the OT canon would suggest that there were fewer than twenty prophets in Jewish history, but this is far from the case. We first hear of Jewish prophecy in the time of Saul (died 1000 BC) when he associated with a group of wandering *nebi'im* who prophesied after they had worked themselves into an ecstasy with singing and dancing. Each local shrine had its resident prophet who, for a suitable fee, woud 'inquire of the Lord' (1 Sam. 23: 4). There developed whole schools of cultic prophets just as there were detachments of priests and when these prophets were attached to the court in Jerusalem they became in effect theocratic civil servants. Not surprisingly, they often became yes-men who told the king what he wanted to hear, as is clear from the story of Micaiah and the obnoxious King Ahab (1 Kgs 22). Ahab proposed an alliance with King Jehoshophat of Judah against Syria. Jehoshophat insisted that they consult their prophets, 'about four hundred men', who said predictably, 'Go up; for the Lord will give it into the hand of the king'. Jehoshophat asked whether there was any other prophet and Ahab replied, 'There is yet one man by whom we may inquire of the Lord, Micaiah the son of Imlah; but I hate him, for he never prophesies good concerning me, but evil'. Micaiah was warned to conform with the other prophets but he said that he would speak only what the Lord told him, and the story relates how Micaiah warned the king that he would be killed if he went to war, how the prophet was thrown into prison for his pains, and how in battle 'a certain man drew his bow and struck the king of Israel between the scale armour and the breastplate'.

With all these cultic prophets around there was the major problem of how to identify a true prophet. The function of authentic prophecy is indicated in 2 Kings 17: 13-8, 'Yet the Lord warned Israel and Judah by every prophet and every seer, saying, "Turn from your evil ways and keep my commandments and my statutes in accordance with all the law which I commanded your fathers, and which I sent to you by my servants the prophets".' So a prophet had to sustain faithfulness to Yahweh and the observance of his commandments. False prophecy, then, could be identified if the hearer was told to ally himself to other gods (Deut. 13: 1-6). It could also be identified if a prophetic warning was not fulfilled, though this was never a very practical method for committing oneself to a prophecy: 'And if you say in your heart, "How may we know the word which the Lord has not spoken?" – when a prophet speaks in the name of the Lord, if the word does not come to pass or come true, that is a word which the Lord has not spoken; the prophet has spoken it presumptuously, you need not be afraid of him' (Deut. 18: 21-2). The canonical prophets railed against the false prophets for crying 'Peace' when they were given something to eat (Micah 3: 5), for being drunk and 'erring in vision' and 'stumbling in giving judgment' (Is. 28: 7). Jeremiah condemned them for telling lies and predicted that they would come to a nasty end (Jer. 14: 13-6; and 23): 'both priest and prophet ply their trade through the land, and have no knowledge' (Jer. 14:18). The writing prophets with whom we are familiar were great not because Hebrew prophecy was great in itself, but because the canonical prophets – although they were sustained by the tradition of cultic prophecy – reacted against that tradition. Amos, Hosea, Isaiah, Jeremiah, Ezekiel and a few others were the great ones; the rest have been consigned to the ash-heap of history.

While most prophets were earning a living, 'plying their trade' as Jeremiah puts it, the true prophet had a clear sense of having been called by God (Amos 7: 10 ff), often in a vision (Is. 6; Ezek. 1), and sometimes recruited with enormous reluctance (Jer. 1). Jeremiah often aruged with God because his life as a prophet seemed so futile, no one listened (Jer. 12: 1 ff; 20: 7 ff). With Jeremiah particularly, suffering became a hallmark of the true prophet. He tells us about Uriah, a prophet about whom we would not otherwise know anything, who had to escape to Egypt when he discovered that his prophecies were not going down very well, but who was pursued and murdered (Jer. 26:20-3). Early in his own career he had to flee his home town of Anathoth because his family were going to kill him. Then when the Babylonians attacked Jerusalem after the death of King Josiah he proved to be not just an embarrassment but a political subversive in warning the Israelites to surrender because they would not be able to resist inexorable punishment through God's instrument of the invading army. He was thrown into prison, put in the stocks, and later dropped into a muddy cistern and forgotten about until Ebed-melech, an Ethiopian eunuch, pulled him out.

In so far as they separated themselves from the cultic prophets, the canonical prophets, far from being innovators, were appealing to the ancient covenant traditions of Israel. The identity of the Jews as a holy community, the people of God, was determined by the alliance they believed they had with Yahweh. At an early stage in their history Yahweh was seen as a tribal god in competition with other gods but who was, the Jews believed, stronger than they were. He would be their God, he would free them from slavery, lead them to their promised land, protect them, and bring prosperity. He would establish laws to ensure stability in the community, and the Jews for their part would obey these laws and Yahweh's religious ordinances. The covenant tradition to which the prophets usually appealed was the Mosaic covenant established on Mount Sinai; and the guarantee of God's righteousness to which the prophets pointed was Israel's exodus from Egypt:

> When Israel was a child, I loved him, and out of Egypt I called my son.
>
> The more I called them, the more they went from me; they kept sacrificing to the Baals, and burning incense to idols.
>
> Yet it was I who taught Ephraim to walk,
> I took them up in my arms;
> but they did not know that I healed them.
>
> I led them with chords of compassion, with the bands of love,
> and I became to them as one who eases the yoke on their jaws,
> and I bent down to them and fed them (Hos. 11: 1-4).

What the Jews were not always conscious of were the religious and moral requirements of the covenant that *they* were obliged to fulfil: 'Hear the words of this covenant, and speak to the men of Judah and the inhabitants of Jerusalem. You shall say to them, Thus says the Lord, the God of Israel: Cursed be the man who does not heed the words of this covenant which I commanded your fathers when I brought them out of the land of Egypt, from the iron furnace, saying, Listen to my voice, and do all that I command you. So shall you be my people, and I will be your God' (Jer. 11: 2-4).

The covenant was a reciprocal arrangement; Yahweh was a righteous God who could be trusted to keep the covenant, but would Israel remain faithful? Predictably, sexual imagery was used by the prophets to picture the covenant. The covenant is, as it were, a marriage and Israel's whoring after foreign gods is described in vivid metaphors of infidelity (Hos 1-3). Ezekiel was most explicit. Of Israel he said: 'She did not give up her harlotry which she had practised since her days in Egypt; for in her youth men had lain with her and handled her virgin breast and poured out their lust upon her. Therefore I delivered her into the hands of her lovers, into the hands of the Assyrians'. And of Judah, the southern kingdom: 'The Babylonians came to her into the bed of love, and they defiled her with their lust; and after she was polluted by them, she turned from them in disgust. When she carried on her harlotry so openly and flaunted her nakedness, I turned in disgust from her, as I had turned from her sister. Yet she doted on her paramours there, whose members were like those of asses. Thus you longed for the lewdness of your youth, when the Egyptians handled your bosom and pressed your young breasts' (Ezek. 23: 8, 9, 17, 18, 20, 21).

Whereas Ezekiel, who was himself a priest, and Hosea specifically attacked the corruptions associated with the cult, all were concerned with the moral and social obligations of the law and the oppression, exploitation and injustice they saw about them. Micah described Judah as a demoralized authoritarian State:

> The godly man has perished from the earth, and there is none upright among men;
> they all lie in wait for blood, and each hunts his brother with a net.
> Their hands are upon what is evil, to do it diligently:
> the prince and the judge ask for a bribe, and the great man utters the evil desire of his soul;
> thus they weave it together.
> The best of them is like a briar, the most upright of them a thorn hedge.
> Put no trust in a neighbour, have no confidence in a friend;
> guard the doors of your mouth from her who lies in your bosom (Mic. 7: 2-5).

The poor were crushed (Is. 3: 15), there was lying, killing, stealing, adultery and murder (Hos. 4: 12). The prophets, however, made it clear what was required of the people:

> Wash yourselves; make yourselves clean;
> remove the evil of your doings from before my eyes;
> cease to do evil, learn to do good;
> seek justice, correct oppression;
> defend the fatherless, plead for the widow. (Is. 1: 16-17)

Jeremiah announced that 'if you truly amend your ways and your doings, if you truly execute justice with another, if you do not oppress the alien, the fatherless or the widow, or shed innocent blood in this place, and if you do not go after other gods to your hurt, then I will let you dwell in this place, in the land that I gave of old to your fathers for ever' (Jer. 7: 5-7). The mark of the prophet, then, is that he is critical of the religious and moral purity of his society and that he is up to his neck in politics, which makes life very risky for him.

The popular understanding of prophecy is that it is a matter of predicting the future, but this is a half truth at best. The prophets were interpreters of contemporary events. Their preoccupation in the first place was forthtelling rather than foretelling. They had a specific view of history; current historical events were controlled by Yahweh to reward the virtuous or, in the case of Israel between 750 and 587 BC, punish the recalcitrant. The message of the prophets was that the Jews had a covenant with Yahweh; they were breaking their part of the agreement; and if they continued Yahweh would certainly punish them. It was in this sense that the prophets predicted the future. They did not speculate on the likely outcome of political developments; they *assured* the Jews that they would not escape punishment and joined this with concrete political judgments. The canonical prophets, furthermore, were hated not simply because they predicted national disaster but because in a sense they caused it. They spoke in the name of Yahweh and his word could not fail (Is. 55: 10-1). So if a true prophet warned of destruction it had to happen (Is. 14: 24, 27). The prophet created the future.

The prophets had no confidence that the Jews would repent and their words became a hammer to break rock (Jer. 23: 29), a devouring fire (Jer. 5: 14) to slay them (Hos. 6: 5). Prophetic warnings were usually given as oracles which connected the ideas of sin and divine punishment:

> Woe to those who decree iniquitous decrees, and the writers who keep writing oppression,
> to turn aside the needy from justice and to rob the poor of my people of their right,
> that widows may be their spoil, and that they may make the fatherless their prey!

> What will you do on the day of punishment, in the storm
> which will come from afar?
> To whom will you flee for help, and where will you leave
> your wealth?
> Nothing remains but to crouch among the prisoners or fall
> among the slain.
> For all this his anger is not turned away and his hand is
> stretched out still. (Is. 10: 1-4)

Or warnings recounted the history of Israel's covenant with Yahweh from the beginning to the punishment still to come (Is. 5). Sometimes the prophets performed symbolic actions which with Ezekiel became almost street-theatre and which must have branded the prophet as a lunatic (Ezek. 4 and 5). Elsewhere Ahijah the Shilonite tore his garment into twelve strips and presented them to the king (1 Kgs 11: 29 ff); Jeremiah broke an earthenware flask (Jer. 19: 1 ff), bought a field (32: 6 ff) and wore a yoke of wood (27: 2 ff). Hosea and Isaiah for their part were commanded to give names to their children symbolizing the fate of Israel: *Lo-ruhamah,* Not pitied and *Lo-ammi,* Not my people (Hos 1.6, 9); *Shear-jashub,* A remnant shall return and *Maher-shalal-hashbaz,* The spoil speeds the prey hastes (Is. 7: 3; 8: 3). So prophetic activity embodied a variety of styles and techniques.

In all this the future had been determined; the prophet had been present in God's secret council (Jer. 23: 22), the prophet knows (Amos 3: 7) and everything is foretold (Is. 42:9; 48: 5). The prophet was appointed watchman (Ezek. 33: 1-9) to look out and warn of the approaching enemy in the hope that the people might prepare themselves and repent. Although it is not mentioned often because the prophets seem to have had little hope that Israel would mend its ways, repentance was always a possibility. After Isaiah's intervention and his subsequent repentance, the dying Hezekiah was restored to health and given fifteen more years of life (Is. 38: 1-6). And Jeremiah pleaded with Jerusalem to 'wash your heart from wickedness, that you may be saved' (Jer. 4: 14). Whereas shared guilt and communal punishment were the theme of early prophecy, the later prophets tempered their expectation of national destruction with a new sense of personal responsibility for sin whereby each man would suffer for his own offences alone (Ezek. 18).

There is no doctrine of God in the prophetic literature. God reveals himself in his historical actions. The prophets were convinced that Yahweh would perform 'new things' (Is. 42:9; Jer. 31: 22) and some of them portrayed the coming judgment as 'the Day of Yahweh', but the Jews were warned not to expect a day of salvation but 'a day of darkness and gloom, a day of clouds and thick darkness' (Joel 2: 2). In fact the *Dies irae* is derived from these prophecies (Zeph. 1: 7-18).

The canonical prophets, however, did not look forward to a *last* judgment at the end of history, but to a future judgment *in* history. Prophetic eschatology was not concerned with the last things, but with the next things which would lead to a restructuring of societies in a new historical age. The prophets' remembrance of their covenant traditions was not frozen in the past but actively created a future discontinuous with the recent past. Yahweh gave his people 'a future and a hope' (Jer 29: 11); he was the 'hope of Israel' (Jer. 14: 8).

Their vision of the future was limited, however. They looked for: (a) a return from exile (Ezek. 36: 8-15), (b) their formation once more as a nation (Is. 49: 6), (c) the restoration of the king (Ezek. 34: 23), (d) with Zion as the centre of a kingdom of peace (Is. 65: 17-25). Most important was Jeremiah's account of the new covenant between Yahweh and Israel: 'Behold the days are coming, says the Lord, when I will make a new covenant with the house of Israel and the house of Judah, not like the covenant I made with their fathers when I took them by the hand to bring them out of the land of Egypt, my covenant which they broke, though I was their husband, says the Lord. But this is the covenant which I will make with the house of Israel after those days, says the Lord: I will put my law within them, and will write it upon their hearts; and I will be their God, and they shall be my people. And no longer shall each man teach his neighbour and each his brother, saying, "Know the Lord," for they shall all know me, from the least of them to the greatest, says the Lord; for I will forgive their iniquity, and I will remember their sin no more' (Jer. 31: 31-4). And Ezekiel added, 'A new heart I will give you, and a new spirit I will put within you; and I will take out of your flesh the heart of stone and give you a heart of flesh. And I will put my spirit within you, and cause you to walk in my statutes and be careful to observe my ordinances' (Ezek 36: 26-7).

The earliest prophetic hope for the future was a suggestion that after their punishment a remnant of the people might be left to renew the nation's life (Is. 7: 3; 10: 20; 11: 11 and various other passages). The restored nation would have a new king, a new messiah, and the prophets described his characteristics: 'his name will be called Wonderful Counsellor, Mighty God, Everlasting Father, Prince of Peace. Of the increase of his government and of peace there will be no end, upon the throne of David, and over his kingdom, to establish it, and to uphold it with justice and righteousness from this time forth and for evermore'. 'And the spirit of the Lord shall rest upon him, a spirit of wisdom and understanding, the spirit of counsel and might, the spirit of knowledge and the fear of the Lord' (Is. 9: 6-7; 11:2).

Second Isaiah later assured the exiles in Babylon that they would return home because God would appoint a servant, 'the servant of the Lord', who would bear the guilt of their sins and who would suffer on their behalf to redeem them (Is. 42: 2-4; 49: 1-6; 50: 4-9; 52: 13 – 53: 12). The Jews did not get a king after their return from exile, not until 104 BC at any rate, and they certainly did not have a king like the suffering servant portrayed in Isaiah's songs. But these prophecies had their fulfilment, so the early Christians believed, in Jesus of Nazareth:

> He was despised and rejected by men; a man of sorrows and acquainted with grief;
> and as one from whom men hide their faces he was despised and we esteemed him not.
> Surely he has born our griefs and carried our sorrows;
> yet we esteemed him stricken, smitten by God, and afflicted.
> But he was wounded for our transgressions, he was bruised for our iniquities;
> upon him was the chastisement that made us whole, and with his stripes we are healed.
> He was oppressed, and he was afflicted, yet he opened not his mouth;
> like a lamb that is led to the slaughter, and like a sheep before its shearers is dumb,
> so he opened not his mouth.

> Therefore I will divide him a portion with the great, and he shall divide the spoil with the strong;
> because he poured out his soul to death, and was numbered with the transgressors;
> yet he bore the sin of many, and made intercession for the transgressors (Is. 53: 4, 5, 7, 12).

With the return from exile, the golden age of prophecy was past. The life of those who had returned was never very glamorous, and when Ezra arrived in the fourth century BC he hardened Judaism into a religion of the book rather than the spoken word. The old prophetic traditions were recorded and incorporated into the Old Testament canon, while post-exilic prophecy became integrated into temple worship in Jerusalem (1 Chron. 25: 1) and the old prophetic guilds may well have developed into guilds of temple singers. Several late texts speak of prophecy as a thing of the past (Ps. 74: 9; 1 Macc. 9: 27; 4: 46; 14: 41) and as Yahwism became Judaism, a religion of the book, priests ceased to be teachers of the law and became offerers of animal sacrifices in the temple (at least until its destruction in 70 AD), scribes acquired a new significance, and prophecy was reduced to the interpretation of and commenting on the writings of the OT. Targums were produced and eventually rabbis took on the importance formerly held by prophets. Prophetic predictions of the next things in history became apocalyptic visions of the last things beyond history.

Christianity brought a brief revival of prophecy but the institution of an ecclesiastical hierarchy at the end of the first century did not permit the spontaneity and unpredictability of prophets. Yet the marks of authentic prophecy can be recognized: criticism of decadence in established religion, condemnation of immoral social behaviour, warnings of divine punishment for oppressive political action. And we can see that prophecy has continued in the history of the Church, though infrequently and perhaps not with the power of OT prophecy. This mixture of religious, moral and political criticism which looks to the future and calls on the righteousness of God can be seen in, among others, St Francis, Savonarola, St Teresa of Avila and Luther, and none of them was treated gently by the Church. Today we may see it in the Nicaraguan priest, poet and politician Ernesto Cardenal and the recently murdered Archbishop Romero of El Salvador. As the Apostles once saw it, of course, in Jesus, the archetypal prophet:

> 'Would that all the Lord's people were prophets,
> that the Lord would put his spirit upon them' (Num. 11:29).

The relevance of the Old Testament for Christians

CECILY BENNETT

Almost from the beginning, there were versions of Christianity which rejected the OT and the God of whom it speaks as alien to Jesus and the Gospel. Their most important spokesman, Marcion of Sinope (about 150), reduced the Scriptures to an edited version of the Gospel of Luke and ten letters of Paul. It is significant that rejecting the OT led unavoidably to rejecting most of the New. But though the Church, from East to West and from that second century onwards, never wavered in its insistence that the books of the Jewish canon[1] are as truly its scriptures as those of the NT, the difficulties to which Marcion gave such an unacceptable solution have not gone away, and most of us seem to be to some degree in danger of practical if not theoretical Marcionism. Not that we would subscribe to the second-century dualist notion of a separate God, distinct from the Father of Jesus Christ, who is the imperfect Creator of this imperfect world and the subject of OT Scripture: we merely do not seem quite immune to the anti-biblical idea that what we read in the Old Testament isn't really about *our* God.

I find myself unable to deal with this question without making some reference to Nazism. Confronted with the appalling accusation implied in Hitler's Final Solution, Christians have been apt to dissociate Nazi anti-Semitism as far as possible from the dark side of Christian-Jewish relations down the centuries by claiming that Christian anti-Jewish attitudes and crimes were (in a perverted sense of the word) religious, not racist, whereas Nazi genocide was inspired wholly by racist mythology; and that the Nazis also persecuted the Christian Churches. There is some truth in this, but little comfort. The Final Solution is hideously linked to the history of the Jews in Christendom at both the practical and theoretical levels: practical, because the Nazi policies, beginning with open discrimination and ending with partially-concealed genocide, presupposed, as a necessary condition for their functioning, the widespread anti-Jewish attitudes which a certain kind of pseudo-Christianity, embedded at all levels in the Christian population, had made respectable for centuries; and theoretical because Nazism also had a religious policy, intended to incorporate Christianity as an ally, which was largely an explicitation and exaggeration of those attitudes towards Jews, and towards the Old Testament as the 'Jewish' Scriptures, which I have called implicit Marcionism. None of the German scholars[2] whose 'Marcionite' interpretations of the Scriptures assisted the Nazis in their attempted construction of a 'German Christianity' and an 'Aryan Christ' was a Catholic. Nevertheless, what Emanuel Hirsch made explicit is not unlike something which I constantly find beginning to emerge in discussions with fellow-Catholics unless they are already very familiar with Scripture.

It seems to start from wanting to see Christ's uniqueness in terms of devaluing everything that went before him. 'He revealed the God of Love to people who knew him only as a God of Wrath'. 'He taught a morality of love as against the OT morality of legalism and fear'. 'His standards were above anything known before — to love your neighbour as yourself and to love your enemies'. None of these formulations ought to be possible for a person at all familiar with the *New* Testament, even if he has no knowledge of the Old and its interpretation in the Judaism of our Lord's time. To equate the God of Love-God of Wrath contrast with an NT-OT contrast is to ignore not only Hosea, Second Isaiah and Jonah (this is not an exhaustive list) but equally Matthew 23, the Book of Revelation and indeed a whole side of the NT teaching from Paul to John. Again, when our Lord gave his summary of 'law' in the double commandment of love of God and of neighbour, he did it by quoting Deuteronomy and Leviticus: Mark tells us (12: 28-34) that he did it in a happily harmonious dialogue with a learned representative of the Judaism of his day.[3] And when Paul wanted to remind the Romans of their Christian duty to love their enemies, he did it by quoting Proverbs 8: 15 (Rom. 12: 20).

We do not enhance Christ by devaluing the OT. Are not these writings, which we sometimes seem to be *opposing* to Christ's teaching, presented to us by his Church as God's word – a message to us from Jesus' Father? We cannot simultaneously hold that, while the OT is (1), as the Church teaches, the inerrant product of God's inspiration (so that no-one is to upset us, please, by a critical approach to it), it is also (2) irremediably unbelievable (so for my faith's sake I had better not read it); and while it is (3) the divinely-inspired record of how unfaithful and unteachable the Jews always were (so different from us, God's *faithful* people) it is also (4) the Scriptures of *the Jews*, whose inferior or even evil religion and morality it displays.

In fact, we receive the OT from the Church as the Word of God, to be listened to as God speaking to us. On (1) and (2), this does *not* mean reading it uncritically: to insist, for instance, on taking what is not factual history as factual history, because of some notion that this somehow involves more faith in God's word, is, on the contrary, to put up a thick barrier against God's word: if we try to make it be what it is not, it has no hope of getting through to us as what it is. On (3), it is God's word addressed to *us*: to the extent that it is indeed a record of deafness and infidelity it is *our* record, a mirror of us, of every age of the Church and of ourselves personally, in our deafness and infidelity, persistently resisting God's endlessly patient working out of his purpose; and on (4), it confronts us with insights we shall never exhaust and standards we have never reached, along with, *also*, the faithful expression of all the distortions of God's meaning and purpose of which his People has proved itself capable, both before and since the coming of Christ.

As soon as we do begin to realize that we should take our OT seriously, it is natural for us, as Christians, to approach it from the NT end. If we are NT readers, the weakness of Marcion's position that will strike us first is the presence, everywhere in the NT, of what to its writers were simply 'the Scriptures': to us 'the OT'. The more we know, the more we shall become aware of this: it is not simply a question of the explicit quotations which we meet at every step. The NT authors were writing (in conjunction with the still more important activity of preaching) in order to present to the world an event, a Person, who was the full meaning and completion of what God had been doing for centuries and saying for centuries in the Scriptures. Almost everything they have to say about Christ, almost every way they have of thinking about him at all, of coping with this event which must be proclaimed to the world, is provided by their understanding of the Scriptures. It is worth noting that for them it is the opposite way round to the way we are apt to put it. They were not searching the OT for relevance to Christ, himself seen as self-authenticating. For them, it was a question of establishing the relevance of Jesus of Nazareth to the Scriptures, as being the Chosen One of the God of Scripture, Scripture itself being taken as 'given', as already known to be divine truth.

Am I saying that what we must do is get ourselves into the mentality of the NT writers, read and use the OT Scriptures as they read and used them, because only then shall we be able to understand the NT as it was intended? I am not, and it would be impossible. There is in any case not just one way in which the NT lives off the OT for its expression of the Christ event, nor is any one author confined to just one method of interpretation and application. Sometimes we shall be able to take their use of Scripture straight, as it were; sometimes we shall need to adapt and transpose it; sometimes (in 1 Cor. 11: 7-9 or Gal. 3: 16 for instance?) we are perhaps unable to use it at all. But we should not exaggerate this. Take, for example, the quotation in Matthew 2: 14 of Hosea 11: 1: 'Out of Egypt I called my son'. If, when we discover for the first time that Hosea was not talking about a future event, more than seven hundred years ahead of him, but about the exodus, we think that we now know too much to be able to connect this part of the Scripture with Christ as Matthew did, we are not being very intelligent. Matthew surely knew as well as we do what Hosea's plain reference was: we are not *merely* being invited to wonder at a prophet's giving a small bit of advance information (though that aspect does seem to have meant something to Matthew that it can scarcely mean to us), but to see the connection of the exodus, of Israel's whole existence as God's Son-People, with Christ: in fact to see something of the *real* relevance of the OT and its revelation of God the Deliverer to Christ.[4]

But we cannot simply assume a first-century mentality. We are of the twentieth century, and our century (even if our personal knowledge may lag behind) has acquired an enormous amount of knowledge (whatever huge areas of dispute and uncertainty it includes) about the gradual formation of the OT, which first-century people did not have: and such knowledge does and must modify the way one understands texts and sees the relevance of them to God's final self-revelation. Indeed, we should rejoice at the knowledge available to us, and hasten to get at least some sort of acquaintance with it. This will save us from getting stuck in that sterile misunderstanding of the relevance of the OT to the New which was not (in the crude version I have in mind) the idea of any NT writer (even Matthew) nor characteristic of the Fathers of the Church, but can be read in some of the least valuable versions of the most superficial apologetics: the notion that the point of the OT is that by relating in advance a large number of the details of Christ's life and death, it provides us with 'objective proof' of the divine origin of our religion, since only God could so have described things before they happened. The more we know, on the basis of the broadly agreed findings of modern biblical scholarship, the more we shall realize that not one single one of the instances set out in such books and pamphlets is in fact a prediction in the sense proposed: and the less we shall be distracted from getting at what the Bible, OT and NT alike, actually is saying to us.

One of the simplest ways, then, of realizing that we must become familiar with the OT seems to consist in seeing that without it we cannot understand the writings of those who drew from it their concepts for understanding Christ and what God had done in him. And this is perfectly sound. But let us be clear about what we mean.

It is a historical fact about the first preachers of the Christian Gospel that their culture was Judaism, with the Scriptures as its richest and most important part. Just as an atheist, or someone from a non-Christian culture, or even a modern Christian, would be well-advised to study medieval Catholic religion if he wanted to appreciate European medieval literature, so we could hardly hope to understand our NT without knowing something of the religious culture in which it is rooted. But is this purely human fact of cultural history all we are talking about? If it were, then there are other things we need to study at least as much as the OT: the type of OT interpretation that characterized the various schools and currents of first-century Judaism; the non-canonical literature produced during the last couple of centuries before Christ (some of it is quoted in the NT, and it is arguable that some of the ideas found in it, for instance, about an imminent crisis in God's direction of history, were actually more important to the beginnings of Christianity than a great many strictly OT ideas); and the culture and ideas of the Hellenistic world in which Christianity was preached, of which first-century Judaism was both a part and a contradiction. All these things, and the mere narrative outline of first-century events, especially in Palestine, are as much the relevant background to the NT as the OT is. Indeed, it is arguable that modern critical and historical methods of studying the OT (which we should use, or we are fleeing from the truth) are entirely irrelevant to understanding the theology which the NT writers drew from the Scriptures and elaborated in order to give their message: what we need for that is the totally different kind of scholarship characteristic of the different forms of first-century Judaism, which completely ignored the key modern idea, the concept of the historical development of a literature.

I am not saying anything against the study of these aspects of the background to the NT. They are absolutely essential to any serious study of it, and some acquaintance with each of them would be desirable for any literate Christian who wants to read the NT at all.[5] But I want to underline the difference in what we say about the OT. It too belongs in the list of things which provide the cultural background to the NT. But it also belongs in a list which does not include these other things at all: the Church's Canon of Holy Scripture.

The Church, by its maintenance of the Canon of Scripture, assures us that the OT is relevant to us as Christians not only as cultural background but as the Word of God addressed to us. We do not have to establish *whether* it is relevant: we can take that as given. We want to see *how,* once we have grasped that it is not supposed to function as some kind of trick 'proof' of Christianity by its ability to predict first-century events, and once we have recognized that we can sympathize with Marcion to the extent of seeing that there is a great deal in it which does not seem to be in harmony with the God revealed to us in Christ. The letter to the Hebrews (1: 1-2) assures us that it is the same God who 'in many and various ways spoke of old to our fathers by the prophets' and 'in these last days has spoken to us by a Son'. Very well, we accept it. But how do we come to *see* it?

For several decades now, the most usual key word in tackling this question has been 'history', and though it has proved to have its inadequacies it remains the most helpful of keys: none the worse for having arisen from the discovery of history, of the historical conditioning of everything human, which has been one of the great insights of western culture since the nineteenth century.[6] The great truth to grasp about the God of the Bible is that he is the God of history,[7] acting and revealing himself in the concrete, unrepeatable events of human history and showing us that history itself has a purpose and meaning, not going round and round or nowhere but towards a divinely-intended fulfilment in which the human race and all creation will be redeemed. Since God is genuinely, without any sort of cheating, acting (including inspiring the Scriptures) in the real history of real human beings, of course his literature, the Bible (not only the OT), reflects all the misunderstandings, the failure to receive and express his self-revelation, the forcing of it into religious and moral categories into which it does not fit, which are part of that human history. That it does include all this human distorting effect is not a contradiction of its truth, making God a liar: on the contrary, it is the process which sometimes seems to be imagined as what God ought to have done, the elimination of all human error and misunderstanding, which would have been the lie: the falsification, because dehumanization, of what was in truth going on in God's dialogue with real human beings.

Now this recognition may 'solve' some difficulties with parts of the OT. But it leaves us instead with a difficulty to which I can offer no solution. We have no criterion for winnowing out the human confusions to leave the sheer grain of God's message. Nothing could be more disastrous than, while reading the Bible, to label everything of which we find ourselves approving (on the basis of our own current cultural and personal values) 'divine communication' and everything of which we disapprove 'human confusion'. On the contrary, we have to take it whole: it is human literature, with all its failings and limitations, *being* God's word to us, not God's word wrapped in a detachable shell of human literature. The limitations and distortions are not just impediments to the message: they are part of the message. As James Barr says: 'Scripture does not come into existence by direct action of God, but by a human action which is a reflex of contact with God. Should we doubt that this human action shares in the distortion and inadequacy which applies to other human acts, and especially to those human acts which claim to relate themselves to the will of God? May we dare to assert that Scripture meets the needs of sinful men just because it is itself not free from its sinful element?'[8]

This is the reverse of an invitation to sit in judgment on the Scriptures: recognizing that the element of human deafness enters into them means praying and struggling against our own deafness as we read: but it does also mean not tying ourselves in knots with efforts to construe absolute theological truth or eternal values where they are simply not to be found.

The discovery of the God of the Bible as the God of history can, however, lead to an idea of 'salvation history' located, as it were, behind Scripture rather than in it.[9] Since he is the God who acts in history, we are asked to see his self-revelation as, essentially, the events, the 'mighty deeds', which *happened* in Israel. Scripture relates these events, but we have to recognize, using all the resources of biblical criticism, that they are related with very varying degrees of factuality: David's reign, for instance, fairly factually portrayed, the exodus perhaps a very small core of fact in a huge theological dramatization. But this involves us in seeing Scripture only as raw material from which, by critical study of the texts and with the help of whatever historical information we can get from elsewhere (archaeology and so on), we *reconstruct* the events of saving history, the deeds of God which are his self-revelation. But then we can never get at that revelation at all. For however interesting, exciting and indeed valuable for helping us to understand the Scriptures these historical reconstructions of the original events can be, we can never be even moderately sure of having got them right. Here we get really huge variations between scholars, even at any one time. And if one reconstruction of a stage of Israel's early history seems for a while to be at least very widely (never unanimously) accepted in critical circles, it is sure to be radically called in question in the following decade. Learned and valuable histories of Israel go out-of-date. The heart of God's self-communication cannot lie in something so inaccessible.

One does not want to deny that God *was* at work (and in a

special sense, over and above his presence in all history) in the sheer events (whatever they were) of Israel's historical existence. If we accept the Scriptures as God speaking to us, we accept his action in those events too, both because his action in Israel is something that those Scriptures are constantly asserting and because those Scriptures, whether narrating events or not, are themselves events: products of Israel's history and of God's inspiration. God was at work in Israel's history getting the books of Exodus and Jonah written, whether or not the book of Jonah narrates events that happened (it doesn't) or the book of Exodus events that partly did and partly didn't (a matter of dispute).

Scripture assures us that God was at work in Israel, in events which we cannot fully reconstruct, nor need we: it is the literature produced by that history which is God's word to us: *in* these writings, not in a salvation history *behind* them, we meet his self-revelation. How does it enrich us over and above his self-revelation in the NT, after allowing for the importance of OT study for understanding the NT? How does reading the OT in its own right bring us face to face with God?

The trouble with this question, now that at last I have asked it, is that it can only be answered with 'Take and read'. But I will try a few questions. Is it clear to you, on the basis of your sense of NT Christianity, that God's meaning for humanity includes passionate concern not only for mercy towards the poor, nor only for social justice, but, more radically, for the final resolution of the power struggle in humanity's political history by liberation of all who are oppressed – despite the manifest readiness of liberators and liberated to turn into tyrants in their turn? If not, you need to meet the God of the law, the prophets and the psalms. Do you expect satirical humour in God's message? Try the book of Jonah. Do you see eroticism as related to him? Try the Song of Songs. If you think there is an 'answer' to the problem of suffering you need the book of Job to tell you that there isn't (it may teach you not to mind so much that there isn't, but that's different). Do you see the whole grandeur of creation filled with God's glory and the whole sordid, moving, noble, degraded, inspiring, horrifying process of human history as man crying out for salvation and resisting it, God at work providing it but refusing to insult man by taking over and making him a puppet? It is possible that, even though you read the NT, your God is too small. You need to meet him where the authors of the NT had met him, in the pages of *their* Scriptures.[10]

Notes

1. I am leaving aside the question of the few books generally (not unwaveringly) included in the Christian OT but not in the Jewish canon.
2. Of pre-Nazi scholars, chiefly Friedrich Delitzsch and, alas, the great Adolf Harnack. In the Nazi period itself, Emanuel Hirsch, who however would certainly have been horrified to think that anything he wrote could have any connection with anything like the Final Solution. Cf D.L. Baker, *Two Testaments, One Bible* (Leicester, 1976), pp. 79-81 and 202; A.H.J. Gunneweg, *Understanding the Old Testament* (London, 1978; German ed. Göttingen, 1977), pp. 153-7.
3. What are usually called the 'antitheses' in Jesus' radical renovation of OT moral teaching in Mt. 5: 21-48 are not antitheses in the sense of contradictions, but expositions of the depth and scope of God's ancient demands, reaching beyond any minimal interpretation which human meanness might prefer: analogies can be found in other Jewish moral teaching of that and other periods. (The 'and hate your enemy' phrase, Mt. 5: 43, which occurs nowhere in the OT, remains a problem in the interpretation of Matthew's gospel which cannot be examined here).
4. For a wonderfully rich demonstration of how our knowing that an OT passage 'isn't really about Christ' does not prevent our entering into a NT writer's Christological use of it, and how this does not require us to read some artificial significance into it, see Brevard S. Childs' study of Psalm 8, in its original meaning and in its use in Hebrews 2: 6-8, in *Biblical Theology in Crisis* (Philadelphia, 1970), pp. 151-63.
5. I mean the kind of acquaintance given by any good popular commentary on the NT books, such as the Pelican Gospel Commentaries.
6. None the worse, that is, so long as we do not misapply it by projecting our twentieth-century sense of history onto ancient Israel: not so much in the sense of expecting the narratives in the OT to conform to our meaning of history-writing as the most accurate possible reconstruction of the past — we soon learn better than that; but in the sense of attributing to Israel our recently-acquired insight into the importance of a sense of history for understanding everything human, and hence also God's dealings with humanity. It would be very unhistorical to assume that the men who produced the OT would have understood what we mean by calling God the God of history.
7. One pitfall is to press too far the contrast of the God of history (Hebrew) with a 'god of the philosophers' (Greek) who is outside history because he is a timeless Absolute; and on the other hand of the God of history with the gods of nature and myth seen as non-historical forces in an endless cycle. There is

much in the contrast that needs to be recognized: but not to the point of denying that Israel's neighbours had any sense of their gods' being active in history, or that there is myth in the Bible. Reading the Bible historically involves seeing that historically-conditioned Israel was part of the ancient near-eastern world with its myths: both part of it and differentiated from it, not only the latter.

8. *Old and New in Interpretation* (London, 1966), p. 163.

9. George Ernest Wright's approach is open to this criticism. But this is almost the opposite of what is meant by 'salvation history' in the work of Gerhard von Rad, with whom the term is especially associated.

10. 'For the irrelevance and impotence of the Church is the inevitable result of failure to understand man as a creature responsible before God, whose creatureliness and responsibility are neither resolved nor negated, but redeemed, by the gospel message of the NT. Where the OT is ignored, such an understanding of man as creature, indeed as historical and societal creature, usually disappears, and the NT is wrongly regarded as only a handbook of personal piety and religion.' D. Moody Smith, Jr, in the title essay of *The Use of the Old Testament in the New and Other Essays* ed. J.M. Efird (Durham, North Carolina, 1972), p. 65.

The writing of the New Testament

HENRY WANSBROUGH

There are two erroneous impressions of how the New Testament came to be written which it would be as well to laugh out of court from the start: the first is the telephone-line theory, that the authors of Scripture wrote with a pen in one hand and a telephone line to heaven in the other; this is often representd in medieval pictures of the evangelist at his table with an ear cocked for a voice from heaven. The second theory is the newspaper-reporter theory, that the evangelists followed Jesus round, notebook in hand, carefully jotting down all his sayings and recording all his deeds, afterwards merely writing up these notes and adding one page to another. Each of these is an over-simplification of a complicated process in which the Holy Spirit was at work among men.

A third assumption about the genesis of the New Testament, which very often simply lies unexamined and unexpressed at the back of the mind, is that the gospels were written first and the Book of Revelation last, with the other writings in the order in which they are printed. The truth is far more complicated. The first group of New Testament writings is the letters of Paul (though some would put earlier the Letter of James), but again the order of these is far other than the order in which they occur in printed editions. The printed order is a decreasing order of length, in two groups, first letters written to communities and then letters written to individuals. Once this monolith of the Pauline epistles has been shattered, it is possible to look at each of the fragments for itself, and see how widely they vary in character. Some, such as the earliest, the two letters to the Thessalonians, are letters of circumstance, written to answer questions and worries of the community which Paul founded there. The extent to which they are occasional writings is shown by the fact that in the second letter Paul can be very concerned to correct an impression given in the first; this is typical of his lively and vibrant letters, for one can see his thought developing as time passes and as he responds to various challenges and errors put to him; indeed it is by the development of thought that the letters are dated. Two epistles are almost certainly collections of short letters, namely Second Corinthians and Philippians; one can imagine that when Paul's letters came to be collected a series of short, affectionate notes to the Philippians was simply joined into one bundle. Another letter is more formal, written to the Romans, a community Paul had not yet even visited, let alone founded, and for which he clearly has a somewhat distant respect.

Others of the letters we know as Paul's epistles are not in fact Pauline, and here we encounter the convention known as 'pseudepigraphy'. It was a literary convention in the ancient world, and especially in Jewish circles, that a writing could be attributed to a well-known figure (who had in fact nothing to do with its composition), to put it under his authority. Well-known examples of this are the Book of Wisdom in the Bible, in fact written about 100 BC but put under the name of Solomon; the so-called Psalms of Solomon, which are in fact hymns stemming from the party of the Pharisees shortly before the time of Jesus; and the 'Testaments of the Twelve Patriarchs', which purport to be the last will and testament of the twelve sons of Jacob, but are in fact documents from about the beginning of the Christian era. This convention was almost certainly the means by which the Pastoral Epistles, the letters to Timothy and Titus, were fathered on Paul. Attempts have been made to show that they are the work of Paul in old age, making far more use of a secretary than he had formerly done. He has lost his elasticity of mind, it is claimed, his confidence and his restless searching for a new synthesis; he is full of the worries and fuss of an old man, preoccupied with his loneliness and with petty details such as a cloak he left behind. The differences of vocabulary could be due to a different secretary who was given very free rein in the actual wording of the letters. But there are more difficulties yet, such as the absence of many of the theological themes so characteristic of Paul, and the difficulty of fitting the letters into any historical framework known from Paul's life: another journey in the eastern Mediterranean after release from captivity in Rome has to be postulated without any further evidence. Perhaps the greatest difficulty is that the ecclesiastical structure seen in these letters does seem much later than any known in Paul, and well on the way to the concept of a monarchical bishop which appears in the next century. It is probably best to accept that these letters are pseudepigraphical, written towards the end of the first century, and therefore exciting evidence that succeeding Christian generations could go on experimenting and developing so soon after the disappearance of the founding generation. An intriguing suggestion is that the three letters were in fact written by Luke as a third element to conclude his two-volume history consisting of the gospel and the Acts of the Apostles.

It has also been suggested that more than one of the gospels is pseudepigraphical as well. This, however, is a completely different situation, for the gospels as we have them come at the end of such a complicated process of evolution that the identity of the actual literary author may remain almost a matter of indifference. One thing that is clear is that we do not, in any of the gospels, have the direct testimony of an eye-witness. The case of the synoptic gospels and that of John must be considered separately. The generally accepted modern theory, from which few serious modern scholars depart, is that the earliest of the synoptic gospels is Mark, and that Matthew and Luke at least partly depend on Mark. Mark does not, of course, even claim to be an eye-witness of the events of Jesus' life, and the suggestion has traditionally been made only in connection with the curious incident in Gethsemane of the young man who fled away naked. Recently quite different, symbolic, explanations of this incident have been put forward. In any case the traditional identification of this young man with Mark is sheer guesswork, and there are some geographical data in the gospel which make it unlikely that the author had ever been to Palestine (for example, Gadara is a dozen miles from the Lake of Galilee, and more from any other lake, which makes the plunge of the Gadarene swine into the lake highly problematical: Mark 5: 13).

Moreover, comparison with popular literature of the ancient world, both within and outside Judaism, has left no doubt that the stories reflect the story-telling techniques seen in a well-worn and well-loved story which has passed through several hands. This does not in itself say anything about its truth value — a well-worn story is just as likely, if not more likely, to be true as a fresh, new story — and certainly in the Jewish world stories and sayings were handed on for generations by word of mouth with quite remarkable exactness and fidelity. Careful research has even established the circumstances in which many of the stories might have been handed down: for example stories about Jesus' disciples fasting, or about Jesus paying the temple-tax as a free offering, might well have been told to guide Christian action when the question arose what a Christian should do in these circumstances. The picture which emerges is of a society which treasures the memory and the words of Christ and turns to them for guidance when problems arise. As in all popular story-telling, the stories do not remain entirely stable, but details develop. One particular way in which the gospel stories developed was by allusion to the Old Testament; such allusions were incorporated to bring out the sense of the incident, to show how Jesus here fulfilled the Old Testament. Indeed in some cases the story-telling is so minutely modelled on its Old Testament predecessor that it is barely possible to reconstruct the historical incident on which it was based (for example, the feeding of the five thousand, whose narrative is now based on the similar but far less spectacular event in 2 Kings 4: 42-4). The communities which handed down the stories did not merely parrot them but thought about them and had at least some part in their formation into the stories we have now.

It is tempting to say that this view destroys the reliability of the gospels: by the time Mark came to process the stories they had already lost any claim to credibility. But why should authorship by Mark be any more guarantee of respectability than loving tradition at the hands of an intervening generation of Christians striving to preserve faithfully the message of Christ? A healthy notion of inspiration demands that the inspiration of individuals within the Church, such as bishops or evangelists, should be seen as part of the inspiration of the Church as a whole. The guidance of the Holy Spirit was to lead the whole Church in the way of truth, and this assistance must surely have been given to the Church in a special way in the crucial founding generations, when the directions of the Church and the implications of

Christ's life and message were being worked out in all their novelty and freshness. For this the guidance of the Spirit must have extended at least to all those who handled the message. It might be objected that certain individuals like Mark and Luke and Paul, though not of the Twelve nor among the other personal disciples of the Lord, were picked out for their task and so received special help. But if these individuals received special help for their task, why should not all those who were engaged on this task of handing on the Lord's message, each according to the nature of their function? This is especially important now that it is granted that some of the writings of the New Testament, like the Letter to the Hebrews, are wholly anonymous, not even pseudonymous. They do not derive their authority from any known or marked figure in the Church. This guidance of the Spirit on all those engaged in handing on the gospel teaching is largely the point of the traditional insistence of the Church that revelation ended with the death of the last apostle: this is a convenient theoretical marker by which to differentiate the crucial foundation-period of specifically scriptural inspiration from later generations for whom the guidance of the Spirit had a different function.

By the time the gospel material reached Mark it had, then, gone through a long process of formation and development. Some of the incidents may already have been grouped or joined together, such as the long 'Section on Bread' (Mark 6: 30 – 8: 21) each incident of which has some mention of bread; it is suggested that this was originally joined up to be ued as an aid in eucharistic instruction. But Mark himself was no mere compiler. Apart from the momentous step of inventing the literary genre of 'gospel', never before known, neither philosophical treatise nor biography but a message of the Good News of Jesus Christ, apart from this stroke of genius he also left his signature on the gospel by means of the points he stresses – the humanity and gentleness of Jesus, the uncompromisingness of his demands, the slowness of the disciples to understand. His very simple Greek was the language spoken by the lower classes and slaves all over the eastern Mediterranean. The small sums of money in which his characters deal also suggest that it is in this company that he should be sought. The extent to which Mark's own inspired initiative is responsible for details is not easy to assess (a good deal more difficult than it is with the subsequent writers Matthew and Luke who use Mark), but it must have been considerable for the gospel to maintain such unity and coherence.

So far, there is general* agreement among scholars; there is also general agreement that Matthew and Luke used Mark. One obvious lack in Mark is a large body of teaching, especially moral teaching and guidance. We may assume that Matthew and Luke, or the communities behind them — for at this stage too it is essential to retain the connection with the early communities — felt that Mark needed supplementing in this and other ways to give a more detailed view of the Good News. A hypothesis, which until very recently had secured very widespread approval, was that both Matthew and Luke used a collection of sayings of the Lord which has since disappeared. This collection would account for the fact that there are large passages where the two evangelists give sayings of Jesus in identical form, or with minor changes which are obviously typical of their own interests. This collection, first analyzed by German scholars, is nicknamed 'Q' *(die Quelle* = the source). But Q has its opponents, perhaps increasing in numbers.

One objection to Q is that no ancient author mentions it, except perhaps Bishop Papias of Hierapolis, whose evidence will bear other interpretations at least as well as this one. Another is that the whole concept of Q and its limits is said to be insufficiently defined. But the main objection comes from those who hold that there is sufficient evidence to show that the author of one gospel knew and used the other, which makes a third, common source, wholly superfluous. The discussion here clearly becomes highly technical, but attractive arguments have recently been put forward to show that Matthew can best be explained as a coherent whole, whose only written source is Mark, that there is running through Matthew's editorial changes to Mark and his other additions such a unity of theme, theology, imagery and style as to exclude any other written source. This explanation must be, and has been, supplemented by similar work on Luke, to show that he is working on Mark and Matthew, rather than on Mark and Q. In both cases recent work has tended to reinforce

*but not universal. Some maintain that Matthew (in an earlier form) was the first gospel. Others deny the possibility of ascribing priority to any of the gospels in their present form.

the view that neither Matthew nor Luke used written sources other than Mark (and possibly Q). The parts which each alone has are shot through with his own special interests and personal vocabulary. Although they may have drawn on oral tradition in some form, the stories and incidents must be specifically shaped by each evangelist himself. Especially typical examples would be, among parables, the darnel for Matthew and the good Samaritan for Luke, or more generally the death of Judas for Matthew and Jesus before Herod for Luke.

It is clear that, at any rate if there is no room for Q, these two writers must have spoken with an authority comparable to that of Paul; especially great must have been Matthew's authority, since he would be responsible for such a large initiative. Rather than rely on the slender and often repetitive evidence of the early church Fathers, we can gather a good deal about these two authors from their own gospels. Matthew is both very familiar with things Jewish and very concerned with the problem of the inter-relationship of Christians and Jews. Although he is writing at a time when the break between Christianity and Judaism has already occurred, his own thinking and habits of teaching and writing are ineradicably Jewish and his teaching methods reminiscent of the rabbinic schools. He must surely be a convert Jewish teacher, well versed in rabbinic argument and instruction. Traditionally this gospel is accepted as having been written by Matthew-Levi the tax-collector, whose conversion is narrated in Mark 2: 15 and Matthew 9: 9; but there are difficulties in this position. First, the relationships of hostility between Christians and Jews visible in the gospel suggests a date of about 90 AD, by which time the tax-collector would have been a very old man, hardly capable of this kind of literary work. Secondly, it is hard to believe that anyone would narrate his own conversion exclusively in terms borrowed from someone else's account; and yet this is how Matthew uses Mark's account. Third, the sort of rabbinic frame of mind and training suggested by the gospel would not be expected of a tax-collector. Therefore it is attractive to look for another reason why the gospel has been connected with the name Matthew. The presence of the name in the conversion story, and the insertion of 'the tax-collector' after this name in the list of the Twelve (Mt. 10: 3) are hardly sufficient reasons. Is it perhaps that the gospel was somehow put under Matthew's patronage or authority, rather as traditionally Mark stands somehow under Peter's authority?

The problem with Luke is in a way less burning; as Luke is not one of the disciples it does not really matter who he is. On the other hand, it is complicated by the question of the authorship of the Acts of the Apostles. The two works were certainly written by the same hand. The question is, whether the author of Acts was a companion of Paul or not. Some sections of Paul's journeys are narrated in the first person ('*we* embarked . . . *we* lodged' and so on in such a way as to yield a coherent route on which the author travelled with Paul. On the other hand the Acts show a theology and attitude which is at some points so much at variance with Paul's that it is hard to believe that the author of Acts had travelled for long with him. To suggest that the author of the '*we*-passages' was a companion of Paul but that a different author incorporated them in his work without changing the personal pronoun is not a satisfactory solution either. Again, the question is less important since a broader understanding of inspiration has removed the worry that somehow the author of a gospel should be at least closely connected with an apostle.

Whatever the solution to this puzzle may be, it is possible from his writings to form a picture of Luke. He moves in a quite different world to either Mark or Matthew, an educated world where style and a sophisticated vocabulary are appreciated, a world rich enough to make frequent warnings about the dangers of wealth and its misuse appropriate. He is at home in the Greco-Roman world rather than the Semitic world, and is well conversant with the legal and constitutional niceties of a number of varied city states of the eastern Mediterranean. He comes from the sort of background which makes him concerned to underline the respectability of Christianity in the eyes both of Roman and of Jew. He is more concerned than Mark or Matthew with the fate of the individual as opposed to the nation, and stresses personal qualities such as generosity and repentance. He is careful to integrate his gospel into the framework of world history.

With three gospels written by three personalities so diverse, and with backgrounds and readership so varied, it is not surprising that the aspects from which they see the Good News differ also. But they do share a common structure, which is not the case with John. The Johannine literature, consisting of the gospel, three letters and the Book of Revelation, stands in a tradition all its own. There is a marked similarity between them all, a similarity of approach, theology and language, and yet enough diversity, both of theological emphasis and of language, to suggest that they cannot be the work of one author. The best solution seems to be that they are the work of a school of writers, all strongly marked by the same spirituality of their master. This has been called by Raymond E. Brown, the scholar whose research into the subject is universally acclaimed, 'the community of the Beloved Disciple'. Traditionally this Beloved Disciple is identified with John, who is certainly one of the inner group of Jesus' disciples; but here again there are some difficulties, in that the Beloved Disciple features first in the Jerusalem stories and the end of the gospel, and is known in the High Priest's household, which would be unlikely for the Galilean fisherman that John was.

Again it makes little difference to the value or appreciation of the gospel whether the author was the apostle John (about whom so little is known personally). The important thing is that it, together with the other 'Johannine' writings, stems from a school who claimed as their initiator the Beloved Disciple, and whose deep but straightforward spirituality was founded on love. Literary studies have suggested that the gospel was compiled and edited not by the Beloved Disciple himself but by his disciples using the tradition of his preaching, which he had left behind in several closely-related versions. This would account for the circling, repetitious nature of the thought which is such a feature of this work. By the time the epistles came to be written the Beloved Disciple was long dead and new tensions had developed within the community, now led by a revered figure known as John the Presbyter; it was to win the separated brethren back to the fulness of fraternal love and to a true view of Christ's saving humanity that the letters were written.

There remain still other writings in the New Testament which have not been considered in this survey. They may be thought to be less important, but even the fact that they were written is often itself of major interest. The Second Letter of Peter may well be the latest document of the New Testament, written long after the death of the apostle Peter (so again a pseudepigraph), since it presupposes that the letters of Paul have already been collected together, and the first generation of Christians is referred to as long past. One of the most interesting things about it is that the letter shows the survival to write this letter of a strongly Jewish-Christian current in the Church, present also in the Epistle of Jude (with which 2 Peter has a number of parallels), for the interests, symbolism and theology of both letters are strongly Jewish. There is no other sign of the survival within the Church of such a strong Jewish interest right into the second century. Both the history of Judaism and of its split from Christianity and the blossoming of the gentile Church might have suggested that this current within the Church was long dead.

The interest of considering the question of the writing of the New Testament, how and by whom the various documents came to be written, lies in the variety of Christian life which it reveals. We do not have apostles and evangelists merely sitting at their desks in prayer and writing. We have a wide variety and a large number of people responding to the many colourful situations of Christian living: crises, questions, controversies, bewilderment, depression, joy. The characters are different and their responses are different; their milieux are different and they are geographically widespread all over the mediterranean world. How many were aware, in their response to everyday problems, that their written reaction would become part of the foundation deposit of the Church? How many were more than dimly aware – as Paul once says he is – that they were being guided by the Holy Spirit? Such richness of life, all (as we can now see) under the guidance of the Spirit, cannot but give confidence that the same Spirit will guide the present Church, so varied in its attitudes and responses, into solutions which hand on intact the message of the Good News.

New Testament morality

JOHN GREEHY

At the end of the parables of the Kingdom coming, the author of the gospel according to Matthew brings the third book to an end with a question which Jesus asks his disciples: 'Have you understood all this?'. They said to him, 'Yes'. And he said to them, 'Therefore every scribe who has been trained for the kingdom of heaven is like a householder who brings out of his treasure what is new and what is old' (13: 51 f).

We have here a challenge to every Christian preacher and teacher, not just a once-for-all statement to Jewish scribes. We bring forth in word and deed the new things of our testamental era and what is perennial from the old covenant dispensation. Our study of OT ethics will have shown us a great stress on justice. It would be wrong, however, to think of this as a kind of balancing act performed by a Greek figure over our law courts with a sword in one hand and a scales in the other. The OT concept of justice is rather one of a God initiating freely a gift of life out of love for his people. We call it covenant. This cannot be an agreement. After all, who can make a contract with the Absolute? Out of mother-love, God calls his people to a fulness of life. A kind of father-love then emerges, an expectancy for a response. Yet we cannot add to the glory of God. He has no need of us. We can only achieve our salvation through his continuing help, which encourages us to be fair in our dealings with one another. Hence our worship of our ever-present caring, healing God leads us to a way of life which embraces our neighbours as much as ourselves.

The element of truth must accompany this justice. We must be trustworthy as our God is faithful to us. Social breakdown follows a lack of these two basic virtues. 'Justice is turned back, and righteousness stands afar off; for truth has fallen in the public squares, and uprightness cannot enter' (Is. 59: 14). The great 'freedom' texts of Exodus speak of a people being let go from Egypt to sacrifice, to celebrate with a feast, and to serve (Ex. 3: 18; 5: 1; 7: 16). It is a service of Yahweh (the first commandment) and a worthy service of the neighbour for his sake (the other nine).

Love, also, has its place in the values of the older covenant. The holy God of Lev. 19 looks not only for a love of neighbour as ourselves in verse 18, but also a similar sharing of life together with strangers as a result of our concern and understanding: 'for you were strangers in the land of Egypt' (v. 34), surely an indictment of our own treatment of itinerants. We even have approach towards the enemy in bringing back his straying cow or donkey, or helping him to lift up his pack-horse lying under its burden (cf. Ex. 23: 4 f).

Justice, truth, freedom, love are the four constitutives of *Shalom,* the fulness of God's promise. It involves bringing tranquility where there is spiritual anxiety, stability where there is mental disquiet, security where there is emotional deprivation, healing presence where there is physical illness, helpful aid where there is material need. *Shalom* comprises everything that makes for human contentment. The peace-maker also reaches out to everybody. Thus, for me, the high point of the old covenant lies in the author of Jonah castigating the exclusiveness of his contemporaries and insisting that the message of fulfilment should be preached even to destructive enemies (like the Assyrians).

I have dwelt on this background to the NT because I firmly believe in the truth of the Japanese proverb: 'We must study the old to understand the new'. L. John Topel, S.J., writes in *The Way to Peace,* in a summary to a chapter on 'The Christian Response (ibility)': 'In the final analysis, the ethical message of the NT (its "law", so to speak) is similar to that of the OT: what God wants is interhuman justice. The NT advances the OT message by speaking of the love of a Father given to us in his Son Jesus, who gave us his own death as a model for the kind of love we should have for one another. Our response to this love is to be converted to the neighbour so totally, beginning from the spontaneous desires of our heart, that we share all of this world's goods with those who are poor. In this way we incarnate the suffering Servant in our world and really enter into that community in poverty that makes us blessedly happy and brings justice to those less fortunate than we. This message is the only salvation of our world'. The norm of morality in the New Testament is the person of Jesus himself.

We find writers on the moral teaching of the NT at variance in their approach. Thus J. L. Houlden's criticism of the monumental work of Rudolf Schnackenburg. 'He sets out to show what Jesus and the early Church taught. His book has three parts: (i) the moral teaching of Jesus; (ii) the moral teaching of the early Church in general; (iii) the teaching of prominent individuals, for instance, Paul, John and James. His scheme is open to serious objection. When we come to the NT and endeavour to come to terms with it, we are confronted with a set of writings, and these alone are our primary evidence. That for which they are primary evidence is, strictly, the thought of the writer concerned, or at the most the circle which he represents. Here then is our proper starting-point: that which for Schnackenburg is the finishing-point. Behind particular writers, we can discern, with varying degrees of confidence, something of the attitudes of groups in the early Church' *(Ethics and the New Testament,* London & Oxford, 1973).

I would suggest in all this discussion that the person of Jesus, the Christ, is a constant basis of all NT moral writing and that the *diakonia* (service) of following him will provide a continually unifying theme. I would propose that Christianity is an extension of a particular form of Judaism. One of the central issues in Palestine during the time of Jesus was the question about what constituted the Torah. It is within this context that Jesus criticizes what he regarded as the human-made elements of the law which get in the way of the close relationship between God and the individual that is intended by the Torah. In order to bring about a return to the Torah, Jesus preached repentance and *metanoia*. This in turn would prepare the people for the coming Reign of God. For Jesus the really important thing in life was adherence to the Torah which consisted in doing God's will. Thus, far from diminishing the centre-piece of Judaism, Jesus is the champion of the Torah as a particular way of life that unites the individual with God. This dimension of the Jewishness of Jesus and his teaching must surely figure prominently in the Jewish-Christian dialogue. The Jewishness of early Christianity and Christian-ness of first-century Judaism has much to contribute to the understanding of both traditions. This position would be very clear from a study of the Gospel according to Matthew (cf e.g. 3: 15 '. . . it is fitting for us to fulfil all righteousness', and 5: 17 'I have not come to abolish the law and the prophets but to fulfil them'). Obviously, a tension exists with Paul. While he admits that the law is 'holy and just and good' (Rom. 7: 12), its practice degenerated into formalism and the opposition of Judaizers led him to be wary about it, unlike Peter and Barnabas (Gal. 2: 11-4). We might also remember that Paul did not desert all of his Jewish patrimony. His continuing usage of the OT following rabbinical methods, and his belief in the bodily resurrection (a Pharisee tradition) which helped in his presentation of soteriology, make this point.

In our new covenant times, our pattern of living is now Jesus, whose Spirit is at work within us. He is the fulness of God's gift to us and revelation of himself (Jn 1: 14). All morality gives thanks to the Father by following his Son, Jesus. The Jesuit moralist, Josef Fuchs, writing on the absoluteness of moral terms, emphasizes that holy Scripture was never meant to be a handbook of morality, though in as much as it speaks of God's ways with mankind, it must also speak of man's behaviour, his religio-moral behaviour towards God. He writes: 'Since Scripture is concerned with the conversion and salvation of the sinner, and therefore with his personal transformation, statements regarding the religio-moral situation of man are central to the Bible. Nevertheless it is not the particular moral imperatives which have this central position, but the fundamental imperative of fidelity and obedience to God, of the following of Christ, of life according to faith and baptism, or, as with John, according to faith and love. But *these* moral-religious imperatives are transcendental, that is, they refer to the personal human being as a whole and not to specific moral conduct. And even though holy Scripture speaks also of particular attitudes and values – goodness, mildness, mercy, justice, modesty – these are still not "operative" norms of behaviour, since it has yet to be determined which actions are to be regarded as just, modest and kind' (*Gregorianum,* 1972). This is where right judgment enters in.

Our moral imperative is *belief in Jesus Christ* – belief in the full biblical sense which includes loving response in hopeful activity. The older observances which cocooned the law have no longer any place. 'I have been crucified with Christ', Paul tells the Galatians; 'it is no longer I who live, but Christ who lives in me, and the life I now live in the flesh I live by faith in the Son of God, who loved me and gave himself for me' (2: 20). Our union with him gives us, through adoption, a special relationship of sonship with the Father and frees us from the harsh tutoring (the *paidagogos*) of the law. 'And because you are sons, God has sent the Spirit of his Son into our hearts, crying, "Abba! Father!". So through God you are no longer a slave but a son, and if a son then an heir' (Gal. 4: 6 f; cf also Rom. 8: 9-17). It would be stupid to translate this *Abba* at a childish 'Daddy' level. The freedom thus freely given by our Father should lead to a continuing growth, a more mature adulthood. We have been freed from the slavery of sin and legal observance of the old dispensation to become, through love, slaves of one another. We should love our neighbours as ourselves, the fulfilment of the law, rather than devouring each other. Now it is true that while enunciating this general principle of love Paul adds in Galatians 5 a list of sins and virtues. What he means is this: Look! In our situation the presence or absence of these actions and attitudes is a sign of the presence or absence of genuine belief in Jesus Christ (our absolute norm). He recognizes that such a service is a continuing, demanding process and encourages us not to grow weary in well-doing, 'for in due season we shall reap, if we do not lose heart' (6: 9).

In our growth in moral living we are guided by the Holy Spirit through our conscience. 'I am speaking the truth in Christ, I am not lying; my conscience bears me witness in the Holy Spirit . . .' (Rom. 9: 1). It is the same faculty of which the second Vatican Council speaks: 'Always summoning man to love good and avoid evil, the voice of conscience can, when necessary, speak to his heart more specifically: do this, shun that' *(Gaudium et Spes,* 16). Paul takes up the notion of conscience for the first time in the pastoral situation of the Christian Corinthians and food offered to idols. He tells them that even though they know in their own conscience that they can buy and eat this meat, yet for the sake of the conscience of the weaker brethren who believe that this would involve a worship of idols they should not do so. Such an attitude will redound to the glory of God. 'So whether you eat or drink, or whatever you do, do all to the glory of God' (1 Cor. 10: 31). The conscience is educated through wisdom. 'For he has made known to us in all wisdom and insight the mystery of his will. . .' (Eph. 1: 9). The best description of this wisdom, as found in men, is delineated in James 3: 17: 'But the wisdom from above is first pure, then peaceable, gentle, open to reason, full of mercy and good fruits, without uncertainty or insincerity'. I would describe it as a virtue of discernment which guides man into a correct evaluation of the real situation (persons, places and things) in conformity to the will of God.

Paul will continually pray for his communities that they may receive this gift of discerning not merely the good from the evil, but the best of many possible good actions. Thus, before the Pauline 'Sermon on the Mount' of Romans 12-15 we read: 'Do not be conformed to this world but be transformed by the renewal of your mind, that you may prove what is the good and acceptable and perfect will of God' (12: 2). I paraphrase from Philippians: It is my prayer that your love may abound more and more, with a profound knowledge of every situation and a moral discrimination, so that you may in a fitting manner choose what is excellent (1: 9; cf also Col. 1: 9-10). He prays that they may always approve of the best among good things. Such a morality is not a conscience about what is merely good, as against evil, a 'morality of brinkmanship', but rather a conscience of what is the better, indeed the best, thing to do.

We might ask whether there is any need for external authority due to this interior guidance of the Holy Spirit. The experience of sinfulness in the community (cf e.g., 1 Cor. 5) forced Paul to exercise such an authority in a very definite manner. He fought also the pretensions of the so-called 'Party of Christ' who refused to subject themselves to the moral teaching of the apostles, claiming that they were servants of Christ alone. He continues to provide us with lists of sins. Sin is idolatry. It is a turning away from the grace of the Holy Spirit which has put an attitude of self-giving in place of the egoism caused by original sin. It is a return to self-seeking. It is the very negation of conscience towards others. It is the slogan: 'Don't delay. Grab to-day'.

In his lists, the specific sin which Paul calls idolatry is *pleonexia* (covetousness). It is so named in Colossians 3: 5, followed by Ephesians 5: 5. It is the crime of always grasping for more, and obviously of that which belongs to somebody else. Why identify this sin with idolatry? Lyonnet answers: 'The reason is that Paul saw in "greediness" the vice *par excellence* of paganism, the exact opposite of *agape* "charity" which defines the Christian "born of God". For Paul, Christians are by definition those who through love are servants of one another (Gal. 5: 13), while the pagan exploits his fellow men as instruments of gain (sins against justice) or of pleasure (sexual sins)'. (Lyonnet-Sabourin, *Sin, Redemption and Sacrifice,* Rome, 1970). Over against the list of vices in Colossians 3, he contrasts the richness of Easter living of those who forgive, love, are at peace, and at all times give thanks to God the Father through the Lord Jesus (cf Col. 3: 1-4 and 12-7).

For some, external law is very necessary: those who easily reject positive grace in favour of things opposed to God's will. Such law states the limits of friendship or enmity with God. We must understand this, 'that the law is not laid down for the just but for the lawless and disobedient, for . . . murderers . . . immoral persons . . . kidnappers, liars, perjurers, and whatever else is contrary to sound doctrine' (1 Tim. 1: 8-11). For others, they are conscious of two forces at work within them. Thus, the young men of the Johannine epistle are strong because they have been anointed by the holy one. The Word of God abides in them. They have overcome the evil one (cf. 1 Jn 2: 14, 20). Yet, they feel the pull of the world, and there is danger that the Father's love may be obliterated. They encounter the lust of the flesh — I call it pleasure; the lust of the eyes — I call it power; the pride of life — I call it the pomp and prestige of possessions. Yet all the while there can be a gradual development to full liberty. The Spirit of Christ moves us not only towards the fulfilment of the precepts of the law, laid down in the external forum for all of us, but also beyond the limits of law, he leads each of us individually towards what is perfect. 'You, therefore, must be perfect, as your heavenly Father is perfect' (Mt. 5: 48) can be a frightening ideal, something which led Luke to express the Lord's word in a more human way. 'Become you merciful, even as your Father is merciful' (6: 36). He is aware that it is a process which goes on all through our lives with its successes and failures. This brings us to the Sermon on the Mount.

All of the Beatitudes can be summed up in the statement

which Jesus made about authority in Mark's gospel when James and John sought the posts of Treasurer and Secretary of State in the political kingdom they thought he was about to inaugurate '. . . whoever would be great among you must be your servant . . . For the son of man also came not to be served but to serve, and to give his life as a ransom for many' (cf 10: 35-45). Jesus gives his life to make us all at one with the Father, freed from sin (cf. Is. 53: 10-11 and 1 Tim. 2: 6). Blessed are those who serve their fellow man even to death, these are indeed the children of God!

The Beatitudes are a complete reversal of worldly attitudes, an ideal which sets the tone for all of the Sermon. The Lord's statement about the OT *anaw* (poor man — often poor in this world's goods, always open to the will of God) is taken up in a social way by Luke, and a catechetical way by Matthew. Luke speaks of those actually poor, hungry and weeping in this life. They will be rewarded in the next. The heavenly only matters. So in his gospel he will seek to achieve the Matthaean beatitudes of 'poverty' in spirit through an apostolate to the rich. It is an attempt to make them less selfish, less self-possessed, and to make them more involved with the community of mankind and its many needs. Thus specific to Luke we meet the social message of the Baptist in ch. 3, the parables of the Good Samaritan, the Rich Man of the Barns, the Prodigal Son and the Resourceful Steward. Above all we have the conversion of the rich 'Outsider' Zacchaeus (cf also for an address to the wealthy 1 Tim. 6: 9-10 and 17-9). We recall the word of my favourite patristic exegete, St John Chrysostom: 'Give God the honour he asks for, that is give your money generously to the poor. God has no need of golden vessels but of golden hearts'. The poor in spirit, then, are those who are selfless in a covetous society and open to the Spirit of God.

Those who mourn do not just perform a *caoine* (a lament) about the evil in the world around us, but also express a genuine contrition about their own deficiencies. The meek man is the person of courage, who speaks firmly but does not react violently to the animal attacks of angry men: like Jesus before Annas (Jn 18: 23). We cannot understand the hunger and thirst of righteousness fully without the experience of a desert thirst, or the kind of hunger suffered in recent years by people in places like Ethiopia and Bangladesh. It is a craving in one's whole being to carry out the will of God totally. The whole word and work of Jesus was about this respect for the will of his Father even to death '. . . not my will, but thine, be done' (cf Lk. 22: 41-4). The merciful are primarily those who forgive others who have offended them, the test of the Our Father (Mt. 6: 14-15) and the awesome threat of the unforgiving servant (Mt. 18: 23-35). Then it also means, and obviously, a generosity to those caught up in need especially the continually deprived (cf. the last judgment parable of Mt 25: 31-46). The pure in heart are those who pursue the work of God with a single-minded purpose, and have a genuine quality about their living over against Pharisee hypocrisy. The peace-maker does not lie low but engages himself actively in bringing the fulness of God's promise to men wherever the need arises. This can only be achieved by people of *kenosis,* self-emptying, the people who are not looking for anything themselves. The early Christians suffered persecution from worldy people because they followed such a right design for life. They were reviled because they followed the way of Jesus Christ. They were blessed in that they continued to love such enemies and even pray for them. In fact, this is the only way which really works in the end. It has been often said: 'The trouble with the idea of an eye for an eye and a tooth for a tooth is that it leaves everyone in the end blind and toothless'. St Polycarp sums up this antithesis in Matthew between the laws of retaliation and love in his words to the Philippians: 'Pray for all God's people. Pray too for our sovereign lord, and for all governors and rulers; for any who ill-use you or dislike you; and for the enemies of the cross. Thus the fruits of your faith will be plain for all to see, and you will be perfected in him'.

As we see, the specific difference between OT and NT lies, not so much in commandment, but in the person of Jesus himself. The love of enemies, already suggested in passages like Exodus 23: 4 and Proverbs 25: 21 and stated in Bhakti Hinduism, becomes real in the continuing forgiveness of Jesus on the cross (cf Lk. 23: 34). Here we have the 'overflowing righteousness', that total response to the God who has always done the right thing by us, of which Matthew speaks (5: 20). 'This abundance is not a bigger and better Pharisaism, an ever more precise observance of legal niceties. It is radical gift of self to God and neighbour in both inner thought and outward action. It pursues the Law to its ultimate intention, even if that means abnegation of the letter.' Six times we meet the contrasting formula between Sinai and Jesus, 'it was said . . . but I say'. 'The opposition may take a mild form of deepending, spiritualizing, or radicalizing the Torah. This is the case with murder, adultery, and love of neighbour; the pattern is "not only . . . but also". But the radicalizing can be pushed so far that the letter of the Torah (some important command, permission, or institution) is revoked. This is the case with divorce, oaths and vows, and retaliation; the pattern is "not this . . . but that". When there is a *conflict* over what is the genuine will of God, the words of the Torah must cede to the word of Jesus' (cf J.P. Meier, *Matthew,* Dublin, 1980, pp. 46-55).

With our modern women's liberation organizations, we need to approach the *Haustafeln* (or kitchen-sink observances) of Titus 2 and 1 Peter 5 rather cautiously. Even the assumption of slavery in the postcard to Philemon may jar. Circumstances change of course, but the starting-point always holds. It is the *koinonia* (sharing, fellowship) of the Acts of the Apostles (cf 2: 42 and 4: 32-7) which would lead to the political freedom of Onesimus and the substitution of liberality for extravagance on the part of the women.

If the whole basis of the OT lay in the original 'passover' from Egypt to Sinai, so the foundation for our NT lies in the saving death and resurrection of Jesus. The way in which this was achieved marks off the new commandment. 'A new commandment I give to you, that you love one another' (Jn. 13: 34). As yet there is nothing new in this NT statement. It is the follow-through which is new and deepens the meaning of all such loving. 'Even as I have loved you, that you also love one another'. Jesus had shown this kind of loving by washing the very feet of his disciples, the service of a slave. Again, if we are to abide in the love of Father and Son and live full of joy in his Holy Spirit, we must keep his commandment. 'This is my commandment, that you love one another as I have loved you. Greater love has no man than this, than a man lay down his life for his friends' (Jn. 15: 12-13). The same Johannine tradition will spell out these 'friends' in terms of all mankind. This type of loving involves a readiness to give up one's life for the sake of all men. 'If anyone does sin, we have an advocate with the Father, Jesus Christ the righteous; and he is the expiation for our sins, and not for ours only but also for the sins of the whole world' (1 Jn 2: 1-2). The centre of Christianity must lie in that supreme moment of self-abnegation, even dereliction, when we are ready to die for others. In another way, this kind of dying may go on every day. Thus Luke, in his presentation of the word of the cross: 'If any man would come after me, let him deny himself and take up his cross daily and follow me' (9: 23). Such a continuing Christian living arises out of our hopeful prayer, 'Come, Lord Jesus' (Rev. 22: 20).

Belief in a Son of God?

HANS KÜNG

When asked 'What is Christmas?' most people would say: 'The feast of the birth of Jesus Christ'. That is correct and also vivid, clear and concrete. Nowadays few people would say: 'The feast of the descent of the Son of God to earth'. And fewer still would answer: 'The feast of the Incarnation of God'. Both these statments are appropriate to believing Christians. They are theologically accurate, yet we find them rather abstract, vague and general. As people of our own time we have difficulties with this kind of elevated theological discourse. Many people nowadays say: 'Jesus, yes — God, all right — but the Son of God, can we believe in God's Son, that God had a Son? Surely all that is mythology, ideas which are no longer meaningful for the modern mind'. Some are afraid to repeat the old Christian credal formulas, which they no longer understand; whereas others are afraid of the disappearance of just those formulas, in which they have always believed. Certainly, today people want to understand what they believe. And so what does it mean to say that 'Jesus is the Son of God'? Can we believe in a Son of God?

Of course the description of Jesus as the Son of God is an ancient article of Christian belief which is already laid down in the NT. Yet this statement is not something merely to be repeated thoughtlessly, to be recited, but something that has to be understood and interpreted for the present day.

My intention here is to try to elucidate the difficult pronouncements of Scripture in terms of the 'infancy narratives' of the NT, for we often combine the divine sonship of Jesus with his miraculous birth. There are three Holy Nights in the great world religions. In Buddhism we have the enlightenment of the Buddha; in Islam the bestowal of the Qur'an; and in Christianity the birth of Jesus. Of course they cannot, as sometimes happens, but put on the same level. But we cannot overlook the fact that extraordinary events regarding the birth of the founders of the great non-Christian religions, especially of the Buddha and of Mohammed, have also been handed down in tradition and can therefore hardly be said to offer evidence for the uniqueness of Jesus of Nazareth. Conception by a virgin, a miraculous birth, angelic visitations, and even satanic temptations are also related of the great founders of non-Christian religions; they are not reserved to Jesus. Miracles surround the birth of the Buddha, of Confucius, of Zarathustra and of Mohammed. The birth of the prophet Mohammed was also announced to his mother by an angel. The conception of Zarathustra was already accompanied by miraculous circumstances. Zarathustra's seed in a virgin produced the Persian world-saviour Saoshyant. The Buddha also had a virginal conception, since the Buddha entered Maya's body in the shape of a white elephant and made his exit from her side in the same form. Angels appear at the birth of Mohammed and Confucius, and all sorts of miraculous achievements are related not only of the infant Jesus but of the young Prince Siddharta. And the Buddha and Zarathustra were tempted by the evil one, just like Jesus. If, therefore, the divine Sonhood of Jesus were to be reduced to such extraordinary events associated with his birth or to miraculous deeds in his life, he might be ranged alongside the founders of the non-Christian religions, and other heroes, to say nothing of more or less dubious miracle-workers of ancient times.

What then is distinctively Christian? The answer is and remains the cross. As the Crucified, Jesus is different from the other founders of religions, and all the heroes and geniuses of world history. It is the crucified Jesus in whom we believe as the living one who was raised up from death and taken into divine glory. It was from the cross of this resurrected Jesus that the first witnesses looked back and took an interest in the beginning of his life: the start of Jesus' life, his birth. Hence the cross and crib go together. In the infancy narratives of Matthew and Luke, Jesus' divine Sonhood is portrayed in the popular form of a few stories that we all know well. They were important for the later development of Christian piety and the Church's calendar. From Christmas, with four weeks of Advent, we go back nine months: the Annunication on 25 March, and as a pendant to Christmas the feast of the Holy Innocents on 28 December, the Circumcision on 1 January, and the Magi on 6 January, and finally the Presentation in the Temple on 2 February. Matthew and Luke tell the reader about things in which the first evangelist, Mark, surprisingly showed no interest. It is just as striking to note that what no longer interested the last of the evangelists, John, both Matthew and Luke used as a miraculous introduction to their gospels: the accounts of Jesus' genealogy and parents, his conception by the Holy Spirit and his virgin birth, the events in Bethlehem and the summary account of his youth in Nazareth. Nowadays Protestant and Catholic exegetes accept (and this is something that we have to realize calmly and without any anxiety) that these infancy narratives, in contradistinction to the accounts of Jesus' public life and above all of his passion, are stories which are for the most part without any historical warranty, often contradict one another, are to a great extent legendary, and are ultimately theological in intention.

These are stories and narratives of a specific kind. The life of Jesus as we know it does not otherwise feature so many dream-events and all these comings-and-goings of angels. At that time they were taken as God's heavenly messengers for important events. Those contradictions which cannot be resolved concern not only the two branches of Jesus's lineage which are read in churches at Christmas time, and which accord with Jewish tables only from Abraham to David. They also concern numerous other points. Whereas Matthew appears to know nothing about Nazareth as the residence of Jesus' mother, Luke in his turn mentions nothing about the admittedly sensational but certainly legendary events of the visit of the Magi, the murder of the innocents in Bethlehem and the flight into Egypt, which no secular source confirms. Well-founded historical doubts also occur in the case of Jesus as a relative of John the Baptist, the census taking place at precisely that time, and even Bethlehem as Jesus' birthplace. In spite of the possibility that historical material has actually been used, we are not faced here with specific historical accounts, with police reports, so to speak. What then do we have? Something more. What we have is religious stories, preaching narratives which probably came from Jewish-Christian communities, were embellished by Matthew and Luke and placed at the start of their gospels. Hence there is an additional intention: to look back in the perspective of the Easter faith in order to proclaim and establish Jesus' status as Messiah in two ways.

In these stories Jesus is proclaimed first of all as the 'son of David' and second as the new Moses. A genealogical table is evidence of the providential descent and justification of the title 'son of David', which was foretold by the prophets. The table reaches from David up to Jesus' legal father Joseph, not to Mary. The symbolic accounting allows Jesus three times fourteen ancestors in the case of Matthew, and eleven times seven in that of Luke. Furthermore, Jesus is proclaimed as the new Moses. The providential destiny of the little child as predetermined by God is represented in the style of the early Jewish tales of Moses. The story of Jesus' birth features both the motif of the rescue of Moses from Pharaoh (in this case from Herod) and the theme of the flight into Egypt. The tale of the coming of the heathen Magi is in most effective counterpoint to that of the killing of the innocents by Herod; it has an irrefutable basis in human historical experience, for Israel and the heathen take up contrary attitudes to the news of the messiah Jesus proclaimed by the community: Israel rejects it and the heathen accept it. Matthew stresses this by citing the OT so as to bring out the salvific nature of events. Whereas Israel rejects the Messiah Jesus, the second Moses, the heathen come to him. That is the meaning of the narrative of the three kings or magi. The very different infancy narratives of Luke are also constructed in accordance with the OT model: the annunciation scene even literally. This is also true of the three songs of Mary, Zachary and Simeon, which probably originate in Judaeo-Christian tradition and reflect OT poetry.

Therefore it is important to realize that, even if the infancy narratives are not an historian's accounts, they can offer their own kind of truth. As preaching narratives or formularies of faith, these infancy stories are not intended primarily as accounts of historical truth but to reveal a saving truth, to offer truth for our salvation: that is, the news of human salvation in this Jesus. This can be done much more impressively, with much more visual effect, as a uniform account of the babe in the crib in Bethlehem than by means of a notice of birth, however historically exact as to time and place it may be. It is not historical criticism looking for the fundamental message that has emptied the news and feast of Christmas of its essential quality; that has been done by the tendency to reduce it to romantic pastoral and private devotion, and above all by superficial secularization and commercial interests. It has been done as though the fetching infant with the golden locks (not of course as in Luke and Matthew, but as in pious representations) had always smiled and never cried out wretchedly in a quite human way — which of course is what the crib and swaddling clothes indicate without any trace of social criticism or similar protest. As though, indeed, the saviour of the heavy-laden, born in a manger, had not clearly revealed his support for the nameless little people, for the shepherds and against the great names of world history, Augustus and Quirinius. As though the magnificat of Mary, the girl full of grace, which speaks of the fall of the mighty and the elevation of the lowly, and of the feeding of the hungry and the neglect of the mighty, did not militantly announce a reversal of estimation of the high and the low; and as though the gracious night of the new-born Child anticipated his activity and fate three decades later, as though this night and not the child himself in the crib already bore the sign of the cross on its forehead! As though (just as later in the trial before the Jewish tribunal) the scenes of annunciation to Mary and the shepherds, which form the very centre of the Christmas story, did not express the complete confession of faith of the community by means of several associated titles of dignity, such as Son of God, Saviour, Messiah, King and Lord, titles given to this small child instead of to the Roman Emperor, who is cited by name. As though there were no reference here to a peace quite other than the Pax Romana, the deceitful peace of the Roman Empire which was paid for with higher taxation, escalating armaments, the oppression of minorities and prosperous pessimism! But now the true peace of Christ was announced: that peace which consists in a new arrangement of relations between human beings in the light of human friendship with God and the fraternity of mankind.

It is obvious that even the apparently idyllic Christmas story has very real, socio-critical, and in the broadest sense political implications and consequences. True peace is set against the political saviour and the political theology of the Roman Empire, which ideologized and supported the imperial peace policy. The true peace referred to is that which cannot be expected wherever divine honour is paid to a man and autocrat. It is the true peace that we can expect wherever God in the highest is honoured and his loving-kindness is imparted to mankind. One has only to compare the Lukan Christmas gospel with the archaeologically discovered gospel of Augustus in the famous inscription found at Priene, to see how the rôles are reversed in the gospel. An end to wars, humane living conditions, common happiness and in short universal well-being, the salvation of men and of the world are no longer awaited from the all-powerful Roman Caesars but from this powerless child with no forces at his command.

In other words, we have to realize today that the stories of Christ's birth, properly understood, are quite different from some impotent little devotional tale about the infant Jesus. They are theologically highly-nuanced narratives of Christ intended to serve a quite specific form of proclamation: one which is designed to make the true meaning of Jesus as the saving Messiah for all the nations of the world apparent, with artistry and in a concrete and highly critical form. He is shown as Jesus the son of David and as the new Moses, the one who fulfils the old covenant and initiates the new, as the Saviour of the poor and as the true Son of God. These stories are obviously not the first stage of a biography of Jesus of or an exact family tree. All this is instead an authentic gospel: that is, a call and proclamation, according to which the OT promises have been fulfilled in Jesus, God's chosen one, the Son of God who does not offer a detailed political theory and programme, but in his talk, actions and suffering provides a very practical standard by which men and women can orientate themselves with assurance in their individual and social behaviour.

The foregoing is also, in essence, the meaning of the notion of the Incarnation of God, or rather, of the Son of God. Not the Father but the Son of God became man in accordance with the Scriptures, as the Word and Logos. The Incarnation of the Son of God should not be interpreted only in terms of the single mathematical or mystical point of the conception or birth of Jesus. What is meant by 'incarnation' here has to be understood in terms of the whole life and death of Jesus. The Incarnation of the Son of God in Jesus means that in all Jesus' talk, in his whole preaching, behaviour and destiny, God's word and will took on human form. In all his words and actions, in his suffering and death, in his whole person Jesus announced, manifested and revealed God's word and will. We might say that he in whom word and deed, teaching and life, being and behaviour were fully accordant, was the living word of God, the living will of God, and the living Son of God: 'And the Word became flesh and dwelt among us and we saw his glory, full of grace and truth'.

What therefore does it mean for us today when we say that we believe in the Son of God? In spite of all the time I have spent studying the God of the philosophers, and in spite of his importance for me, I must confess that the God of the philosophers – however impressive – remains intellectually and emotionally unsatisfactory. Even the God of the OT is, as far as I am concerned, and without any compulsion thereby to surrender my philosophical insights, the more divine God, the real God with characteristics, the God with a human face. The human Jesus of Nazareth in his whole being and activity, speaking and behaviour, suffering and dying, shows, manifests and reveals to me this divine countenance which is still hidden and sometimes polyvalent in the OT. When I contemplate Jesus and precisely the infant Jesus, I have the unusually firm assurance that before this God, in spite of all his infinite distance, I have no need to shake and tremble with fear. Before this God, this child Jesus, I do not need to make myself small or to cringe. Nor do I have to consider God's mysterious decrees and anxiously search out his inscrutable will. Instead I should be grateful to those who taught me to recognize this more friendly God, instead of embittering me against him, as a psychologist put it recently. I know that where Jesus is, there is God too. He tells me what God's will is. Where Jesus acts and speaks, God is on his side; where Jesus suffers and dies, God is secretly present. Therefore I can look on him as the countenance or face of God, but also as the word and Son of God. For me, all these images serve to express the unique relationship of God to Jesus and Jesus to God, his Father: his unity with God, the Father; his significance as the one who reveals this God.

Surely it is more comprehensible now why I wish to see what Jesus really means and is only from the basis of God: why precisely Jesus and no other great teacher, not Buddha, Confucius or Mohammed, and not Marx or Freud, can summon me unconditionally to follow him. In Jesus I am summoned by the one, true God himself to follow him. I am as little inclined to say Lord, Lord, as to say Son of God, Son of God. But it is supremely important for me that man and God are truly involved in the history of Jesus Christ. On the basis of the NT, I could not substantiate any interpretation of the history of Jesus Christ in which Jesus Christ was only a man, only a preacher, prophet or soothsayer, let alone only a symbol or a cypher for general, fundamental human experiences. That is not the message of the Bible. But on the NT basis, I am also unable to substantiate any interpretation of the history of Jesus Christ in which Jesus Christ is only God or simply God: as though he were God, the Father, and a God who traverses the earth removed from human weaknesses and inadequacies.

For me Jesus of Nazareth is the Son of God. The whole significance of the events that took place in and around him relies on the fact that in Jesus the God who loves mankind is himself at hand. The God who loves mankind is himself at work in Jesus. Through him God himself spoke, acted and finally revealed himself. Here I am as little in need of mythological and semi-mythological semblances as in the case of belief in the Creator God or the eschatological God. But I do stand by the uniqueness, the underivability and insurpassable nature of his person, and the summons, offer and claim it expresses. Because God himself speaks and acts through Jesus, for me he and no other is the Christ of God, his revelation and his likeness, his word and his Son. He is the only-begotten Son of God. For that reason, it is proper for me to maintain against all piously intended attempts to divinize him, that Jesus precisely as the Son of God was fully and entirely man, and indeed a child with all the consequences that that entails, and like men could suffer, felt lonely and uncertain, and was not free from temptations, doubts and errors in his later life. But, unlike men – all other men, and even all saints and founders of religions – he is not a mere man but, because he is God's word and Son, true man. He is the true man in whom theory and practice, being and acting, teaching and living form a unity. As true man he offered his proclamation, his behaviour and indeed his whole life and death for me as a model of human existence that, if I trust in it, ever and again, enables me to discover and realize the meaning of my humanity, my freedom and my life, the meaning in being here and for my fellow men.

Jesus Christ as the one confirmed by God therefore represents for me the lastingly trustworthy, the ultimate standard of human existence. Christology or Christ-theory may be important, but belief in Christ and following Christ are more important. It is a matter of being a Christ-ian. That is something that Jesus Christ makes possible for me, and therefore I do not hesitate to say, even as a man of the twentieth century: '*Credo in Jesus Christum filium Dei unigenitum*' – 'I believe in Jesus Christ, the only-begotten Son of God'.

The resurrection and Christian belief

BRIAN DAVIES, OP

Consider the following account, which more or less represents what my schoolteachers taught me about the resurrection: 'Christian belief in the resurrection is based on the New Testament, which gives us an accurate, historical picture of what actually happened in the past. According to the NT, to believe in the resurrection is to believe that Jesus was physically raised from the dead at a certain point in time. This means that he is divine, and, therefore, to be trusted (you don't argue with God). It also means that our own future resurrection is guaranteed'.

What I want to do in this chapter is briefly to consider the credibility of this view. Were my teachers right about Christian belief and the resurrection? Or should their position be rejected?

One thing, at least, is perfectly clear. Belief in the resurrection certainly includes the belief that Jesus is alive, even though there was a time at which he died (cf Lk. 24: 5, 23; Acts 1: 3, 25: 9; 2 Cor. 13: 4). But anyone who says this will quickly realize that he has only gone so far. Jesus is alive, but so are dogs and cats. And so are dandelions. The question is, what does it mean to say that Jesus is alive? I shall be moving in a moment to some of the things that NT writers say about this question; to begin with, however, let us consider it in more general or philosophical terms. In other words, let us start by asking what must be true if Jesus is indeed alive.

One thing, I think, that cannot be true is that Jesus is now around as some kind of disembodied mind or soul or spirit. You may, or course, find my view strange, for there is a widespread tendency to think that people are basically identical with something other than their bodies, something intangible, something that can survive corporeal dissolution. And this view, indeed, is not without a long and impressive pedigree. Poets have traded off it (think of John Donne), and it has also been defended by some of the most famous philosophers. You can find it, for example, in Plato's *Phaedo* and in later works like Descartes' *Meditations* and the *Discourse on Method*. But it is still very misguided.

It is, to be sure, easily come by. In many contexts it is natural to think of ourselves as composite creatures, as being, or having, a mind and a body. But we also need to remember that much of our understanding of human beings involves an ineradicable reference to the existence and processes of their bodies. To be alive as a human being is to be able to engage in all sorts of activities which are impossible in the absence of a body. Consider, for instance, thinking. That is not just a process of silently reciting sentences to oneself; it involves reflecting about what one is doing, taking in one's enviornment, acting with a purpose, doing things precisely, and so forth. Then there is seeing. Anyone who tries to explain what this involves will soon have to take notice of sentences like 'I can't see, it's too dark', 'Look and see', 'Let's see if he's finished', 'I saw her in the park yesterday'. The point is that if we are really talking about human life and human activity, we cannot be talking about anything less than bodily life and bodily activity. That is not, of course, to say that there cannot be human life which is more than bodily life as we have to think of it when we think of people being alive. It is just that there cannot be human life which is less than this.

It seems, then, that if Jesus is alive, he cannot be alive in anything less than bodily form. Or is that really so? It might be said that the argument has already moved too quickly. Jesus cannot be alive as a disembodied mind; but does this have to mean that he is actually alive with a body? Ought we not to be more sophisticated in our thinking about the living Jesus? Why not say that Jesus is alive in a sense that involves neither spiritual survival nor bodily existence?

That kind of view has certainly been supported, though it takes more forms than can be documented here. Usually, however, the argument goes something like this: 'To say that Jesus is alive is not to say something about Jesus himself. It is not, for instance, like saying that Queen Elizabeth is alive. In fact, it is really a way of talking about ourselves or some abstract principle. It is, for example, to say that we are committed to Jesus, or that the power of love is stronger than that of evil, or that the life and work of Jesus is deeply significant.'

Another view is that talk about the present life of Jesus is a way of speaking about the Christian community. Hubert Richards endorses this opinion in his book *The First Easter: What Really Happened?*. According to Richards, to believe in the resurrection is to believe in the bodily life of Jesus. But, says Richards, to talk about bodies is to talk about 'communicability'. In fact, it is to say that Christians can come to a certain level of 'communicability' with each other. 'If anyone', says Richards, 'is asked today where the body of Jesus is, he can only point to a group of people. They *are* the way in which he is now embodied'.[1]

The trouble, however, with views like this is that they are basically silly. If I say that there is a pig in my room, and if it turns out that what I am telling you is that pigs are a good thing, or that there is an important point to grasp about pigs, or that the world contains pig addicts, you will rightly upbraid me for failing to say what I mean. More precisely, you will tick me off for talking nonsense. Similarly, if one says that Jesus is alive, and if one only means by that the sort of thing mentioned in the last two paragraphs, one is simply being disingenuous, or, at least, trying to say what one means in a very misleading way. Jesus was a human being, and to say that he is now alive must, therefore, be to say that a human being is now alive, for otherwise we would not be talking about Jesus, but about something else. As we have seen, however, to be alive as a human being is to be a bodily individual, which is something quite different from a bright idea, a verdict on the past, an abstract truth, or a group of people. Such things cannot be identified with a living person, and it is sheer sophistry to say otherwise. You might just as well argue that Napoleon was a puff of smoke or that Hitler was the twelve apostles. We can, of course, make sense of statements like 'Shakespeare is immortal', and that might be urged as a point on the other side. But it also needs to be said that, however immortal Shakespeare may be, if he is physically dead, then he (Shakespeare in the fullest sense) is not alive.

So if we are to take seriously the view that Jesus lives, we will have to start thinking in terms of his bodily life after death. And at this point we can turn directly to the NT, for that is how the NT thinks of the resurrection.

Take, for example, 1 Cor. 15. Here Paul talks about the resurrection of Jesus and the resurrection of Christians. And it is obvious that he thinks that the Christian's resurrection resembles that of Jesus (cf Phil. 3: 21). How, then, does Paul think of the Christian's resurrection? The answer is: 'In bodily terms'. According to Paul, whose position at this point has a background in Jewish thinking,[2] the notion of resurrection is the notion of the raising up of the body that has died. Paul certainly does not confuse resurrection with mere resuscitation. 'What is sown', he says 'is perishable, what is raised is imperishable. It is sown in dishonour, it is raised in glory. It is sown in weakness, it is raised in power. It is sown a physical body, it is raised a spiritual body' (1 Cor. 15: 42-4). But Paul still holds that when a person is raised then a body is raised, and he is clear enough that, though this body is spiritual, it is still a body. So his conclusion on the resurrection of Jesus is that it involves the continuation of Jesus' bodily life.

The same view can be found in the gospels, particularly in the tradition that the tomb of Jesus was found to be empty. Why do the evangelists hand on this tradition? The most natural answer is that they want to say that Jesus has been restored to life in a way that excludes his body remaining in its grave. And that, presumably, is what other NT writers would want to say. It has been argued otherwise, for Paul does not mention the empty tomb though he obviously believes in the resurrection. But this fact hardly establishes that Paul does not accept or presuppose the tradition of the empty tomb. He never does say much about traditions concerning the historical Jesus, but he may well have been familiar with and in agreement with several of these. And he certainly does not reject the empty tomb tradition. What he says is actually consistent both with it and with the overall position of the evangelists on the resurrection. Both Paul and the evangelists think of the resurrection in bodily terms. They also hold that Jesus was buried, and that the real reason for believing in the resurrection lies in the appearances of Jesus after his death (of which more below). It is important to remember that the evangelists do not endorse a straight inference from the empty tomb to the resurrection. In Mark the discovery of the empty tomb leads only to fear and confusion (Mk 16: 8). Matthew mentions the supposition that the body of Jesus was stolen (Mt. 28: 13-5), from which one imagines that he was aware that various explanations of an empty tomb are possible, which indeed they are, and which seems also to have been realized by Luke and John. Luke says that women find the tomb of Jesus empty and 'were perplexed about this' (Lk 24: 4). According to John, Mary Magdalene jumps to the conclusion that someone has removed Jesus' corpse. 'They have taken away my Lord', she says, 'and I do not know where they have laid him' (Jn 20: 13).

The physicality of Jesus' resurrection is also brought out in some of the gospel appearance stories: to be precise, in those of Luke and John. Both these evangelists talk about the way in which the risen Jesus presented himself to his disciples, and both evidently want us to suppose that he did so as a figure materially continuous with the Jesus who died and was buried. Luke makes the point by actually saying that Jesus drew attention to his flesh and bones (Lk. 24: 39). And in John, of course, there is the famous story of doubting Thomas. What Thomas doubts is that Jesus is actually risen. According to John, the matter is settled for him empirically (Jn 20: 24-9).

But there is more to the NT view of the resurrection than a simple emphasis on the raising of the body of the dead. We have already seen that Paul does not believe simply in a mere resuscitation of Jesus; but neither do other NT writers.

Consider again the gospel appearance stories. We have just been looking at the way in which they stress the continuity between the Jesus of before and after Easter. But they also stress discontinuity or transformation. Thus, for example, Luke says that the disciples only recognized the risen Jesus after a very long time in his presence, whereupon 'he vanished out of their sight' (Lk. 24: 31). And, on Luke's account, Jesus does not appear in Jerusalem simply by walking into a room. The disciples are talking among themselves when suddenly 'Jesus himself stood among them' (Lk. 24: 36). Afterwards, he is actually capable of ascending into heaven (Lk. 24: 51; cf Acts 1: 6-11; cf Jn 20: 17).

This stress on the transformation of Jesus is also something that emerges in the various ways in which NT writers talk when they are concerned not with the business of resurrection appearances but rather with what we might call the life of the risen Jesus. They think of this in terms of exaltation. Consider, for instance, Luke's account of Peter's speech on the day of Pentecost: 'This Jesus God raised up, and of that we are all witnesses. Being therefore exalted at the right hand of God, and having received from the Father the promise of the Holy Spirit, he has poured out this which you see and hear . . . Let all the house of Israel therefore know assuredly that God has made him both Lord and Christ, this Jesus whom you crucified' (Acts 2: 32-3, 36). Notice in particular the reference here to the lordship of the risen Jesus. It is echoed throughout the NT. Jesus, says Paul, died on the cross. 'Therefore', he immediately adds, 'God has highly exalted him and bestowed on him the name which is above every name, that at the name of Jesus every knee should bow, in heaven and on earth and under the earth, and every tongue confess that Jesus Christ is Lord to the glory of God the Father' (Phil. 2: 9-11). For Paul, the resurrection is something final and transcendent, something belonging as much to the world of God as it does to the world of men, a point which is also emphasized by the author of Hebrews. According to him, Jesus is 'a great high priest who has passed through the heavens' (Heb. 4:14).

But now for another question. At the beginning of this chapter I referred to the view that Christian belief in the resurrection is based on the NT considered as an historically accurate account of events in the past. But can we now think of the NT in this way? And can we now think of its references to the resurrection as statements of an historical kind?

It has been maintained that the answer to this question is perfectly simple. On this view, which is a very familiar one, everything that the NT authors say can be understood in a literal manner. In talking about the resurrection, so the argument continues, the NT offers a straight historical account of what actually happened at some time past.

But this conclusion will obviously not do as it stands, anxious though many people are to think otherwise. One reason for saying so (and it is only one reason) brings us to the question of the nature of the gospels, and especially to the nature of their resurrection narratives. It is generally agreed by modern NT scholars (though there are still a few dissenting voices) that

Matthew and Luke were both aware of Mark's gospel, which they used as a source for their own writings. But they certainly do not follow it slavishly, and they also disagree with it on various matters of detail. They also disagree with each other, particularly in their resurrection narratives. These cannot be convincingly harmonized either with each other or with the resurrection narrative found in John. As Christopher Evans puts it. 'It is not simply difficult to harmonize these traditions, but quite impossible. Attempts to combine them by means of inspired guesses and hypotheses, of which F. F. Morrison's *Who Moved the Stone?* has been for so long an outstanding and brilliant example, are really defeated from the start. For what have to be combined are not a number of scattered pieces from an originally single matrix, but separate expressions of the Easter faith. Each of these is complete in itself; each has developed along its own lines so as to serve in the end as a proper conclusion for an evangelist of his own particular version of the gospel. Behind and within all the traditions, of course, is the conviction that Jesus of Nazareth continues to be and to operate, and that in him past, present and future are somehow related; but the mode of this continuation is differently conceived in the four gospels, and in each case is closely related to the theology of the particular gospel concerned. Each evangelist gives his own version as a total version, which is not intended to stand up only if it stood alongside another, or was supplemented by another'.[3]

The reader must obviously decide for himself how far he agrees with Evans here, ideally by working through a synopsis of the gospels. But the general drift of his remarks would currently be regarded as a commonplace of modern biblical scholarship, both Protestant and Catholic. Evans, as it happens, is a Protestant, but much the same as he says is also affirmed by, for example, the Catholic writer Xavier Léon-Dufour. Talking of the gospel resurrection narratives he says: 'Every biography assumes that coordinates of place and time have been established at least in outline, for without them the narrative has no firm basis. Now an attentive reading of the texts defies us to harmonize the various narratives in time and space'.[4] According to Dufour, the gospel resurrection narratives 'are the result of literary constructions'.[5]

So we cannot think about the resurrection simply by repeating the words of the NT on the assumption that they are all to be taken as parts of the latest doctoral thesis on ancient history. But we also need to avoid going too far in the other direction. If the NT is not a bald piece of history writing, it is not an early novel either. From what I have just been saying it might be inferred that one cannot regard the NT as providing us with reports of what actually occurred. But that is far from obviously true.

For one thing, although the gospels are not to be thought of as straight historiography, they are not obviously unconcerned with history. As many contemporary specialists argue, it is possible to use them in trying to say something about the actual words and works of Jesus. Some years ago there was a great deal of scepticism aout the possibility of any historical reconstruction based on the gospels. As R. H. Lightfoot put it (in a particularly famous remark): 'The form of the earthly no less than of the heavenly Christ is for the most part hidden from us. For all the inestimable value of the gospels, they yield us little more than a whisper of his voice; we trace in them but the outskirts of his ways'.[6] But this view has not gone unchallenged in recent literature. The last thirty years have thrown up a number of studies devoted to what is sometimes called the New Quest for the Historical Jesus, involved in which have been some of the twentieth century's most widely read students of the NT, figures like Günther Bornkamm, C. H. Dodd, J. Jeremias, Ernst Käsemann, Norman Perrin, J. M. Robinson, and Eduard Schweitzer.[7] It cannot be said that all these writers agree with each other in detail, and the whole project of a New Quest has not gone unchallenged. But it cannot now be regarded as idiosyncratic to argue that the gospels are not flatly unconcerned with historical fact. They may be a curious mixture of accurate historical reporting and personal elaboration and reflection. Documents of this kind are, of course, perfectly familiar to secular historians. Particularly worth noting with reference to the gospels are the earliest accounts of the death of Thomas Becket. There are several of these, and they can all be taken as recording the absolutely certain historical fact that Becket was murdered in Canterbury. But they disagree with each other in some remarkable ways, especially over details concerning people, dates and chronology. Some of them also show signs of being affected in their narrative by theological reflection on Becket.[8]

It might still, of course, be urged that the NT talks of the resurrection in ways rather different from those in which we might normally talk about an event in the past. But even if this is so, it is important not to make too much of the fact. For, as we have seen, for all their insistence on the transformation of the risen Jesus, writers like Luke and John also give us passages which pull the other way. Could these not be interpreted as emphasizing that it was really the historical Jesus who was transformed and, therefore, that the transformed Jesus is continuous with the historical one? Can one not reasonably infer that, for Luke and John at least, the resurrection is also part of the history of an historical individual?

That other NT writers think of the resurrection in these terms is certainly a plausible conclusion. Consider, for example, the NT assertion that Jesus was raised 'on the third day' (1 Cor. 15: 4; cf Mt. 16: 21; 17: 23; 20: 19; 27: 63; Lk. 9: 22; 18: 33; 24: 7, 46; Acts 10: 40). It has recently been argued that 'the third day' entered the NT because it was already believed that the resurrection fulfilled OT expectations, or for some reason other than that the NT writers (or their sources) are anxious to hand on a chronological detail which they take to be historical. And in support of this view one might appeal to passages like Hos. 6: 2 and Jonah 2: 1, as well as to other non-biblical Jewish writings which would enable one to make theological (as opposed to chronological) sense of the expression 'the third day'. But Hos. 6: is not cited as a proof text in the NT, while Jonah 2: 1 (with its reference to 'three days and three nights') is incompatible, when applied to the resurrection, with the gospel's statement that Jesus was found to have been raised 'on the first day of the week' (cf Mt. 28: 1; Mk 16: 2; Lk. 24: 1; Jn 20: 1). And, even if 'the third day' had a theological significance for writers at the time when the NT was produced, this significance is not drawn out in any obvious way by NT writers. Perhaps 'the third day' is, for them, a theological and not a chronological phrase, but I do not see that there is any compulsion on us to suppose that this is so. And, of course, there is always the possibility that the expression serves both a theological and a chronological purpose.[9]

A related point can be made with reference to the whole of 1 Cor. 15: 3-8. Here Paul says that Jesus was raised. What could he mean by that? Could he mean something other than that an event took place involving the historical Jesus? If he does, it is strange to find him later talking in terms that suggest that resurrection involves a change in people (cf. 1 Cor. 15: 35-58). And his very use of the word 'raised' (*egēgertai*) is significant. The Greek word *egēgertai* comes from the transitive verb *egeirein,* and it denotes waking up and rousing from sleep. Paul also talks of the resurrection by using the verb *anistēmi*, which denotes being put on one's feet, being made to stand up. He evidently does not suppose that when one is raised from the dead one just gets up and walks away as if nothing has happened, rather like Lazarus (Jn 11) or the widow's son at Nain (Lk. 7: 11-7). But his talk about resurrection does not overtly and absolutely exclude this idea and its associations. If anything, it could be regarded as taking them up and adding to them.

I should argue, then, that, in the view of the NT, belief in the resurrection is founded on a matter of history — the fact that at some time past Jesus was raised from the dead, not in any metaphorical sense, but in the sense implied by Paul in his discussion of resurrection in 1 Corinthians. Yet no sooner has one said this than an obvious question arises. Why does it all matter? Why should one make anything of the resurrection?

As I have said, my teachers took the view that if Jesus has been raised, then Jesus is divine. But here one must definitely part company with them. Apart from the fact that there is no obviously sound inference from 'X is raised' to 'X is divine' (why not just move from 'X is raised' to 'X is very lucky'?), there is no NT writer who claims that Jesus is divine because he has been raised.

But this is not to say that the NT does not maintain that conclusions can be drawn from the resurrection. Indeed, the opposite is true, for there are at least three NT views about the significance of the resurrection.

The first concerns what we can say of Jesus in the light of the resurrection. According to the NT, the resurrection indicates the endorsement of Jesus by God. This point can easily be confirmed by looking, for example, at NT assertions to the effect that Jesus 'was raised' (cf 1 Cor. 15: 4; Rom. 10: 9; 1 Cor. 6: 14; 2 Cor. 4: 14; Eph. 1: 20; 1 Thess. 1: 10; 1 Pet. 1: 21). To say that Jesus 'was raised' is another way of saying that God raised Jesus, and it reflects the language of Jewish apocalyptic, which also presents the idea of a resurrection brought about by God (cf Is. 26: 19; Dan. 12: 2). In its NT context, used with reference to Jesus, the meaning of such language is clear enough: God has acted on behalf of Jesus and is therefore, so to speak, behind him. As St Paul puts it in 2 Cor: 13: 'For he was crucified in weakness, but raised by the power of God' (v. 4).

Another way of presenting this view can be seen in NT appeals to the OT, in particular in the appeal made in some of the speeches in Acts. Take, for example, the speech of Paul in Acts 13. First we get a reference to the death and resurrection of Jesus; then comes the climax: 'And we bring you the good news that what God promised to the fathers, this he has fulfilled to us their children by raising Jesus; as also it is written in the second psalm, "Thou art my Son, today I have begotten thee". And as for the fact that he raised him from the dead, no more to return to corruption, he spoke in this way, "I will give you the holy and sure blessings of David". Therefore he says also in another psalm, "Thou wilt not let thy Holy One see corruption" ' (Acts 13: 32-5). The drift of this argument is not hard to fathom: since Jesus is raised he can, in accordance with the OT, safely be regarded as the Messiah.

But NT writers are interested in the resurrection as more than an indication of Jesus' special status. For they also want to regard it as part of the story of man's salvation. Much Christian thinking about salvation concentrates almost exclusively on the fact of the crucifixion. The idea here is that it is basically by means of the cross that men are saved. And there is no doubt that the saving significance of the crucifixion is given some prominence by NT writers, especially Paul (cf Rom. 3: 21-6; 1 Cor. 15: 3; Gal. 1: 4). But this fact ought not to make us forget the sort of thing Paul says about the resurrection in texts like Romans 4. Here he talks about faith being reckoned to Abraham as righteousness. 'It will', he adds, 'be reckoned to us who believe in him that raised from the dead Jesus our Lord, who was put to death for our trespasses and raised for our justification' (vs. 24-5). Later in Romans, Paul explains that Christ 'has been raised from the dead in order that we may bear fruit for God' (Rom. 7: 4). The point lurking around here becomes explicit in 1 Cor. 15: 17: 'If Christ has not been raised, your faith is futile and you are still in your sins'. In Paul's view, Christians have something to be thankful about precisely because Christ has been raised (cf Col. 2: 6-15).

A variation on this theme receives a particularly detailed exposition in the letter to the Hebrews. For the author of Hebrews, Christ is the great high priest whose work brings salvation. But this work is not to be thought of as over and done with at the crucifixion. Christ is to be understood as currently exercising his priestly role: 'Although he was a Son, he learned obedience through what he suffered; and being made perfect he became the source of eternal salvation to all who obey him, being designated by God a high priest after the order of Melchizedek' (Heb. 5: 8-9).

Nor is the author of Hebrews the only NT writer to support the idea that Christ, being raised, now works on behalf of people. In John's gospel Christ talks of his death (and therefore, for John, of his resurrection). He says that he goes 'to prepare a place for you' (Jn 14: 2). Later he adds: 'It is to your advantage that I go away, for if I do not go away, the counsellor will not come to you; but if I go, I will send him to you' (Jn 16: 7). A related comment occurs in 1 Jn 2: 1: 'If anyone does sin, we have an advocate with the Father, Jesus Christ the righteous'. And the presence of the risen lord as a source of salvation cannot be far from St Paul's mind when he says that Christians are 'in Christ'. As F. X. Durrwell puts it: 'In the Apostle's earliest writings, where the phrase is used to express some relationship with Christ not clearly defined (I Thess. iii. 8; iv. 1; v. 12, 18; 2 Thess. iii. 4), the Christ indicated is the Lord present to the Church through his resurrection. Later, as the phrase grew in depth to mean some mysterious way in which the believer was present in Christ, it does not seem as though Christ was ever thought of except as in his present state of glory; the union it indicated was above all a sharing in the new life into which Christ was born through his resurrection. Such is certainly the sense of the great majority of these texts: "In Christ all shall be made alive" (1 Cor. xv. 22): "Anyone who is in Christ is a new creature" (2 Cor. v. 17): "The law of the spirit of life in Jesus Christ hath delivered me" (Rom. viii. 2): "He . . . hath raised us up together and hath made us sit together in the heavenly places, in Christ's Jesus." (Eph. ii. 6)'.[10]

So, in reading the NT, we also have to reckon with the notion that the Christian's salvation depends on the resurrection. But there is yet another point to note, and with that we come to a final major NT attempt to make theological capital out of the resurrection. It is found in the view that the resurrection of Christ is a ground of hope for the future resurrection of the Christian.

The view is simply stated by St Paul, and again it is 1 Cor: 15 that proves decisive. Here Paul copes with the assertion that 'there is no resurrection of the dead' (v. 12). The assertion is evidently intended as a general one: nobody is raised. But, Paul argues, that cannot be, for Christ is raised. The implication is that Christ's resurrection is a reason for supposing that people other than Christ are raised: 'If Christ has not been raised, your faith is futile and you are still in your sins. Then those also who have fallen asleep have perished. If for this life only we have hoped in Christ, we are of all men most to be pitied. But in fact Christ has been raised from the dead, the first fruits of those who have fallen asleep' (vs. 17-20). The idea here is that, just as the first part of a crop is an assurance that the whole crop will follow, so the resurrection of Jesus is an assurance that the resurrection of those in Christ will follow. As Paul goes on to say: 'For as in Adam all die, so also in Christ shall all be made alive. But each in his own order: Christ the first fruits; then at his coming those who belong to Christ' (v. 22).

More or less the same point emerges in Romans 6. First Paul brings together the death of Christ and the death to sin of the Christian. Then comes a parallel relating to resurrection (Rom. 6: 4-5). According to Paul, the resurrection of Christ is not just something that concerns Christ; it also concerns the Christian, for it is something akin to what Christians can hope to participate in themselves.

But only, says Paul, because Christ is raised; and here Paul agrees with John, who is also emphatic that the resurrection of Christ is a condition of a general resurrection. 'Truly, truly', says Christ in John, 'the hour is coming, and now is, when the dead will hear the voice of the Son of God, and those who hear will live. For as the Father has life in himself, so he has granted the Son also to have life in himself . . . the hour is coming when all who are in the tombs will hear his voice and come forth . . . '(Jn 5: 25-9).

John is in no doubt that it is the risen Christ who calls the dead to life. He is also certain that the risen Christ is the Christ who died. We have now seen that his certainty is shared by other NT writers; and, though I have only touched on some of their ways of expressing it, though the topic of the resurrection raises philosophical questions which I have not here gone into, and though there are prolems of exegesis that I have ignored altogether, perhaps I can now leave the reader with the suggestion that the view with which we started is not entirely wrong. It might be worth adding that, if such is the case, then life, however it may appear, can also be said to be something about which to rejoice. To put it another way, if the NT is right, then what we value most, our humanity, is pregnant with its own glory. In this connection it is worth ending with some remarks of Ludwig Wittgenstein: 'What inclines even me to believe in Christ's Resurrection? It is as though I play with the thought. – If he did not rise from the dead, then he decomposed in the grave like any other man. *He is dead and decomposed*. In that case he is a teacher like any other and can no longer *help*; and once more we are orphaned and alone. So we have to content ourselves with wisdom and speculation. We are in a sort of hell where we can do nothing but dream, roofed in, as it were, and cut off from heaven. But if I am to be REALLY saved, – what I need is *certainty* – not wisdom, dreams or speculation – and this certainty is faith. And faith is faith in what is needed by my *heart*, my *soul*, not my speculative intelligence. For it is my soul with its passions, as it were with its flesh and blood, that has to be saved, not my abstract mind'.[11]

Notes

1. H. Richards, *The First Easter: What Really Happened?* (Glasgow, 1976), p. 92.
2. Cf W. D. Davies, *Paul and Rabbinic Judaism* (London[3], 1970), ch. 10.
3. C. F. Evans, *Resurrection and the New Testament* (London, 1970), p. 128.
4. X. Léon-Dufour, *Resurrection and the Message of Easter* (London, 1974), p. xiv.
5. *ibid.*
6. R. H. Lightfoot, *History and Interpretation in the Gospels* (London, 1935), p.225

7. G. Bornkamm, *Jesus of Nazareth* (London, 1960); C. H. Dodd, *The Founder of Christianity* (London, 1971); J. Jeremias, *New Testament Theology* I (London, 1971); Ernst Käsemann, *Essays on New Testament Themes* (London, 1964); Norman Perrin, *Rediscovering the Teaching of Jesus* (London, 1959); Eduard Schweitzer, *Jesus* (London, 1971). Cf also G. Vermes, *Jesus the Jew* (London 1973).
8. Cf *St Thomas of Canterbury* by Edwin A. Abbott (London, 1898).
9. There is a detailed discussion of 'the third day' in K. Lehmann, *Auferweckt am dritten Tag nach der Schrift* (Freiburg, 1968). See also Edward Schillebeeckx, *Jesus — An Experiment in Christology* (London, 1979), pp. 526 ff.
10. F. X. Durrwell, *The Resurrection* (London and New York, 1960), p. 29.
11. Ludwig Wittgenstein, *Culture and Value*, trans. Peter Winch (Oxford, 1980), p. 33e.

Teaching the Bible

DORIS K. HAYES

Recently a teacher in a primary school was telling the children in her class of seven-year-olds the story of the six days of creation. A bright little boy who, like many children today, had enjoyed picture-books illustrating the origin of the earth and the planets and stories of dinosaurs and ape-men, put up his hand. 'Please, Miss, it didn't happen like that at all. It took millions of years before man appeared, and he was descended from the animals'. — 'Sit down, Peter Smith, you think you know everything just because you read', said the teacher.

In a secondary school which I visited recently a very devout Catholic was teaching the creation story in Genesis in the same fundamentalist way to a class, most of whom, as I discovered later, watched David Attenbrough's TV series *Life on Earth,* each week. 'But they will lose their faith', I protested in discussion with him afterwards. 'I don't mind if they lose their faith in evolution', he retorted.

These isolated and extreme but true examples illustrate the very grave responsibility of the teacher: if the faith in which children are educated is presented in a way which is incredible in the modern world, they may discard it only a little later than fairy stories.

A teacher of even small children has to take the study of the Bible very seriously. No escape into a 'simple-faith' approach is possible. If faith today is to remain simple it must not be complicated by the intellectual dichotomy required of the children in the classes I have described.

Teachers are rightly nervous about bible teaching. They fear that if they depart from the extreme of fundamentalism they may be unable to avoid the extreme of liberalism and will undermine their pupils' faith in the divinity of Christ. That fear can only be dispelled if they are willing to undertake the difficult but immensely rewarding task of studying the Bible in the light of modern scholarship, as they have been encouraged to do by papal and conciliar documents during the last forty years.[1] Priests prepare for their task of preaching by an intensive course of study lasting at least six years, during which, Vatican II recommends: 'Students should receive a most careful training in holy Scripture, which should be the soul, as it were, of all theology'.[2] If priests are not expected to be able to teach the Bible without careful study, then teachers should not hope to find the meaning on the surface without availing themselves of the work of scholars. The research of biblical scholars and theologians is in the service of the Christian community, so that the word of God may be received anew in every age, place and culture. It is the task of priests and teachers to make available to ordinary people the understanding gained by this work.

An immense distance separates us from the age, place and culture of the biblical writers. Moreover the collection of writings that make up the Bible arose in the history of a people whose memory had been preserved in ancient traditions going back over some two thousand years. They did not live in isolation from their neighbours, and had been influenced by a variety of cultures. In the Bible we have the word of God in the words of men. God, who willed to save men through men, and supremely through his word made flesh, worked from the beginning in a truly incarnational way. He revealed himself in the history of a people and ultimately in the culmination of that people's history in the life, death and resurrection of Jesus of Nazareth. If we are truly to hear God's word we must understand the language in which he spoke — the language of events. God's word was active and dynamic. It appeared in history.

People nowadays find this difficult to accept, for they conceive of history as based strictly on objective data uncovered by careful research. The over-riding interest of the biblical writers was in the history of their relationship with God. This they preserved in oral tradition and then in a variety of literary forms: folk-tales, songs, poems, prayers, wise sayings and sagas. They were a story-telling people. Even when they preserved their history in books described as historical, their interest in the meaning of the experiences resulted in stories the religious and moral significance of which was paramount. Scientific history in the modern sense was unknown. The Israelite people saw reality as history: God's history, purposeful, linear and moving forward to an ultimate goal.

A teacher who wishes to help pupils to bridge the immense gap separating our age and culture from that of the biblical writers needs information. Biblical geography, history, archaeology, sociology: all are important. The cosmology and cosmogony of the people must be understood. The symbols and imagery they used, drawn from their daily lives and experience, must be interpreted. The nature, origin and history of the texts in their rich variety, related to the living situations in which they arose, must be studied as well.

All of this is very interesting. However, the interest is not in the information for its own sake. It is only when we realize ourselves to be involved personally in that same history in which God 'in many and various ways spoke of old to our fathers by the prophets', and 'in these last days has spoken to us by a Son' (Heb. 1: 1-2), that his word in Scripture reaches us and becomes meaningful and relevant for us today.

Literary and textual criticism helps us to understand the text. This is only a first step to understanding the history behind the text. When that history is seen as God's purposeful activity culminating in the death and resurrection of Jesus and the outpouring of the Spirit, it becomes meaningful for me in this age and for all peoples in every age.

A simple illustration of how a knowledge of the circumstances of the time in which Jesus lived can deepen our understanding of one of the stories he told must suffice.

One of the stories where the meaning may seem obvious and in no way time-conditioned is that of the Good Samaritan in Luke 10: 25-37. It is a story told to illustrate the law of love, and love is surely an idea timeless and so basically human in its appeal that interpretation would seem unnecessary. The relevance of the story seems immediately apparent. If interpretation remains at this level it may just be a story to illustrate the excellent boy-scout rule of doing one good deed a day, as E. Earle Ellis has remarked.[3] Let us look more closely. The 'lawyer' was a Jewish theologian, since theology consisted of interpretation of the law. The lawyer's answer brings together two vital texts central to the law: Deut. 6: 5 and Lev. 19: 18. Luke seems to imply that the rabbis had already brought these two texts together as a summary of the law, although in Mark 12: 28-32 Jesus seems to be the first to bring the two together. The lawyer's 'desiring to justify himself' may indicate the pharisaic obsession with observance of the law as a means of justification. In any case his next question, 'Who is my neighhour?' certainly reflects the legalism inherent in a minimalist morality of carefully delineated prescriptions and prohibitions. The discussion of whom exactly I must regard as neighbour would perhaps extend that category to proselytes. Certainly pagans would not be included. The hated and despised Samaritans would hardly be considered fit objects of the love which the law required a Jew to extend to his fellow-Hebrew. It is important to realize that the Samaritans were hated and despised on grounds of race and religion. They were of mixed race, the products of intermarriage between pagans and Jews. Their religion was also regarded as heterodox. There was a history of mutual hatred and violence between Jews and Samaritans.

The interest of the story is enhanced by a description of the steep, lonely, bandit-infested road and by knowing that Jericho was the residence of many priests, who used this road when journeying to Jerusalem to serve in the temple. It is necessary to appreciate, as the first hearers of the story would have known, that to touch a man 'left half-dead' would render the priest and Levite ritually unclean and so unfit to perform their temple duties. They were 'holy' men who preferred observance of the law and ritual worship to the demands of charity.

When these details and others to be found in any commentary are known, the story is seen to possess depths of meaning which do not appear on the surface. The subtle twist at the end when Jesus corrects the lawyer's question should be noticed too. 'Who *proved* a neighour?', he asks.

The tension between law, concerned with exact legal definitions, and love, extravagant in its demands, occurs in the ethics of every age. It is as relevant today as it was in the infant Church for which Luke wrote. The letters of Paul illustrate its importance in the early Church. In the context of Luke's Gospel, with its message of the universality of salvation, an ethic about the universality of the love-command is particularly appropriate. In the history of humanity strife and hatred on grounds of racial prejudice and religious bigotry are among the evils from which Christ came to redeem us. Christians in every age need to be reminded of a love-command which knows no barriers of race or religion. The self-righteous need to be shown that the one who is despised on grounds of such narrow-minded zeal may be the one who knows how to love. In any case, God's law requires a generous response to any man in need.

I have heard student-teachers use this story in many ways. Sometimes a student has modernized it, and sometimes told it in its biblical setting and asked the pupils to write a modern version. The stories written by the pupils have varied from those set in Handsworth (a multi-racial area of Birmingham), in South Africa, in Northern Ireland or in an American city to stories about mods and rockers with the hero befriending a 'mugged' member of the opposite gang. Martin Luther King has a splendid sermon on this same parable entitled 'On being a good neighbour' in which he applies the lesson of this parable to the evils of segregation and discrimination in America.

I have taken this example of a well-known parable in an attempt to illustrate how information about the life and times of Jesus are needed if the full meaning of a story he told is to be understood, first in its own setting and then in its contemporary relevance.

Jesus was following the true tradition of his people when he used stories to convey his message about his Father's loving plan for mankind. He was also a superb teacher, using illustrations from the familiar life of the people to whom he spoke. It has been said that from his parables alone it would be possible to build up a picture of the life of the ordinary people of his land. The images he uses reflect the daily life of the workman that he was: sheep, shepherd, goats, plough, yoke, seed, salt, leaven, fish, nets. However, these are not part of the daily experience of the city-dwelling children most of us teach today. So that gap has to be bridged too. Ways must be found of making the stories as vivid today as they were when they were first told. Pictures, films, slides must sometimes supply scenes to which Jesus, preaching in the open air, could point as he spoke. Children have lively imaginations; sometimes word-pictures, followed by their own attempts at illustration, may suffice.

The stories were not told, and must not be told today, just 'for their own sake'. They have a meaning. The meaning is profound. It should be remembered that the Bible is essentially for adults. We can only really appreciate the message of redemption when we have experienced the need for it, the word of forgiveness when we have realized our own sinfulness. Some experience of life is needed. Care should be taken to suit the biblical material used in the classroom to the age of the children. If we introduce unsuitable themes too early we may build up a resistance in children so that they may never hear the message, having heard its sound so often that they never really appreciate the meaning.

Another example from a classroom may illustrate this. A friend of mine, trained as a grammar-school teacher, found herself teaching six-year-olds during a period of convalescence. She told them the story of the Prodigal Son, and knowing that the elder son is an important character in the story questioned them about him. 'Who was sorry when the younger son came home?' she asked. 'The fatted calf was, Miss', came the reply. The little animal was the only character in the story who had really captured their imagination. The danger is that when the children are really ready for the message of their Father's forgiveness the story will sound to them like 'kid's stuff' belonging to kindergarten days.

We have not yet reached the heart of the matter in teaching the Bible today. It may be wondered why it should be taught at all if it is so beset with difficulties.

The answer, of course, is that in the Bible we have a unique record of a history which is not yet complete, a history in which God is the chief actor, a history in which we are ourselves involved. It is the history of God's ways with his human creatures, of God's loving invitation to mankind and to every human person.

From the beginning God willed to enter into a relationship with his people, a relationship which he initiates and which invites a free response. In the Bible we have the history of that relationship and of God's fidelity through many vicissitudes arising from the repeated failure of man's response. Then we have the revelation of God's plan to reconcile men to himself in spite of their chronic infidelity.

Although the imagery used to express this relationship, Father-child, Mother-infant, Bridegroom-bride, Husand-wife, is of universal human significance, the word most often used to describe it is one which needs interpretation. The word is *covenant*. We have it in the heart of our eucharistic liturgy as well as in the Bible, so we ought to understand it.

God calls man into a relationship of love. Man's response is to be in a way of life ordained by God. The covenant was the agreement which the twelve tribes entered into with their Sovereign Lord when they said 'All that the Lord hath said we will do' (Ex. 19: 8). Thus they became a people, God's people. The Decalogue prescribes a way of living with God, to be expressed in social relationships. Man's relationship with God is to be made manifest in the way he lives with his fellow human beings. God calls individuals. On Sinai he calls a whole people. That people is to be a sign to all nations of God's intentions for all men. God's love is constant but man's is fragile. There is repeated failure. God will not allow his plan for mankind to be finally frustrated, so he promises a new covenant of the future, when he will send his Spirit into men's hearts (Jer. 31: 31ff). He will take away their hearts of stone and give them hearts of flesh (Ez. 36: 26).

All this history, with its many strands and many colours, is woven in a remarkable way. The pattern is only discerned when all the strands and colours are drawn together in the history of Jesus of Nazareth. Through his life, death and resurrection a new covenant with God is made, the Spirit of God and of the Risen Lord is poured forth and a new people, a Spirit-filled people, emerges: the Christian community, a sign to all peoples of God's loving design for all men. That is the theology of the paschal mystery and of the Church as the people of God, which is central to the teaching of Vatican II. The central theme of that Council's teaching was surely, 'Let the paschal mystery be seen in the living of it'. In his life of loving service of the Father, whom He called 'Abba',[5] Jesus gave from within a human life a total response to the call of God. The Father raised him and the Spirit was sent into the hearts of men, enabling them also to call God 'Abba' (Rom. 8: 15; Gal. 4: 6). The central conviction of that first Spirit-filled community was that after his death a Jew of recent history, Jesus, of Nazareth, a contemporary of many of them, was now alive with the life of the New Age. They acknowledged him as Christ, their Lord. They, Jew and gentile convert alike, used the writings which we call the OT as their Scriptures. They discovered ever more deeply how these Scriptures spoke of him. In worship, in preaching and teaching, and in polemic, his memory was kept alive. Eventually this oral tradition gave rise to the writings which we call the NT. The Gospel of John shows us Jesus praying 'for those who believe in me through their word'. The Christian people of all ages are those who so believe, and 'their word' is to be found in the NT. The NT can and does bring us into touch with God in and through Jesus Christ whom we meet in its history, Jesus of Nazareth, who is one and the same as the Lord of faith, the centre of our Christian liturgy and living.

But a teacher cannot merely assert all this. Students, old and young, will ask many questions. Is it true? How do we know? Who wrote it? What does it mean? Did it really happen? The question of truth deserves to be taken with the utmost seriousness. It cannot be answered by a demand for faith. Faith and reason, including historical reason, are concerned with the same truth and cannot contradict each other. Intellectual honesty is a quality of paramount importance for teachers of all subjects, and supremely so for teachers of religion. Sometimes reason may require that we re-think the way in which we articulate our faith.

Hard work and much study are needed. The researches of the scholars must be used and made available to our students. The Bible is not self-interpreting. An open Bible in a modern translation is not sufficient. The discovery of the culture-gap, and even of the various culture-gaps, between the documents themselves should neither intimidate the teacher nor undermine the confidence of the students. Nor should the discovery that there have been elaborations, accretions and a variety of interpretations in the transmission of the message. The message grows, develops and interacts with the environment in a vital way.

A positive approach is essential. I have seen adult audiences shocked and disturbed by lecturers in Scripture whose approach appeared, to that audience at least, to be negative and sceptical. For instance, if questions about the meaning of a saying of Jesus are met with, 'We are not sure that he said it', followed by a learned discussion about the doubtful historicity of the passage, then the audience feel that their confidence in the words of Scripture is being undermined.

On the other hand, to involve the audience in the serious attempts which scripture scholars make to uncover the actual words of Jesus, and then to show how each evangelist has interpreted and elaborated them, in an effort to answer the needs of his contemporaries or to illustrate his own special theological concerns, can be very illuminating. Unless we deny the work of the Holy Spirit entirely we cannot think that later adaptations are worthless. Indeed subsequent modifications must be of importance too. The concern for historicity does not and should not lead to scepticism.

Nor should the discovery that there are a variety of interpretations of Jesus in the New Testament make us despair of finding any unity amid the diversity. Dr James Dunn, in a book which seeks to illustrate the pluralism in first-century Christianity,[6] nevertheless concludes that amid all the multiplicity of expressions of faith in Jesus there is an 'integrating centre for the diverse expressions of Christianity. That unifying element was the unity between the historical Jesus and the exalted Christ'.

Then as now the living relationship with God brought about by the Spirit was in and through the risen Lord. The constant refrain of early Christian prayer was 'through Jesus Christ our Lord'. The expression 'in Christ' in Paul's letters shows how soon they were aware that they enjoyed a new relationship with God in union with the exalted Lord.[7]

That also applies to us. But the living, risen Lord is not seen or heard by us. Also we are much farther removed from his memory, so recent to the experience of the first Christians. How are we to know him? Surely the Gospels are a unique and authoritative source. They were written in the light of the resurrection, and the life of the earthly Jesus is interpreted in that light.

I once knew a Catholic convert from Methodism and Quakerism. Her Methodist upbringing and subsequent theological studies had given her an intimate knowledge of the Scriptures. Her patristic studies eventually brought her to Roman Catholicism. She said that her chief reason for becoming a Catholic had been her desire for the eucharist. Then she discovered her fellow Catholics' vast ignorance of the Scriptures, even of the gospels (this was some twenty-five years ago). '*Who* do they think they are receiving? What do they know of him?', she asked. She recalled one occasion when she had approached Holy Communion with a keen sense of her own sinfulness. Then she had thought, 'This is the Jesus who was so kind to that horrid little man, Zacchaeus', and she was reassured.

If the image of Jesus that Catholics have is derived from the pictures and statues with which they are surrounded rather than from the gospels, they are deprived of a rich source of spiritual inspiration. Here there is no substitute for reading the gospels themselves, and reading them again and again. The impact of the person of Jesus on his contemporaries was such that his personality and personal traits come through all the layers of tradition uncovered by scholars. Furthermore the stories and sayings of Jesus reveal the character of a highly original mind, even when we allow that they have often been elaborated in the telling. It would be a pity if detailed analysis and careful exegesis, rewarding as that is, robbed the student of the enjoyment of coming to the text fresh and reading it whole. Before detailed study of any one gospel I always ask my students to sit down and read the whole work at a sitting with the sole purpose of receiving an impression of the man Jesus conveyed by the whole gospel.

The immediate impact is of a character far more robust than the 'gentle Jesus, meek and mild' of their childhood prayer. The fictional 'Christ of the gospels' who is mild in manner, endlessly patient, grave in speech, is far removed from the powerful personality, capable of rage, of humour, of witty repartee and of irony verging on sarcasm whom we meet in the writings of the evangelists. Jesus of the gospels challenges us not least by his pithiness of speech and by the incisiveness of his criticism. There is urgency in his preaching about the sovereignty of God. Most of all he challenges us by his total dedication to his mission, by his utterly complete response to the call of his Father, the One whom he calls 'Abba' even in the moment when 'his soul is sorrowful, even to death' (Mk 13: 34). At the beginning of that story Mark told us that it was 'good news' (Mk 1: 1). So it is. The teacher of Scripture should never forget that. Resurrection joy pervades the whole New Testament. The story is interesting, exciting, and joyous. It gives meaning to life, especially to sorrow and to suffering, and promises that there is ultimate joy even in suffering.

The study of Scripture is an enjoyable enterprise. The teacher who cannot convey that should not be teaching it at all.

Notes

1. *Jerome Biblical Commentary* ed. Raymond Brown (London & New York, 1968), Article on 'Church Pronouncements', pp. 624-32. *A New Catholic Commentary on Holy Scripture* ed. Fuller, Johnston and Kearns (London, 1969), Articles on 'The Bible in the Life of the Church', pp. 1-20.
2. Vatican II, *Decree on the Training of Priests*, (*Optatam Totius*) para. 16.
3. *The Gospel of Luke* ed. E. Earle Ellis (London, 1974), p. 160.
4. Martin Luther King, *Strength to Love* (London, 1963). p. 26ff.
5. The mountain of research done by the scholar Joachim Jeremias and his students over many years which established that this word 'Abba', an affectionate familiar term used in the intimacy of the family, was not used as an address to God and that Jesus' use of it was unique, illustrates the contributions made by careful scholarship to our understanding of the Bible.
6. James D. G. Dunn, *Unity and Diversity in the New Testament* (London, 1977).
7. For a scholarly treatment of the theological implications of the Pauline expression 'in Christ' see *The Origin of Christology* by C. F. D. Moule, (Cambridge, 1977). See also *Pauline Pieces* by Morna D. Hooker (London, 1979).

The Bible and liturgy

HAROLD WINSTONE

Jesus Christ was a Jew, which means that he was steeped in the Jewish scriptures. They were read not only in the synagogues but in the home, and the whole of Jewish life was conceived of as a fulfilment of the law and the covenant. The Bible was the equivalent of our modern school text-books. It was history, literature, drama, poetry, law, philosophy, and above all, and pervading all, religion; for the God of the Jews dominated the whole of life. The God of Abraham, Isaac and Jacob was Lord of all.

Hence it is true to say that everything Jesus did was in some measure a reflection of his spiritual upbringing. The revised lectionary used in the Roman Catholic Church throughout the world and in many other Churches, especially in the United States, is an eloquent witness to this. The compilers seem to have found no difficulty in choosing an OT reading which would throw a revealing light on the text of the gospel, and that over a three-year cycle of Sunday readings covering most of the text of Matthew, Mark and Luke, and a considerable portion of John. Most of the well-known images used by Jesus in his parables and many of the events recorded in the gospels are seen to have had their counterpart in the OT scriptures. That Jesus himself was conscious of this is evidenced in his statement: 'Do not imagine that I have come to abolish the law or the prophets. I have come not to abolish but to complete them. I tell you solemnly, till heaven and earth disappear, not one dot, not one little stroke, shall disappear from the law until its purpose is achieved' (Mt. 5: 17-8).

There were two things especially about the mentality of Jesus as we know it from the gospels that were markedly scriptural: his use of symbolism and his prayer; and these are the things which have passed over into the Christian liturgy and form the basis of our Christian worship.

Let us consider first the prayer of Jesus. With the exception of John, the evangelists have not recorded many of the actual prayers of Jesus. Those which are recorded are either direct quotations from the psalms ('My God, my God, why have you forsaken me?' — Ps. 22: 1), or are clearly inspired by the words of the psalmist ('Father, I thank you for hearing my prayer' — cf Ps. 118: 28). We can be quite sure that Jesus prayed the psalms often. He had made them his own. They figure largely in his converse with the Father. And yet in this one significant respect he changed them: he addressed his prayers not to Yahweh (Adonai — my Lord) or to Elohim, but to his Father, and he taught his disciples, and through them his Church, to do likewise: 'When you pray, say this: Our Father . . . '.

Yet the content of that prayer, the 'Our Father', is wholly scriptural. It begins where all Hebrew spirituality begins, with the contemplation and praise of the glory of God in his heaven: 'Our Father in heaven, may your name be held holy' (Mt. 6: 9).

Unlike the gods of the Greeks and Romans, the God of the Hebrews was not conceived of in anthropomorphic terms. He was not a kind of superman. He was inaccessible, unknowable. Even his name was unutterable. The Hebrews could give no answer to Pharaoh when he said to them 'Who is Yahweh?' They could only say: 'The God of the Hebrews has come to meet us' (Ex. 5: 3). He did not live in trees or streams or hills or stones. His throne was above the heavens, yet his glory pervaded the whole of the universe, the work of his creation. He could only be known because he 'had visited his people' and made a covenant with them that they should be his people and he should be their God. His one distinctive quality was his holiness; a term which meant more than the omnipotence and immortality attributed to the Graeco-Roman gods. It comprised all this, but meant, in addition, that he was wholly above any human concept of him. He was 'completely other'. In his presence only one attitude was appropriate on the part of mortal man, that of awe and reverence and wonder and praise. No one could see his face and live.

It was not easy for a primitive people to retain this conceptual understanding of a transcendent God. Again and again the Hebrews had to be forbidden to make 'graven images' of their God. They wanted something tangible which they could relate to and worship. In the end Moses had to settle, not for an image, but for a place which could localize, so to speak, God's meeting with his people. He called it the Tent of Meeting, a focal point for prayer and sacrifice, the tabernacle where his glory dwelt.

Three hundred years later Solomon did the same thing when he built the Temple in Jerusalem and prayed: 'Yet will God really live with men on earth? Why, the heavens and their own heavens cannot contain you, how much less this house that I have built! Listen to the prayer and entreaty of your servant, Yahweh, my God; listen to the cry and prayer your servant makes to you today. Day and night let your eyes watch over this house, over the place of which you have said, "My name shall be there" ' (1 Kings 8: 26-9).

The glory and majesty of God were impossible to describe, even by prophets and visionaries. Instead they concentrated on the perpetual praise and adoration given to God by heavenly beings surrounding his throne. In Isaiah we read: 'I saw the Lord Yahweh seated on a high throne; his train filled the sanctuary; above him stood seraphs, each one with six wings: two to cover its face, two to cover its feet, and two for flying. And they cried out to one another in this way, "Holy, holy, holy is Yahweh Sabaoth. His glory fills the whole earth" ' (Is. 6: 1-3).

This sense of wonder and awe in the contemplation of God's presence is the inspiration of many of the psalms. Yahweh is great; he does marvellous things; we bless his holy name,

> 'in his presence are splendour and majesty,
> in his sanctuary power and beauty' (Ps. 96: 6).

It is also the inspiration of the prayer of Jesus: 'Our Father in heaven; may your name be held holy'. It is the inspiration too of the great eucharistic prayers of the liturgy:

> 'Father, you are holy indeed,
> and all creation rightly gives you praise' (EP III).

The God we address in our Christian liturgy is the God who dwells in unapproachable light, surrounded by countless angels praising him by night and day (cf EP IV).

This sense of the holiness of God, so characteristic of the Bible, is the mark of true Christian worship. Without it our worship would not be authentic; we would in fact be worshipping a false God. Idol-making was not a temptation confined to the Hebrews in Old Testament times. We too, in our more sophisticated ways, often succumb to the temptation of making and worshipping a god in our own image and likeness, a god who in the end is nothing more than a glorification of man, a god shorn of all mystery and height and depth, a god within our reach and at our beck-and-call.

The second element in Hebrew thought about God has already been referred to. It is this: the glory of God is not confined to heaven; it fills both heaven and earth. The God who dwells in inaccessible light is also the God who has visited his people. The Hebrews praised and thanked God not only for his great glory but for the marvellous things he did for them. Their God was a saving God. Every event in their history was a manifestation of his saving presence among them. What he had done for his people in the past he would do now and would always do, 'for his great love is without end'.

When disaster threatened and in times of national calamity when all seemed hopeless, they remembered God's promise to their fathers and prayed that he would once again do 'in our own day' the marvels that he had done for them in the past. Gradually the notion of the messiah gained credence, the one who was to come in the name of the Lord and introduce a new era of peace and prosperity, the kingdom of God on earth. So Christ prayed, and taught his disciples to pray: Thy kingdom come; thy will be done on earth as it is in heaven.

With the incarnation the kingdom has already come. In Christ 'the world was blessed with all the spiritual blessings of heaven' (Eph. 1: 3), for Christ was 'the radiant light of God's glory and the perfect copy of his nature'. Nevertheless, he still had to accomplish his Father's will, in himself and in every human person. Hence his prayer: As thy will is done in heaven, so may it be done on earth.

This too is the constant prayer of the liturgy: 'From age to age you gather a people to yourself, so that from east to west a perfect offering may be made to the glory of your name' (eucharistic prayer III). The incarnation has to be effected in each one of us so that we may become 'one body, one spirit, in Christ'. The liturgy is a calling down of the heavenly Spirit upon earth so that the earth may be transformed into the kingdom of God. This is what is symbolized by the consecration of the eucharistic elements: 'Let your Spirit come upon these gifts to make them holy, that they may become the body and blood of our Lord, Jesus Christ'. It is the fulfilment of the psalmist's prayer: 'Send forth your light and your truth; let these be my guide, to lead me to your holy mountain and to the place where you live' (Ps. 43: 3).

The total effect of the liturgy of the Eucharist and of all the sacraments is this bringing down of heaven to earth so that the Father's will may be done on earth as it is in heaven. Isaiah uses the metaphor of rain. The heavens pour down rain upon the earth and the earth opens up and brings forth the fruit of justice and holiness.

The third element in the spirituality of the Bible is its concern for the human condition. It is a down-to-earth spirituality, all about people, their daily needs, their relationships, and their constant struggle against their enemies and the forces of evil. This is what comes through in nearly all the psalms. The Hebrew did not look to an after-life to redress the misery and injustices of this life. He called upon God to redress them here and now. OT religion was no opium for the people. It was the religion of a people for whom the possession of God is here, not hereafter. There is in fact little evidence in the OT of any clear belief in an after-life. That conviction was part of the good news brought by Christ. Those who believed in him would live for ever. *He* was the resurrection and the life.

The prayer he taught his disciples reflected this biblical concern for the here and now: 'Give us this day our daily bread'. The Church has interpreted this prayer widely, to include all our needs, both bodily and spiritual, and has moreover given it a eucharistic dimension, but it is likely that Jesus was referring literally to man's need for daily bread. There is evidence in the gospels that the people were not infrequently without bread. Jesus complained on one occasion that their only reason for following him was because he had given them all the bread they needed (Jn 6: 26). Nevertheless, the Church is right in giving this prayer a eucharistic connotation, for Christ said: 'Do not work for good that cannot last, but work for food that endures to eternal life, the kind of food the Son of Man is offering you, (Jn 6: 27) . . . The bread that I shall give you is my flesh for the life of the world' (Jn 6: 51). And so in the eucharistic prayer, having praised the eternal holiness of God, we think of our own needs and pray that he may send his Spirit on this bread and wine that it may become for us the body and blood of Jesus Christ.

Returning to the psalms and to the OT writings generally, we cannot fail to be struck by their preoccupation with the problem posed by the sinner. God is rich in mercy, but the sinner he will utterly destroy (Ps. 144). Happiness, peace and prosperity in this world are thought of as being the reward of virtue. If disaster comes, then it can only be that the people have sinned and turned away from God; there can be no other explanation. If the sinner seems to prosper, it can only be for a time. Retribution will follow surely and swiftly. And so the psalmist prays for forgiveness for himself and at the same time vows to have nothing to do with sinners, with the deceitful, the unjust, the scoffers (Ps. 1).

Jesus too teaches us to pray: Forgive us our trespasses; but then he adds something of his own: 'as we forgive those who trespass against us.' If the Christian does not forgive others he dare not ask for God's forgiveness. This thought can be shattering, yet it lies at the heart of all our liturgy. If when we bring our gift to the altar we remember that our brother has something against us, we must leave our gift there at the altar and go back and first be reconciled with our brother. Only then may we come and offer our gift. This is sacramentalized in our liturgy by the kiss of peace. It is an important and indispensable part of Christian worship. Before we dare receive the body that was given for us and the blood that was shed for the forgiveness of sins we must extend that forgiveness to others. Not to do so is to act a lie.

In this whole area what is common to both OT and NT is concern for the brother. 'Am I my brother's keeper?' asked Cain. God does not answer directly. What he says is: 'If anyone kills Cain, sevenfold vengeance shall be taken for him' (Gen. 4:15). It is not for us to exact vengeance; that is God's prerogative. Jesus implied the same thing when he said about the woman taken in adultery: 'Let him who is without sin cast the first stone'.

To this day we have not resolved the eternal question: Why do good people suffer and bad people prosper? The question is repeated in a thousand different ways: 'Who sinned, this man or his parents, that he was born blind?' (Jn 9: 2). The prophet Malachi says we weary God with this question. The question as Malachi reports it is especially ironical. If prosperity is God's gift and the evil-doer prospers, then 'any evil-doer is good as far as Yahweh is concerned, indeed he likes them best' (Mal. 2: 17). Yes, it would seem that he does, for when God sent his messenger, as Malachi foretold, he really was the friend of sinners. The Hebrews could not believe this, and we can scarcely believe it: that the good should suffer for the sins of the wicked. And yet it is the man who was despised and rejected, a man of sorrows and familiar with suffering, whom we offer in the holy sacrifice for the forgiveness of sins, and we do so because 'he was pierced through for our faults, crushed for our sins. On him lies a punishment that brings us peace, and through his wounds we are healed' (Is. 52: 5). We do this week after week, and we still ask: Why do the good suffer and the evil prosper? The message of Jesus and of the whole of Scripture is that we are all sinners in need of the mercy of God. No one is justified in his sight. We are all involved in the sinful human condition, and for this very reason we need to forgive others and to seek their forgiveness. Only Christ was without sin (and his mother who was redeemed through his merits), and if we are to return to the Father it can only be 'through Jesus Christ our Lord'.

Yet evil remains as a very real part of our world, and with it a certain attraction which we call temptation. Jesus was aware of this in his own life. We are told in so many words that he was tempted. The prayer he taught his disciples: 'Lead us not into temptation, but deliver us from evil' must have been his own prayer too. He saw clearly what the consequences of his mission would be and that knowledge must have appalled him: 'Father, let this chalice pass from me'. He was faced with the ultimate temptation, to give up, not to go through with it, to stand aside (apostatize). Peter touched on this nerve when he took Jesus aside and said to him: 'Lord, this (suffering) must not happen to you'. Unwittingly he was doing Satan's work, and Jesus rounded on him and said: 'Get behind me, Satan! You are an obstacle in my path, because the way you think is not God's way, but man's' (Mt. 16: 23). It was with a deadly fear that he approached the final test: 'My soul is sorrowful even unto death.' As he looked at his disciples on the Mount of Olives, he feared for them too, and he said: 'Pray that *you* may not be put to the test" (Lk. 22: 40). We know how he wrestled with the Father until he found peace and strength in the words: 'Let your will be done, not mine' (Lk. 22: 43). 'Thy will be done on earth as it is in heaven'.

In every celebration of the Lord's death the Church too prays not to be put to the test. After the recitation of the Lord's Prayer the celebrant takes up the words of this final petition and amplifies them, praying that as we wait in joyful hope for the coming of the Lord, God may take away the fear and sin that paralyses us, and give us peace.

> Lamb of God, you take away the sins of the world,
> grant us peace.

The liturgy of the Church is not, however, confined to words. It is a sacred action using meaningful signs and symbols to express the faith that is in us and our relationship with God. These symbols are of two kinds. They are bodily gestures used to express the intention of the mind, and they are things of everyday life which, because of their association with significant events in the life of a people, bear a meaning over and above the normal meaning attaching to them. Water, for example, can be regarded as something to drink or to wash in, but to a nation which owed its national and religious identity to the experience of crossing the Red Sea and the Jordan, water could signify liberation and salvation.

There are events in the history of a nation which are regarded as so significant that they are seen to contain in themselves all the events which subsequently transpired. Such an event for the Jews was the passover meal which they shared in their homes in Egypt on the night before they made good their escape from slavery and achieved their identity as a nation. Their liberation was Yahweh's doing. The significant event was not so much their crossing the Red Sea and their victory over opposing tribes, but their celebration of the promise of this victory in the context of the passover meal. Hence in after years, when they wanted to commemorate this turning-point in their history, they did so by re-enacting the significant events of the eve of their liberation.

They sacrificed and ate the paschal lamb, ate the bitter herbs and the bread that symbolized the bitterness of their years of slavery, and drank the cup of Yahweh's promise of salvation. 'That night, when Yahweh kept vigil to bring them out of the land of Egypt, must be kept as a vigil in honour of Yahweh for all their generations' (Ex. 12: 42). They were to do this annually in remembrance of their salvation.

It was this remembrance that Jesus and his disciples were celebrating on the night before he died, and he made of it the meal of his own passover from death to life, and the passover of the new people of God from the slavery of sin to the life of grace. The bread of bitterness that he broke and gave to them became the sacramental sign of his own body, broken and given. The cup of the promise became the blood of the new covenant shed for the forgiveness of sins. And Jesus said: 'Do *this* in remembrance of me'.

For Christians this became the significant event in the history of their salvation. In it was already contained all that was to happen on the morrow: the agonizing crucifixion, the death, the victory over death, his taking possession of the kingdom. And Christians in after years, wishing to celebrate their redemption, did so not so much by rehearsing the actual events of the passion, death, resurrection and ascension of the Lord, but by re-enacting the significant events of that last supper which contained the seeds of all that was to follow. This was what they must do in remembrance of the Saviour.

When we realize this, the whole liturgy of the Mass falls into place. Why the liturgy of the word? Because on that night Jesus opened the scriptures to them and they began to understand. He prayed with them. He preached his law of love, and, as always, in a most dramatic way: he washed their feet and explained to them what that meant. Then, if the Mass is the last supper rite, why is it not more like a meal? Because, as always, it is the significant, not the incidental things that are remembered. Jesus took the bread and blessed God for it. That they remembered. They remembered the vitally significant thing he said over the bread and how he broke it and gave it to them to eat. After that the next significant thing was at the end of the meal when he took the cup of the promise, blessed God for it and gave it to them saying: 'This is the new covenant in my blood, shed for the forgiveness of sins'. Henceforth he woud not drink of the fruit of the vine until all was fulfilled in the kingdom of heaven.

This, therefore, is what we re-enact at Mass; nothing else, only the significant things, for in doing this we are in communion with the body and blood which was sacrificed for the sins of the world, and we are united with Jesus in his offering:

> 'In memory of his death and resurrection,
> we offer you, Father,
> this life-giving bread,
> this saving cup'.

The Bible, evangelization and the world

ADRIAN HASTINGS

Perhaps the central ambiguity in all Christian history, and in Catholic history most particularly, is the relationship of Bible and Church, and it is an ambiguity particularly decisive in its consequences for the character of 'evangelization' – the proclamation of the Christian message outside the frontiers of the Church. The Bible as Bible, a single book containing several score of intensely different pieces of writing, originating in so many times and places, makes no human sense at all except as the book of a community which put it together, cherished it, added to it, decided its boundaries, its inclusions and exclusions.

But here at once one is faced with a vast additional ambiguity: which community? indeed, what Bible? In a way, some would argue, Israel's book was hijacked by its breakaway Christian community and then so added to as to become, with a crucial second half, an essentially different thing: either a thoroughly misguided piece of religious hijacking or a providential messianic revolution, transforming at one and the same time book and community. Yet the new community took time to settle upon its additions: yes, even Revelation and Jude and Philemon, but not 1 Clement or the *Didache* or the Gospel of Thomas. And all of this not as an anthology but as Bible, one totality, somehow standing henceforth to face both Church and world as a new unity, Genesis to Revelation, with two distinct but interlocking parts. Its various authors come and go. Their collective work in all its complexity and ultimate anonymity has become The Bible, something more than even its greatest parts, something far transcending in meaning the thoughts of its writers, something inconceivable apart from the historic community that made it, yet standing at last strangely independent of that community, indeed acknowledged by it as not its own word but primarily God's. It belongs to the Church, yet stands over and above the Church. It is in daily use, but it judges. Ignored at one's peril, its use seems often as dangerous as its reverent ignoring. The Church changes, the Bible remains the same.

There would be no Bible without the Church, but the Church by canonizing the Bible certainly did not thereby resolve all its own ongoing problems. However sincerely Christians search the Bible, they have found time and again that it provides no obviously clear guide in many of the intellectual, moral and institutional problems with which they are faced. The evolving scene of culture, politics, humanity's multi-faceted moral sense, cannot convincingly be coped with by the Bible as a straight and independent authority standing simply by itself. The fundamentalist norm is appealing in its simplicity but it would seem only to be able to work in so far as one settles upon a rather tight and closed community and then applies to that community some rather limited sections of the Scriptures. Fundamentalism involves both a withdrawal from the totality of the contemporary world (into small bits of it which seem to be more biblically recognizable) and from the totality of Scripture into a preoccupation with certain favoured books, texts or just a catena of selected passages.

Effectively every large Church comes to reject fundamentalism – that is to say, the view that all required religious truth lies clearly at hand in the biblical word, and that the task of the Church is no more in each generation than its obvious straight application. It does not suffice in practice; moreover, in theory Christianity has long had at hand an alternative type of authority: belief in the presence of the Holy Spirit in the contemporary Church and not only in Scripture. The action of God in the world is rather two-fingered: word and spirit. And the two-fingeredness has itself a double model, for 'word' can mean the written Scriptures, but 'word' too can mean Christ. Scriptures and Christ. Christ and Spirit. Scriptures and Spirit. Scriptures and Church. There is the objectivity of the external norm in its various modes and the assurance of the inner ongoing divine presence and guidance, again in various modes. If there has been one model of Christian authority, the fundamentalist, which places all the weight upon the one side, there have been various models, ecclesio-institutional and charismatic, which place it all upon the other.

Yet both sides are there and the tension between them does not appear a resolvable one. No one theological or ecclesiastical model really seems to do justice to these contrasting, yet irremovable, strains. Such, maybe, is the divine wisdom. Both sides are God-given, and being so, the divine model cannot be humanly tied up. The scriptural finger upon its own, seen as the whole work of God's redemptive action so that there is nothing more to add of significance after the completion of the last canonical book, would be a belittling of the divine freedom at work in the totality of creation, of human history, of the ongoing believing community. The Church is the Church: no less than Bride of God, Body of Christ, foretaste of the New Jerusalem. The Spirit remains here. We must not forget that.

The ecclesiastical finger, on its own, fully worked out in ultramontane terms, must be no less disastrous. Here the authority of Scripture effectively ceased to matter, devoured by such a growth of 'tradition', 'special revelations' and the authority of the magisterium. Recourse to Scripture simply lost its sense in such an environment, while over the centuries this development produced such absurdities, intellectual and moral, as should make one for ever proclaim the fallibility of the Church. The Church's 'teaching office is not above the Word of God but serves it' (*Constitution on Revelation,* 10). It ought to serve it, yet for centuries the facts of the matter have been only too often otherwise. The history of the relationship of Church and Bible is as a result one of an often strained polarity, with at times almost a sense of deliberate double-talk. For the theoretical authority of the Bible within the Church has seldom been in question. It was too clearly foundational to both belief and worship for theology to get away from it, though increasingly from the Middle Ages canon law would seem to do so. And the canonists would rule the Church. But even in theology, as doctrine and theological method hardened, so did the understanding of Scripture and its uses. What effectively happened as a result within almost every ecclesiastical tradition was the domestication of the Bible — its subordination through the selection of regularly-used passages and an agreed interpretation to a particular and limited form of ecclesiastical life. So much so was this the case in Catholicism that the laity were long discouraged or even prevented from reading it. At a time when Latin was understood by hardly a handful of lay people, church authority was for centuries intensely suspicious of the translation of the Scriptures into the vernacular. The absence, right up to our own day, of a Catholic translation of the Bible in many, many languages long used by Catholics, such as – and particularly revealingly – Irish, is mute witness to the Church's conviction that the Bible was a dangerous book. If it was to be safely domesticated, it really needed not only to be strictly interpreted but also reduced to selected passages. Current ecclesiastical life was likely to be threatened rather than fortified by a free use of the Bible. Nothing symbolizes better the threat of the sixteenth-century Reform to the Church as it then – and long after – stood, than the placing by Henrician order of the Matthew Bible in every English parish church.

Now it has been 'current ecclesiastical life' in all its immediate teaching, canon law and church structure which have provided the effective sending context of missionary preaching. That may sound odd, even scandalous, but it has undoubtedly been true – and as a matter of fact, for Protestants almost as much as for Catholics. While the full character of the belief and practice of a mature church community has many, even conflicting, strands to it and includes levels of experience which may hardly be explicitly mentioned, still less approved of, within the community and especially by its contemporary leadership, all such sides only too easily get left out of the thrust of the missionary enterprise, the message carried abroad to the non-believer. 'Evangelization' and its inevitable correlative 'church building' take very formally the current in-model of Christian orthodoxy as providing the right missionary pattern. The consequence can only be, and in age after age has been, the provision – indeed, most generally, the imposition – of a particularly partial form of Christianity instead of the whole. *Pars pro toto,* one may say. *Pars contra totum* can as well be the case. The Bible stands for the (not immediately realizable) whole. Every subsequent historical form of Christianity offers (rather as one or another bit of the Bible offers on its own) a part, greater or less, more or less open to the whole or cut off from the whole because formed into a closed, lesser system of its own – and that is true even though, at the same time, it may also offer, again to a greater or lesser extent, a true religious advance brought about by the action of the Spirit of God at work in the one historical biblical community now faced and in profound ways necessarily transformed by new social, political and cultural developments.

Missionaries are zealous people, inclined to be narrow in the range of their concern but very much on fire with something: they might never set off on the so often ungrateful task of endeavouring to 'convert' others, if they were not so. They have been gripped, a great deal more powerfully than most of their contemporaries, by a part of the whole, and the very power of that grip may well relate to the narrowness of the part. The wider one's sense of the biblical vision, with all its overtones and complexities, the less likely one may well be to feel it remotely sane to pack one's bags and set off for the Antipodes to communicate it to an unbelieving world. The intensity of Francis Xavier's fervour balanced well enough the narrowness of the message he proclaimed so selflessly and – humanly speaking – so unrealistically.

Quite clearly, if such is the pattern of things, then the Bible is only too likely not to come into it all that much. It must seem a distraction, an apparent counter-authority whose words will time and again have to be explained politely away to the bewildered neophyte. The Church is the evangelizer, not the Bible. But while that may adequately rationalize away historic Catholic missionary practice, what about the Protestants? They did not do it like that, you may well say. They did take the Bible whole, they translated it, they printed it in scores and scores of languages. The great bible societies were set up for nothing else and it worked. Indeed the non-biblical Catholic missionary has been outflanked in his aims time and again, as bibles untranslated by him have seeped into his flock, try as he might to confiscate and burn them as gravely unauthorized. Protestant evangelization was biblical.

It could not have been otherwise seeing that Protestant life in the home Churches was so explicitly biblically-based, and all glory to them for that. Yet the consequent paradox has been remarkable and highly revealing. As a matter of fact the normal non-Catholic missionary – Anglican, Presbyterian, Methodist, Baptist – was, just about as much as the Catholic, preaching as his message the current doctrine and ethical *mores* of his own Church in all its formal clarity, the precision of the 'Westminster Confession', the institutionalized norms solidified in the Victorian age, the established church order. The package offered might well be even neater and tighter than the Catholic, for it was likely to come from a more culturally-homogeneous community, and deviancy from it would no less severely ensure excommunication. Yet they offered the Bible too and believed it, reading it so firmly through their own Church spectacles. Yes, Jacob did have several wives, and so did David and Solomon. Yes, the Bible is God's word, our only absolute authority. No, brother, you may not have two wives. The Bible may not say so, but if you do, you will be an excommunicated back-slider.

In a way the Protestant missionary had domesticated the Bible more completely than the Catholic. He could no longer see that it might sit in judgment upon him; that it might prove a fearful Pandora's Box out of which all sorts of things could jump – angels and dreams, prophets and miracles and an imminent *eschaton,* as well as down-to-earth practices like polygamy – upon his cosy well-ordered Victorian Christianity. He found one thing in that large book while his converts too often found another. The Bible in fact proved a bigger thing than current evangelization from any church or school; it just could not be the latter's running dog. The missionary might well be rejected, and much of his sound message too, some independent Church might well be formed, whether in Africa or the Pacific or wherever, but the Bible went on producing a further chaotic medley of partial Churches, limited and quickly also institutionalized responses to its insufferable wholeness.

Of course it might not do quite that. The danger of schism might be warded off. The domesticated Bible might be accepted as such, read essentially as the missionaries said it should be read. Such remains the main visible response, increasingly a Catholic one too as Catholics come more freely to use and pass on the Scriptures in a missionary situation. Nor is it wrong. For where the Bible stands alone without Church, it ceases fully to be Bible. Yet it can, of course, so stand. It has gone today far beyond the boundaries of any and every Church. It is read and valued by millions of Japanese who are in no conceivable way members of an existing Church. It is, simply as a matter of fact, the world's primary book, printed and read in quantities far beyond any other. The Bible does then in a very real way proclaim its message apart from the Church and the impression made by this 'naked' presentation, standing quite on its own as a piece of unique religious literature, must not be underestimated. It communicates, it may evangelize, simply by being read. And yet, wholly apart from the Church, it is quite certainly out of its natural habitat in which it was formed and flourished and struggled over and made sense of. Take away the church connection and there is no real reason for keeping it as one or seeing it as uniquely authoritative. Certainly it has modes of authoritativeness which are valid outside any church context whatsoever, modes common to the wider field of spiritual literature. But the particular and special sort of authoritativeness, which — however difficult it is to assess and make precise and relate to the varying contents of the Bible — we recognize as being of the very essence of the whole biblical thing, is something meaningless apart from an ongoing historic community which still accepts, as it has always accepted, this package of writings as uniquely normative for itself in a way that the Dialogues of Plato or the Koran or the *Summa* of St Thomas or the decrees of the Council of Trent are not, or should not be. It may be almost impossibly hard to spell out what the authoritativeness does and does not imply in regard to the whole *corpus* of Scripture, and yet the very unity of the Bible, its sheer existence as Bible, implies for it as a whole an ultimate collective authoritativeness which requires as correlative a living Church.

If the Church is unthinkable without the Bible, and the Bible is unthinkable without the Church, then the missionary evangelist has only too clearly to present each as integral to the other. He cannot present the Church without the Bible; but he cannot present the Bible without interpreting it, however much he may do so from the standpoint of his own limitations. It would be impossible for him to offer the Bible without explanation, and he can only explain it as he believes its meaning to be — eschatology and miracles and marriage mores and all. What else would you have him do? His converts will be confused enough as it is, what with one thing and another. They would not thank him for an uninterpreted Bible any more than the Sunday congregation thanks its priest for reading out a particularly odd piece of Scripture and then concentrating its attention for the ten minutes before the creed upon bingo, the new church hall and the diocesan pilgrimage to Lourdes.

Interpret it and be in danger of domesticating it. Fail to interpret it and — effectively — you will be asserting its irrelevance to anything else you do or say. You cannot advise doing the latter. You have then to do the former. How to achieve in evangelization or in any other form of teaching an interpretation which is not a domestication? That is the heart of the matter. How to ensure that across the months and the years the interpreter communicates an ever greater sense that the Bible, so meekly open to our reading and explanation, is not a string of proof texts or a *confirmatur* for the confining clarities of a particular ecclesiastical orthodoxy or contemporary theology, but the imperial word, far above all other human words in its capacity collectively to embody — though at some points far more than others — the inexpressible word of the revealing God. The Bible cannot be and must not be treated as a domesticated tame cat comfortably purring on the hearth rug of a Catholic magisterium any more than of a Protestant fundamentalist sect, else it will at dawn become a tiger to rend you limb from limb, each tooth a two-edged sword. There is a type of interpretation which serves the biblical word in due humility and there is a type which dominates.

Clearly some church situations are far better, others far worse, when it comes to letting the Bible be the Bible, do its thing and be the companion of all evangelization, the guide to new vision, the unsilenceable judge of our misdirections, the sustainer of faith and hope and compassionate living, verbal sacrament of the unavoidability of the living God. To let all this really happen so that the missionary can go forth with a living Bible confidently in his hand the Church must be a very free Church. One cannot have a free Bible in an unfree Church. The Bible challenges the Church to be free because, if it is not, then it can only be that the Bible too is muzzled, domesticated, partialized. A free Church will be, towards the Bible, a listening Church, a questioning Church, a Church consciously *en route* rather than self-satisfiedly *chez soi*. The Bible is so clearly about the world as much as the Church that it really requires to be read within the context of the world and the sense of mission. A free Church at grips with the world is the place to read the Scriptures. And this has, perhaps, never been more practicable than today. Past situations have tended to be, or have been interpreted to be, rather sharply divided between Church and world, Christian and non-Christian, sacred and profane. The pastoral care of the believing community and the evangelization of non-believers have been seen as quite different, contrasting ministries, with between them little overlap. We speak to the Church in one way, address the world in another. In fact the Bible does not relate to either mode of address entirely satisfactorily, being too unbreakable a whole to be properly at home in either half-ministry. But it is a particular characteristic of our modern religious predicament that such half-ministries are really fading into non-existence. We cannot divide them up any more, *didache* from *kerygma*. The believer and the non-believer can no more be separated. All over the world there is such an intermingling of belief and non-belief, both within and without the formal borders of the Church, such a social fusion of the Christian and the non-Christian, such an inseparable range of certainty and scepticism in matters religious to be found everywhere, from religious houses and Italian villages, to student chaplaincies or central African catechumenates, that the distinction between the pastoral and the evangelistic ministry no longer makes any deep sense. The Gospel has everywhere to be proclaimed at one and the same time to a whole uncertain spectrum of belief and disbelief. Whether one is speaking on radio or television, writing a book, addressing a baptism or marriage gathering, one has effectively to be speaking in the mode both of pastor and of evangelizer. The community addressed today is then of necessity a very free one and to it, with its variant shades of faith and doubt, the Bible can speak with all its strength. It is tied far less to some single pattern of theology and order established in a particular church community so unquestionably as to deny the Scriptures and their interpretation any real freedom.

For the characteristic Bible of our age one might point to the Gospel in Solentiname. In that community of peasants and fishermen and students, presided over by Ernesto Cardenal, and their communal interpretation of the gospel during the Sunday Eucharist, we find a situation where the Bible is at work with power in an appropriate context. The community, the interpretation, and the evangelization going with it are not divorced from the Church, hierarchy and all, by any means; but they are not smothered by it either. The word is being listened to here within a community where the degree of formal belief and ecclesial commitment greatly varies, and in which the very internal pedagogy of the Bible makes its sense, including as it does its own wide range of religious and ecclesial commitment: so close and sure in Acts or Ephesians or Titus, so wide in Job or Jonah or Proverbs.

The Bible draws its depth of meaning from its intrinsic historical development and its concentration upon an old and limited covenant prior to the new and unlimited. Now every person, and more still every society, that comes to Christ has some very real and special sort of old covenant of his or its own: the particular religious and cultural dispensation whereby the grace of God has already been mediated. These old covenants cannot and must not be dismissed as minor or irrelevant. They are on the contrary the only lock in which the key of biblical revelation can turn: the old but not untrue word before the new Christ-word, witness to the Spirit's presence in every area of the total people of God. If the old covenant is the covenant of God's people, but all humanity is truly people of God for he 'has no favourites', then all humanity must possess an old covenant. Yet this vast multiplicity of God's pre-Christ covenant does not dispense with the relevance for every man of the Hebraic Old Testament; it does not permit the latter to be dismissed and replaced by Platonic dialogues or Upanishad or Nuer religion or whatever. No, rather the Judaic Old Testament is the necessary epistemological intermediary, the model old covenant for all old covenants, without which not only could Christ's new alliance not be properly appreciated in its own terms, but nor ultimately could any other old alliance. The Bible, NT and OT together, does then constitute an amazing unity in which the process of the divine formation of the world in its wholeness is so revealed that both its Christ-centredness and its vast religious, cultural and ethical multiplicity find their necessary place and meaning. The focal point of biblical interpretation for the missionary evangelist is to relate the multiplicity of the old testaments to the biblically originating OT and then both to the NT. And those almost numberless old testaments are not only the religious systems of the past, they include every contemporary pattern of order and ultimate meaning not grounded in the living Christ. The evangelist's specific biblical rôle is so to enter into the intersection of OT and NT that it is replayed in a thousand different tunes in the continuity and discontinuity between traditional religion or its equivalent and the Christian Gospel, between the *status quo* and the breaking in of the kingdom, between a particular national ethos and the universal communion of the new alliance. The essence of evangelization is to proclaim the Christ, whose finality and novelty establish discontinuity with all that comes before, and yet whose function of fulfilment establishes the necessity of a continuity far profounder than we have ever imagined: a continuity with the Buddha, with every king born to die, with every harvest ritual, with every struggle of mankind for freedom, for light, for happiness. Within a purely church and pastoral context the OT easily withers. It is in the context of evangelization that it should necessarily revive, and reviving make clear anew the basic dual structure of the Bible, with all its implications.

To sum up: The Bible and the living community of the Church require each other, but each must be free. If the Bible speaks of the Church it does so across the interaction of covenants, a model whose implications are world-wide. The further you press into the inside of the Church the further away you get from the crucial interaction. On the frontiers of faith that interaction is renewed and requires interpretation in terms of the original inter-testamental relationship. That is the crucial biblical entry-point for the evangelist. But those frontiers no longer belong, if they ever did, to some limited 'missionary' apostolate, distinct from the regular teaching of the Gospel. We are back today with the NT situation where *kerygma* and *didache* are appropriate in the same city and in practice to a single group of people. Everywhere the Church is faced today with the world; so faced it needs more than ever it did the word of Scripture at its side, but it can only effectively have the word if it is free in its own life, as today still it is not. The more truly free the Church, the greater the power of Scripture; the more servile the Church, the more is the Bible domesticated, canonized and confined. The word of God is not above the teaching office of the

Church but serves it. The teaching office of the Church is not above the word of God but serves it. The efficacity of the Scriptures as evangelizer to the world depends on which of these two opposites — freedom or servility — is demonstrated in practice within church life.

FURTHER READING

Books and articles listed under individual chapter headings are chosen by the respective contributors. Further suggestions will also be found in the Notes at the end of certain chapters.

General

Y. Aharoni, *The Land of the Bible* (London & Philadelphia, 2nd ed. 1980).

B. W. Anderson, *The Living World of the Old Testament* (London & New York, 1967).

M. Black & H. H. Rowley (eds), *Peake's Commentary on the Bible* (London & New York, 1963).

C. K. Barrett, *From First Adam to Last* (London, 1962).

R. E. Brown *et. al.* (eds), *The Jerome Biblical Commentary* (London & New York, 1968).

L. Bright (ed.), *Scripture Discussion Commentary,* 12 vols. (London 1971-2).

J. D. Derrett, *Jesus' Audience* (London, 1973).

'Dogmatic Constitution on Divine Revelation' (*Dei Verbum),* in W. M. Abbott (ed.), *The Documents of Vatican II* (New York & London, 1966).

A. Dulles, *Apologetics and the Biblical Christ* (New York & London, 1966).

P. Grelot, *Introduction to the Bible* (London & New York, 1967).

S. Herrmann, *A History of Israel in Old Testament Times* (London, 1975).

L. Johnston, *A History of Israel* (London, 1964).

J. L. McKenzie, *Dictionary of the Bible* (New York & London, 1965).

J. L. McKenzie, *Vital Concepts of the Bible* (New York & London, 1968).

J. L. McKenzie, *A Theology of the Old Testament* (New York, 1974; London, 1976).

J. Schmidt *et al.*, 'Biblical Exegesis', in *Sacramentum Mundi,* vol. 1 (London & New York, 1968), pp. 191-207.

L. A. Schökel, *Understanding Biblical Research* (New York & London, 1968).

E. Trocmé, *Jesus and his Contemporaries* (London, 1973).

Inspiration and revelation

R. E. Brown, *Biblical Reflections on Crises facing the Church* (New York & London, 1975).

R. E. Brown, *The Sensus Plenior of Sacred Scripture* (Baltimore, 1955).

L. Grollenberg, *A Bible for our Time. Reading the Bible in the Light of Today's Questions* (London, 1979).

A. Jones, *God's Living Word* (London, 1965).

W. S. Lasor, 'The *Sensus Plenior* and Biblical Inspiration', in W. W. Gasque & W. S. Lasor (eds), *Scripture, Tradition and Interpretation* (Grand Rapids, 1978), pp. 260-77.

J. Levie, *The Bible, Word of God in Words of Men* (London, 1961).

T. Radcliffe, 'The Old Testament as Word of God: Canon and Identity', in *New Blackfriars* 61 (1980), pp. 266-75.

K. Rahner, *Inspiration in the Bible* (*Quaest. Disput.*, 1, Freiburg, New York, Edinburgh & London, 1961).

K. Rahner, *Foundations of Christian Faith* (London & New York, 1978).

Literary Categories and Biblical Imagery

G. B. Caird, *The Language and Imagery of the Bible* (London, 1980). Provides a good general treatment of a range of topics.

J. Court, *Myth and History in the Book of Revelation* (London, 1979). Brings out the variety of influences upon a particular text.

D. Daube, *The New Testament and Rabbinic Judaism* (London, 1956). Makes some startling suggestions of correspondence.

H. F. G. Swanston, *Prophets II* (*Scripture Discussion Commentary,* London, 1972). Sketches the pagan and Hebrew liturgical influences in the minor prophets.

A. Wilder, *Early Christian Rhetoric* (London, 1964). Briefly sets out the literary originality of the new community.

The Spirituality of the Bible

Augustine, St, *Confessions* (various edns.). A formidable book, at once philosophical investigation, theological compendium and spiritual testament. As a presentation of

Christian spirituality it is unique, powerful and inexhaustible.

A. Carmichael, *The Sun Dances.* A selection from Carmichael's great 5-vol. *Carmina Gadelica* (in Gaelic and English). A spirituality that has escaped the shadow of Augustine, the reformation conflict and the Enlightenment.

G. Gutiérrez, *A Theology of Liberation* (New York, 1973; London, 1974). One-sided and rhetorical, but still provides the best statement of this contemporary approach to the Bible. The ch. on poverty is especially good.

Imitation of Christ, The (various edns.). Traditionally attributed to Thomas à Kempis, this great classic is an irreplaceable commentary on the 'come, follow me' of Jesus.

N. D. O'Donoghue, *Heaven in Ordinarie* (Edinburgh, 1979). Provides a background to this chapter.

P. Teilhard de Chardin, *Le Milieu Divin* (London & New York, 1960). Provides a good balance to *The Imitation of Christ.* Opens up the cosmic dimensions of biblical spirituality.

Thérèse of Lisieux, St, *The Story of a Soul* (various edns.). The autobiography of the young woman who asked to follow Jesus all the way, into Gethsemane and through the *Lamma Sabachthani.*

The Old Testament in the History of Israel

J. Rhymer (ed.), *The Bible in Order* (London & New York, 1975).

A. Robert & A. Feuillet (eds.), *Introduction to the Old Testament* (Tournai, 1965); cf the essay by P. Grelot.

H. H. Rowley, *The Growth of the Old Testament* (London, 1964).

The Relevance of the Old Testament for Christians

D. L. Baker, *Two Testaments, One Bible* (Leicester, 1976).

J. Barr, *Old and New in Interpretation: a Study of the Two Testaments* (London, 1966).

C. K. Barrett, 'The Interpretation of the Old Testament in the New', in *The Cambridge History of the Bible,* vol. I (Cambridge, 1970), pp. 377-411.

B. S. Childs, *Biblical Theology in Crisis* (Philadelphia, 1970).

C. H. Dodd, *According to the Scriptures* (London, 1952).
A. H. J. Gunneweg, *Understanding the Old Testament* (London, 1978).
D. Moody Smith, Jr., title essay in *The Use of the Old Testament in the New and Other Essays: Studies in Honor of William Franklin Stinespring,* ed., J. M. Efird (Durham, N. Carolina, 1972).
G. E. Wright, *God who acts: Biblical Theology as Recital* (London, 1952).

Prophecy in the Bible

E. W. Heaton, *Old Testament Prophets* (London, 1977).
G. von Rad, *The Message of the Prophets* (London, 1968).
H. Ringgren, *Israelite Religion* (London, 1966); cf Ch. II, 12, 'The writing Prophets', pp. 248-94.
And of course, the OT prophets themselves, especially Amos, Hosea, Micah, Jeremiah and Ezekiel.

New Testament Morality

J. L. Houlden, *Ethics and the New Testament* (Oxford, 1973).
W. Lillie, *Studies in New Testament Ethics* (Edinburgh, 1961).
L. H. Marshall, *The Challenge of New Testament Ethics* (London, 1966).
R. Schnackenburg, *The Moral Teaching of the New Testament* (London, 1965).
R. Schnackenburg, *Christian Existence in the New Testament* (Indiana, 1968).

The Resurrection and Christian Belief

P. Badham, *Christian Beliefs about Life after Death* (London, 1976).
M. Dummett, 'Biblical Exegesis and the Resurrection', in *New Blackfriars* 58 (1977), pp. 58-72.
R. H. Fuller, *The Formation of the Resurrection Narratives* (London, 1972).
P. Geach, 'Immortality', in *God and the Soul* (London, 1969).
J. Hick, *Death and Eternal Life* (London, 1976).
S. H. Hooke, *The Resurrection of Christ* (London, 1967).
F. Kerr, 'Exegesis and Easter', in *New Blackfriars* 58 (1977), pp. 108-21.

G. E. Ladd, *I believe in the Resurrection of Jesus* (London, 1975).

H. D. Lewis, *Persons and Life after Death* (London, 1978).

W. Marxsen, *The Resurrection of Jesus of Nazareth* (London, 1970).

C. F. D. Moule & D. Cupitt, 'The Resurrection: a Disagreement', in *Theology* LXXV (1972), pp. 507-18.

C. F. D. Moule (ed.). *The Significance of the Message of the Resurrection for Faith in Jesus Christ* (London, 1968).

G. O'Collins, *The Easter Jesus* (London, 1973).

N. Perrin, *The Resurrection Narratives* (London, 1977).

D. Z. Phillips, *Death and Immortality* (London, 1970).

K. Rahner, 'Dogmatic Questions on Easter', in *Theological Investigations,* IV (London & New York, 1966).

J. Rohde, *Rediscovering the Teaching of the Evangelists* (London, 1968).

Teaching the Bible

C. H. Dodd, *The Founder of Christianity* (London, 1971).

X. Léon-Dufour, *The Gospels and the History of Jesus* (London, 1963).

C. F. D. Moule, *The Birth of the New Testament* (London, 1966).

R. C. Walton (ed.), *A Source Book of the Bible for Teachers* (London, 1970).

NOTES ON CONTRIBUTORS

Editors

PAUL BURNS: Chairman of Process Workshop. Read Modern Languages at Oxford University; former Publishing Director of Burns & Oates, Publishers to the Holy See; associated with a number of Catholic Renewal groups. A regular translator for *Concilium,* and of several books, mainly concerned with liberation theology, from Spanish and French. Co-editor, with John Cumming, of *The Church Now* (1980).

JOHN CUMMING: Literary and educational editor of *The Tablet*. Co-editor with Lord Bullock of *Fontana Biographical Dictionary of Modern Thought*; executive editor with Karl Rahner of *Encyclopedia of Theology* (1975); author with David Konstant of *Beginnings* (1969); co-editor with Paul Burns of *The Church Now*. Member of the editorial board of *New Blackfriars*; translator and editor of many books from German, French and Dutch.

Contributors

CECILY BENNETT: Lecturer in Religious Studies at St Mary's College, University of London. Born Cecily Hastings in Malaya; read Modern Languages at Oxford University, and developed an interest in theology largely through speaking for the Catholic Evidence Guild and translating various major authors, especially Hans Küng and Karl Rahner. Has lectured in religious studies since 1965, now specializing in OT Biblical Studies.

REV. LAURENCE BRIGHT, OP: Joined the Dominican Order after a distinguished Oxford career as a physicist, and became increasingly well known as lecturer and counsellor. Edited *Life of the Spirit* and *The Newman* for a number of years; general editor of *Scripture Discussion Commentary* (12 vols. to 1972), to which he also contributed several commentaries. Editor at Sheed and Ward Ltd till his recent death.

REV. BRIAN DAVIES, OP: Lecturer in Philosophy at Blackfriars, Oxford. Reviews editor of *New Blackfriars*; has published numerous articles on philosophical and theological topics in *Philosophy, Theology* and other journals. His book, *An Introduction to the Philosophy of Religion* is due to be published by Oxford University Press in 1981.

V. REV. JOHN GREEHY: President of Clonliffe College, Dublin. Studied at University College, Dublin, the Pontifical Biblical Institute, the Lateran and Angelicum Universities in Rome. Lectured in Scripture at Oscott College and the University of Birmingham 1961-7; since then Professor of Sacred Scripture at Clonliffe College. He has contributed numerous articles to theological and catechetical journals in Britain and Ireland, and was made a member of the Pontifical Biblical Commission in 1968.

REV. ADRIAN HASTINGS: Reader in Religious Studies at the University of Aberdeen. Spent twelve years in Africa, mostly in Uganda, as a missionary; author of *Church and Mission* (1968) and *Wiriyamu* (1974). A member of the joint International Roman Catholic/Anglican Preparatory Commission 1966-8. His other books include *The Faces of God* (1975), *In Filial Disobedience* (1978) and *A History of African Christianity, 1950-75.*

DORIS K. HAYES: Principal Lecturer and Head of Theology Department at Newman College, Birmingham. MA in theology from the University of Birmingham. After teaching at various schools she has been lecturing in theology at Colleges of Education for the past fifteen years.

REV. PROF. HANS KÜNG: Professor of Dogmatic and Ecumenical Theology at the University of Tübingen. Member of the Editorial Committee of *Concilium*; known as lecturer throughout the world, including China. Probably the most widely-read theologian in the world today, his major works translated into English include *Justification* (1964), *Structures of the Church* (1964), *The Church* (1968), *On Being a Christian* (1976) and *Does God Exist?* (1980).

REV. JOHN L. McKENZIE, SJ: Professor of Theology at the De Paul University till his retirement in 1978. Previously Professor of History at the University of Chicago and of Theology at the

University of Notre Dame. President of the Catholic Biblical Institute 1964-5 and of the Society of Biblical Literature 1965-6. His many major published works include *Dictionary of the Bible* (1965), *Authority in the Church* (1966) and *Theology of the Old Testament* (1973).

REV. NOEL D. O'DONOGHUE, O. CARM: Lecturer in the Faculty of Divinity in the University of Edinburgh. Holds a doctorate in Philosophy from the University of Louvain. Professor of Ethics in the National University of Ireland (at Maynooth) 1952-6. Author of numerous articles on philosophy, published in Irish, European and American journals, a collection of which has appeared in book form as *Heaven in Ordinarie* (1979).

REV. TIMOTHY RADCLIFFE, OP: Vice-regent of studies at Blackfriars, Oxford. Member of the editorial board of *New Blackfriars*, to which he is also a regular contributor on theological and sociological topics. Author of the chapter 'Relativizing the Relativizers . . . ' in *Sociology and Theology: Alliance and Conflict* (1979).

BERNARD ROBINSON: Head of Religious Studies at St Mary's College, Fenham, Newcastle upon Tyne. A member of the Society for Old Testament Study, he has published numerous articles and reviews in *Scripture, Scripture Bulletin, The Heythrop Journal* and other periodicals. Contributed the commentaries on Daniel, 1 Peter and 1 John to the *Scripture Discussion Commentary*; has recently completed an M. Litt. thesis on the Simon Magus traditions.

LIONEL SWAIN: Teacher of Religious Studies at Beaconsfield High School. A graduate of the Institut Catholique, Paris, the Pontifical Biblical Institute, Rome, and London University, he taught Sacred Scripture at St Edmund's College, Ware, from 1965-75. Has lectured widely on the Bible and his published works include commentaries on Galatians and Hebrews in *Scripture Discussion Commentary* and articles on 'Inspiration', 'Interpretation' and Ephesians in the *New Catholic Commentary on Holy Scripture*.

REV. PROF. HAMISH. F. G. SWANSTON: Professor of Theology at the University of Kent at Canterbury. Has taught at universities in both North and South America; author of half-a-dozen books on matters of systematic and scriptural theology, as well as a recent Pelican, *In Defence of Opera*. He is now completing a study of British theology from the late seventeenth century to the present.

GEOFFREY TURNER: Teacher of theology at The Trinity School, Leamington Spa. Holds a degree in theology from Oxford University and a Doctorate in NT hermeneutics from St Andrews. Has published articles in *Scottish Journal of Theology, Irish Theological Quarterly* and other periodicals; author of *Christianity: a Brief Description of the Present-day Church* (1972) and *Theology after Auschwitz* (1980).

REV. HENRY WANSBROUGH, OSB: Housemaster at Ampleforth College, Yorkshire. Holds degrees from Oxford, Fribourg and Rome; has studied at the Ecole Biblique in Jerusalem and taught in the United States. The author of several books on biblical subjects, he is also a regular contributor to theological journals and general editor of the *Jerusalem Bible*. Catholic chairman of the Roman Catholic/Methodist theological commission.

V. REV. HAROLD WINSTONE: Director of the St Thomas More Centre for Pastoral Liturgy in N. London since 1969. Educated at St Edmund's College, Ware, St Sulpice in Paris and Cambridge University, he served as a POW chaplain in the Second World War, later teaching classics at St Edmund's College. Chairman of the I.C.E.L. Advisory Commission 1965-75; has translated many liturgical works from German; editor of *Pastoral Liturgy* (1975); co-editor of *English Catholic Worship* (1979).